PRIVATE RO

THE LEGAL FRAMEWORK

Third edition

- by -

Andrew Barsby
Barrister
(non-practising)
A. C. I. Arb.
Accredited Mediator

A. W. & C. BARSBY
LEGAL RESEARCH AND PUBLISHING
2003

A. W. & C. Barsby
Legal Research and Publishing

2 Lynwood Avenue, Epsom, Surrey, KT17 4LQ
Tel: +44 (0)1372 742372

www.barsby.com
mail@barsby.com

ISBN 0 9521625 9 8

Copyright

© A. W & C. Barsby 2003

This work is copyright, and all rights in it are reserved. No part of it may be reproduced, whether by photocopying or any other method, save in accordance with the Copyright, Designs and Patents Act 1988 or by permission of the copyright owners. Unauthorised reproduction may result in civil or criminal proceedings or both.

Crown copyright material is reproduced by permission of the Controller of HMSO.

Printed and published in England by A. W. & C. Barsby

Preface

In the six years since the second edition of this book was published, there have been many small changes in the law, and some larger ones. The Countryside and Rights of Way Act 2000 amends the law relating to public rights of way. The Land Registration Act 2002 makes some important changes to land law and will bring in, over the coming years, a new system of electronic conveyancing. There have also been some significant decisions by the courts on rights of way, parking and other issues.

More important, perhaps, have been continuing social changes. Three may be mentioned. First, the pressure to develop means that residents' associations and companies in private roads are increasingly being confronted with problems such as whether further rights of way are needed and (if so) should be granted, in order for development to take place.

Secondly, in relation to sales of existing houses, the guidelines of the Council of Mortgages Lenders, which are used by the major lending institutions, now require a report to be made if arrangements are not in place for maintaining a private road.

Finally, this is becoming an increasingly litigious society. Claims are pressed, to obtain compensation in the event of accidents, when once they would not have been. "No-win-no-fee" agreements by lawyers have contributed to this process. The position is particularly acute for unincorporated residents' associations—those which are not companies—since the individuals running the organisation may find that they are personally liable.

For these and other reasons it is becoming increasingly important for residents to be organised, and to act effectively.

In re-writing the book we have tried to take account of these pressures, and offer as much help on the law, and on the practicalities as we can. The shape of the book has changed somewhat: chapter 1 now summarises the history of the law on roads and public rights of way, ownership is dealt with in chapter 2, and the process of forming an organisation to manage a private road in chapter 12.

As before, the Notes and Queries pages on our internet site, www.barsby.com, provide the opportunity to respond to questions from users about the law, expanding on and clarifying the printed text

0-7 We are sometimes asked whether we can make available the legal materials which the text refers to. Though for copyright reasons we cannot reproduce printed material from textbooks, law reports and journals, the answer is increasingly "Yes"—Acts of Parliament from 1988, and delegated legislation from 1987 are available on the internet, from HMSO. The text of judgments in the higher courts are also often available. Wherever possible, our Notes and Queries pages contain links to these sources.

0-8 We remain extremely grateful to all the individuals and organisations who have raised points with us and given us their views. Feedback of this sort is essential if the book is to serve its purpose of being a practical guide to the law of private roads, for residents associations, local authorities, solicitors, surveyors and other professionals, developers, and indeed all those with an interest in the subject. Mistakes remain our sole responsibility.

0-9 Are private roads a "good thing?" On the whole they are. They offer residents the chance to exercise a degree of control over their immediate area, and so enhance amenity and security. But these advantages come at a price, and it is increasingly important for residents to be organised, so that they can act collectively, and for residents and others involved to understand the workings of the law. We hope that this book will help them to do so.

―――― // ――――

0-10 Changes to the law, both minor and major, are constantly being made, and readers should be alert to the possibility that changes have occurred since publication. It should also be emphasised that this text should not be regarded as a substitute for legal advice when the need arises, and indeed that we cannot give advice.

0-11 The book aims to summarise the law of England and Wales[*] (Scotland has its own distinct legal system) as it stands at the end of April 2003.

[*] But see 1-54.

A. W. & C. Barsby
Epsom, May 2003

Private Roads at a Glance

There is no precise definition of the term "private road". But private roads are different from the majority of roads because the latter are (in the language of the Highways Act 1980) "highways maintainable at the public expense", meaning that there is a public right of way and that the road belongs to and is maintained by the local authority. (0-12)

Private roads are not owned or maintained by the local authority, though they may be highways, i.e. subject to public rights of way. Private roads may be long or short, through-roads or cul-de-sacs, urban, suburban or rural. (0-13)

This book is concerned primarily with private roads which provide access to properties in separate ownership, and with the many legal issues which arise in such circumstances. These include issues relating to maintenance, public and private rights of way, planning, liability for accidents, and services; and also the participation of residents in the ownership and management of the road. (0-14)

Many private roads date back to the end of the 19th century and the first half of the 20th. Often the original ownership of the road has been forgotten; sometimes it may have been acquired by residents, and (with or without ownership) residents will have organised themselves so as to look after the road. In contrast, many new private roads are being built, because of the amenity and security they offer for development, and in particular residential development; but these are much more likely to have been left by developers with a degree of organisation, so as to provide for future maintenance and to cope with problems which may arise. (0-15)

No private road is an exclusively private matter: even if there is no public right of way, local authority and other officials will have an interest in safety and amenity, and the pipes, cables and other equipment of the utility companies will almost certainly located under and over the road. (0-16)

for more information see www.barsby.com

© A. W. & C. Barsby 2003

CONTENTS

Chapter 1: Overview 1
Introduction...................................1
A brief history of roads 1
What is a private road? 3
Nomenclature 4
Classes of private road........................6
How private is private?........................7
Private roads as land 7
   Common land................................8
   Town and village greens 8
   Crown land 8
Possession and occupation of land 9
Licences 9
Civil and criminal courts.....................10
Administrative law...........................10
Conventions..................................11
How to use the book 12
How to use the website 12
Topics not included 13

Chapter 2: ownership 14
Introduction..................................14
Ownership generally 14
History of ownership 14
Presumption of ownership 16
Adverse possession 17
   Background 17
   The present law 17
   Changes to the law.........................18
What land is included in a road?..............20
Land registration 20
   The system of land registration 20
   Electronic conveyancing 21
   Registering title to a private road 21
   Contents of the Land Register 22
   Searching the Land Register 22
   Other registers............................23
Bona vacantia 23
Absence of an owner 24
Assessment 24

Chapter 3: Highways 26

Introduction. 26
Classes of highway. 26
What land is subject to the public right of way? 27
The right to use a highway 28
Dedication and acceptance 28
Evidence of use by the public. 31
Preventing dedication and acceptance 32
Highways Act procedures: highways generally 34
    Section 30. 34
    Section 37. 34
    Section 38. 35
Highways Act procedures: bridleways and footpaths 36
    Section 25 36
    Section 26. 36
Footpaths and bridleways created by dedication and acceptance 37
The definitive map and statement. 37
    Generally 37
    Modifications. 38
    Footpaths and bridleways in private roads 39
    Private roads as RUPPs, restricted byways, and BOATs. 40
Stopping up and diversion of highways. 41
    Procedures 41
    Consequences. 42
Assessment 43

Chapter 4: Private rights of way and other easements 45

Introduction. 45
What is an easement?. 45
Rights of way in a private road 46
Creation of private rights of way 48
    Creation by grant. 48
    Creation by prescription 48
Scope: rights of way created by grant 51
    What land has the benefit of the right of way? 52
    What is the extent of the use allowed?. 53
Scope: rights of way arising by prescription 54
Vehicular Access. 55
Other ways in which easements can arise 57
    The rule in Wheeldon v Burrows. 57
    Section 62 of the Law of Property Act 1925 57
Maintenance and repairs. 57
Access to the road. 58
Breaches of the law. 59
Termination and modification of private rights of way 60
Other easements 61

Registered and unregistered land 61
Assessment 62

Chapter 5: Parking 65

Introduction. 65
Licences 65
Parking as an expressly-granted easement. 66
Parking as a prescriptive easement 67
Parking in connection with a right of way 68
Remedies for unlawful parking 69
   Civil law. 69
   Criminal law 70
   Self-help 70
Private roads which are highways. 71
Assessment 72

Chapter 6: Civil law 73

Introduction. 73
Torts 73
Trespass 73
Nuisance 75
   Land generally 75
   Highways. 76
Occupiers' liability 76
   Who is an occupier?. 77
   The Occupiers' Liability Act 1957: "visitors" 77
   The Occupiers' Liability Act 1984: trespassers, private rights of way 79
Negligence 81
Remedies 81
   Compensation 81
   Injunctions. 81
Access to neighbouring land. 83
Restrictive covenants 84
   Generally 84
   Building schemes 85
   The role of the Lands Tribunal. 85
   Enforcement. 86
Assessment 87

Chapter 7: Offences 89

Introduction. 89
Highways Act offences 89
Public nuisance 92
Theft and criminal damage. 93
Environmental matters 93
   Litter 93

Dumping cars and other things	93
Hedgerows Regulations 1997	94
Noise	96
Motoring offences	96
Criminal trespasses	98
Unauthorised camping and caravanning	98
Old statutes	99
Dogs	99
Assessment	100

Chapter 8: Planning 101

Introduction	101
Development	101
Specific provisions affecting private roads	103
Maintenance of private roads	103
Gates, fences, walls, etc.	103
Access to a highway	104
Services	105
Security cameras	105
Disapplying the General Permitted Development Order	105
Enforcement of planning control	105
Tree preservation orders	106
Control of outdoor advertisements	108
Special areas	110
Conservation areas	110
Other areas	111
Planning decisions and rights of way	111
Assessment	112

Chapter 9: Powers of local authorities 113

Introduction	113
The Highways Act 1980	113
Powers relating only to highways maintainable at the public expense	113
Powers relating to highways	114
Powers relating to roads to which the public has access	115
Powers relating to all "streets"	116
Marking of footpaths, etc.	117
Dangerous trees	117
Traffic regulation	118
Amenity	120
Names and numbers of roads and houses	121
Public entertainments	122
Other powers	123
Assessment	123

Chapter 10: Services 125

Introduction. 125
The New Roads and Street Works Act 1991. 126
Exercise of powers by statutory undertakers. 129
Nature of statutory powers. 130
Electricity. 131
Gas 132
Telecommunications 134
Water and sewerage. 137
   Water 137
   Public sewers 138
   Private sewers and drains 140
The Post Office 140
Assessment 140

Chapter 11: Making up and adoption 142

Introduction. 142
Part XI of the Highways Act 1980 142
Some basic concepts. 143
The private street works code: procedure 144
   First step: initial resolution by the local authority 144
   Second step: preparation of specification, etc. 145
   Third step: resolution of approval 146
   Fourth step: publicity. 146
   Fifth step: objections 147
   Sixth step: carrying out of work 148
The private street works code: financial provisions 148
The advance payments code. 149
Exemptions from the advance payments code 150
The advance payments code: financial provisions 152
Land designated as a private street on a development plan 153
Local land charges 153
Adoption after street works 154
   Local authority's discretion 154
   Majority of residents 155
Special procedures for urgent repairs 155
Adoption when an advance payment has been made 156
Human rights issues. 157
Assessment 158

Chapter 12: Organisation 162

Introduction. 162
Why be organised? 162
Ownership and management 163
Forms of organisation 163
Unincorporated associations. 164

> *Nature* 164
> *Operation* 164
> *Ownership of property* 165
> *Dissolution* 166
> Companies 166
> > *Operation* 167
> > *Ownership of property* 169
> > *Winding up* 169
>
> Trusts 169
> > *Nature* 169
> > *Operation* 170
> > *Ownership of property* 171
> > *Dissolution* 171
>
> Securing an income 171
> > *Rentcharges* 172
> > *Restrictions on transfer* 172
>
> Assessment 173

Appendix 1: Questions and Answers 176

Appendix 2: Tasks for managers 181

Table of Authorities 183

Index 195

Chapter 1: Overview

Introduction

This chapter contains general explanations which will be used in other chapters, starting with the question of what a private road is.

The term "private road" is a convenient one, but it should not be taken to imply that there are just two sorts of road, public and private. In reality the law is more complicated, and "public road" and "private road" are not terms with precise legal meanings.

However, one key term which does have a clear meaning is "highway maintainable at the public expense". This term, defined in the Highways Act 1980, defines roads and paths which are a public responsibility. A brief historical account will explain how the law has evolved, and why the position today is more complicated than might be expected.

A brief history of roads

Under the common law[1] of England and Wales, public rights of way were—and may still be—created by a process known as "dedication and acceptance". A way becomes a highway when:

- The owner dedicates it to the public as a highway, by allowing them to use it; and

- The public accepts the dedication, by using the way[2].

Then, after a period of time, the length of which depends upon the circumstances, a public right of way arises; or (in other words) a highway is created*.

Responsibility for repairing roads which were highways generally lay with the inhabitants of the parish in which the road was situated[3]. The responsibility was open-ended, and extended to any roads which became highways by dedication and acceptance.

*See further 3-11 onwards for dedication and acceptance.

---

1. That is, the law laid down by the courts, over the centuries, in deciding cases.
2. See *Hereford and Worcester County Council v Pick* 12/7/95, 1 CL 1996 424.
3. Some highways were legally maintainable by private bodies, or by individuals.

*The Act did not deal with footpaths and bridleways which have a slightly different history: see 3-47.

1-6 The latter rule was changed by the The Highway Act 1835, which laid down that for roads* which became highways after 1836, there was no public responsibility to maintain them unless a specific decision was taken to do so, this being known as "adoption". (The term is still in use, to mean the process by which a road or path becomes a public responsibility—hence "unadopted road".) But the law on dedication and acceptance was not changed. It thus became possible for the a road to become a highway, by dedication and acceptance, *without* becoming a public responsibility.

1-7 The 1835 Act also provided that parishes should elect officers known as "surveyors of highways" to discharge the public responsibility of maintaining roads. Later Acts (the law was eventually consolidated[4] in the Highways Act 1959, and again in the Highways Act 1980) introduced other procedures for creating highways. They also dealt with public responsibility for maintaining roads. Most of the functions have come to rest in rural areas with County Councils, and in metropolitan areas with Metropolitan District Councils. In rural areas, District Councils[5] may have some functions relating to highways, for example maintaining roads and footpaths. These bodies are known in the Highways Act 1980 as "highway authorities". For some major roads, the highway authority is central government.

1-8 Highways which are a public responsibility are known in the Highways Act 1980 as "highways maintainable at the public expense", and this term includes all highways which were a public responsibility in the past, and any new ones which may be created (s. 36). When a road is a highway maintainable at the public expense:

*But generally only ownership of the top layer: see 2-29.

- Ownership passes to the local authority* (ss. 263 - 268).

- The road is a highway, i.e. there is a public right of way.

- The local authority is under a duty, by virtue of s. 41, to maintain the road.

*See chapter 3 for highways generally.

1-9 Most of the roads which the public use (and many footpaths and bridleways and other cross-country highways*) are highways maintainable at the public expense. This book is not directly concerned with highways maintainable at public expense, but refers to them in passing to show how the law differs; and it also deals with the ways in

---

4. A consolidating Act is one which draws together the law in a number of previous Acts, and sets it out again, sometimes with minor changes.
5. Parish and community councils may also have a role, e.g. in maintaining footpaths and bridleways.

which private roads can become highways maintainable at the public expense and how the process can be reversed by "stopping up"*.

*See particularly chapters 3 and 11.

What is a private road?

Private roads are outside the category of highways maintainable at the public expense: responsibility for their upkeep is not a public matter, and they do not belong to the local authority.

From the history explained above, it will be seen that all private roads either:

- Pre-date the Highway Act 1835, but were not before 1836 used by the public to a sufficient extent to make them highways, and so automatically maintainable at the public expense; or

- Post-date the 1835 Act, and have never been adopted (i.e. have never become highways maintainable at the public expense).

But post-1836 private roads *may nonetheless be highways,* as a result of dedication and acceptance or (occasionally) a statutory procedure. Where a private road is a highway, there is an element of unfairness in the law. The road is subject to public use, and hence wear and tear and a degree of intrusion; but the owners of the road cannot look to the public, as represented by the local authority, to contribute to the upkeep of the road. However, private roads, whether or not highways, can in some circumstances become highways maintainable at the public expense*.

*See chapter 11 on making up and adoption.

Many sorts of road which are not highways maintainable at the public expense could be described as "private roads", for example roads within the grounds of institutions such as factories, hospitals and schools, slip-roads leading to petrol filling stations and other facilities, roads serving industrial estates, or blocks of flats, and so on. Some of the law explained in this book will apply to such roads.

But the book is mainly concerned with private roads which give access to properties in different ownership, and where the use is therefore shared[6]. Private roads may be long or short, metalled or unmetalled, through-roads or cul-de-sacs. They are often suburban, but the same legal issues apply to private roads in city centres and in rural areas. They are often wholly or mainly residential, and this book

---

6. In some cases—for example, roads which service blocks of flats or other leasehold housing, or leased commercial or industrial property—the position may be regulated by agreements between landlord and tenant.

makes the simplifying assumption that the properties in a private road are all houses, and refers to the owners of property in the road as "residents". But much of the law will be the same whether the properties served by a private road are houses, or commercial or industrial properties.

Nomenclature

1-15   "Road" is used generally in this book, as a convenient although not very precise term*. In practice, usage differs. Some local authorities distinguish between "streets" which have houses in them, and "roads" which do not, or between "streets" which are subject to a public right of way, and "roads" which are not. Terms such as "estate road" and "accommodation road" are sometimes encountered, but have no special legal significance[7].

*But "street" is used in chapter 11, to accord with the wording of the legislation.

1-16   Private roads are sometimes referred to as being "unadopted", echoing the language of the Highway Act 1835 and meaning that they have not become maintainable at the public expense*.

*See 1-6.

1-17   As far as the law is concerned, "highway" has the technical meaning explained above, namely that the road or path in question is subject to a public right of way. Ironically, perhaps, "highway" is not defined in the Highways Act 1980[8], so continues to have its common law meaning.

1-18   A frequent problem, in framing legislation, is that there are not enough ordinary words with precise meanings. Legislation therefore has to give words special meanings; and the same word in different contexts may bear different meanings. Several specialised meanings can usefully be noted here; though terms such as "road" and "street" do not always have special meanings in legislation*.

*See for example 8-2.

1-19   "Street" is given a special, and very wide, meaning by the New Roads and Street Works Act 1991*; and this same meaning has been inserted into the Highways Act 1980 and some other legislation. A "street" for these purposes includes:

*See particularly 10-4 onwards for this Act.

> "......the whole or any part of any of the following, irrespective of whether it is a thoroughfare—
>
> (a) any highway, road, lane, footway, alley or passage,
>
> (b) any square or court, and

---

7. The Highways Act 1980 used to include a reference (in s. 38) to "occupation roads", but this was removed by later legislation.
8. Though s. 328 makes clear that "highway" includes bridges and tunnels.

© A. W. & C. Barsby 2003

(c) any land laid out as a way whether it is for the time being formed as a way or not."

The term is thus useful for legislation which is intended to apply to any road, path or other piece of land which is used for getting from one place to another.

"Road" in the Road Traffic Act 1988*, by s. 192(1):

1-20   *See particularly 7-21 for this Act. And see also the Road Traffic Regulation Act 1984, at 9-14 onwards.

"[a] in relation to England and Wales, means any highway and any other road to which the public has access, and includes bridges over which a road passes".

1-21

In what circumstances does the public have access for these purposes? There must be use by substantial numbers of the public. The courts have generally taken the view that the public has access to a road if members of the public actually use it and the use is tolerated, even if there is no actual right to use the road[9]. A physical barrier, or a notice making it clear that the public has no right to use a road, is relevant but not conclusive—it may be that, despite a notice or barrier, use by the public is in fact tolerated[10]. In the absence of such measures, a private road which was actually used by the public would be within the definition of a "road" for these purposes, even if it was not (or not yet) a highway.

1-22

This definition of "road" enables legislation to apply to all highways, including private roads which are highways, and to some other roads, which are in fact used by the public. The latter may be in the course of becoming highways, by the process of dedication and acceptance. Including roads which are subject to public use makes it easier to enforce the law, and especially the criminal law, since proving that a road is currently subject to public use is easier than proving that it has become a highway because of public use over a period of time[11].

1-23

Whether a private road comes within the Road Traffic Act 1988 will be a matter of choice on the part of those managing the road: they can stop public use if they wish, provided the road has not become a highway through prolonged public use*.

*See 1-8.

1-24

A private road which comes within the definition in the Road Traffic Act and which has lamp posts at intervals of 200 yards or less will generally be a "restricted road", and subject to a 30 m.p.h. speed limit*.

*See 9-17.

1-25

One other definition should be noted, namely "made-up carriageway"*, which by s. 329 of the Highways Act 1980 means:

*See 3-3 for the meaning of "carriageway".

---

9. See *Kreft v Rawcliffe, The Times* 12 May 1984.
10. See *Hogg v Nicholson* [1968] SLT 265—a Scottish case.
11. The same principle is sometimes adopted by legislation in different language, for example that a road or other place is "open" to the public.

"...a carriageway, or a part thereof, which has been metalled or in any other way provided with a surface suitable for passage of vehicles".

Classes of private road

1-26 To summarise what emerges from the above paragraphs, there are for legal purposes three main sorts of private road:

- Private roads which are highways, and so "roads" for the purposes of the Road Traffic Act 1988.

- Private roads which are subject to public use and so "roads" for the purposes of the Road Traffic Act 1988, but not (or not yet) highways.

- Private roads which are neither highways nor subject to public use.

1-27 Establishing that a road is private, rather than a highway maintainable at the public expense, is relatively simple. Local authorities must keep a list of highways maintainable at the public expense, and this list must be open to the public (s. 36(6) of the Highways Act 1980). If a road is on the list, it is a highway maintainable at the public expense.

1-28 Establishing whether a private road has become a highway through dedication and acceptance, or whether it is one to which the public has access for the purposes of the Road Traffic Act 1988, may be more difficult, since this will depend upon questions of fact, and there may a dispute about the facts. Ultimately, only a decision by a court can resolve the question, as between two parties who are in dispute, of the status of the road.

1-29 The status of a private road is important since this affects the law which applies to the road. If the road is a highway, the public have a right to use it, and the local authority have a duty to uphold the public's interest, exercising their powers and enforcing the criminal law[*]. The liability of the managers of the road, and their freedom of action, are also affected. If the road is a highway, or subject to public use and hence within the Road Traffic Act 1988, a good deal of motoring law applies, and other consequences ensue, including the fact that the local authority will be entitled to make traffic regulation orders under the Road Traffic Regulation Act 1984[*].

[*]See 7-1 onwards and 9-1.

[*]See 9-15.

How private is private?

The public interest—and hence the ability of local and central government to intervene—is naturally greater for private roads which are highways or otherwise subject to public use.

But even where a private road is not a highway, or subject to public use, it will not in reality be as private as other areas of private property, such as the garden of a private house, since, for example:

- The Highways Act 1980, and other legislation, gives local authorities a few powers which apply to all roads*.

    *See 9-8.

- Legislation often gives the utility companies special powers to install pipes, cables and other equipment under and over all types of road*.

    *See chapter 10 generally.

It is in any event true that there is a legitimate public interest in all land, and that its use is regulated by planning law and other legislation, and local authority staff and other officials have many powers enabling them to enter on to land for inspection and other purposes. The extent to which these powers are exercised will depend upon the circumstances of the case; and the interest which a local authority shows in a particular private road will (quite properly) depend upon the circumstances.

In short, private roads are private only in a relative sense. But a private road nonetheless confers on those owning and managing it an important and worthwhile degree of control. They may be able to regulate such matters as parking, and the grant or refusal of further rights of way.

Private roads as land

Although private roads are subject to many different areas of law*, they are, for legal purposes, land, or "real" property and in that sense are not in a different class from any other sort of land. The law contains rules which govern dealings with land and interests in land*, and these rules are in many respects different from the rules which apply to other sorts of property. In particular, land and many rights over land can be created and transferred only by means of a deed.

*See 1-56.

*See also 2-30 onwards for land registration.

Special rules apply to some sorts of land, of which the following may be noted.

1-36 *Common land* Common land has a long history, dating back to the time when land was cultivated in accordance with the manorial system. The use of land was often shared, by means of rights of common, such as the right to graze livestock, or to take firewood and other materials. These rights would exist both over the large common fields which were characteristic of the manorial system, and over uncultivated land surrounding settlements.

1-37 During the latter part of the eighteenth century and the first part of the nineteenth, much common land was "enclosed"—divided up and fenced, and transferred into separate ownership and cultivated according to more modern methods of agriculture. But towards the end of the nineteenth century, the legislation which allowed this to happen was given a new purpose, namely protecting common land as a recreational resource for the population of large industrial towns. The Commons Acts 1876 and 1899 provide for the regulation of common land, and many areas of common land are regulated under schemes made by District Councils under the 1899 Act[12].

1-38 Furthermore, the Law of Property Act 1925, in s. 193, protects much common land by forbidding unlawful driving over the land, and other activities. Commons must be registered under the Commons Registration Act 1965.

1-39 Although a good deal of common land is owned publicly, it may also be owned by private individuals, whether or not subject to schemes under the Commons Acts. The prohibition on driving over common land has led to legal difficulties now addressed by regulations made under the Countryside and Rights of Way Act 2000*.

*See 4-36 onwards.

1-40 *Town and village greens* These also have a long history[13]. They too must be registered under the Commons Registration Act 1965, and indeed the same land may be both a common and a town or village green. Even if this is not the case, there may be legal difficulties in using a green for access.

1-41 *Crown land* Government in the United Kingdom is carried on in the name of the Crown (i.e. the reigning monarch) and land belonging to government departments is thus Crown land. More significantly, a certain amount of land belongs to the Crown for historical reasons; and this is administered by the Crown Estate Commissioners.

1-42 The law differs in some respects in relation to Crown land. In particular, it is more difficult to acquire land by adverse possession* and the Highways Act 1980 does not apply automatically to Crown land (s. 327).

*See 2-12 onwards for adverse possession.

---

12. And the Commons (Schemes) Regulations 1982, SI 1982/209, which set out a model scheme for District Councils to use.
13. For an interesting and informative account see particularly *The English Village Green* (1985) by Brian Bailey.

Possession and occupation of land

In giving rights and imposing responsibility, the law is concerned not merely with the ownership of land, but with the question of who is in control of it. The law uses the concepts of *possession* and *occupation* of land to identify the person in control. A person occupies land if she is in physical control of it. Possession is technically a wider concept, but for the purposes of this book can be regarded as meaning the same thing. Usually the person occupying or possessing land will be the owner; but it may be some other person, including in some circumstances a trespasser.

1-43

The law of trespass, for example, protects not just the owner of land, but any person who is in possession of the land*. And the Occupiers Liability Acts 1957 and 1984 impose civil liability not just on the owner of land but on any person who is in occupation of it*.

1-44

*See 6-5.

*See 6-15 onwards.

These concepts are particularly important in relation to private roads, since the ownership of the road is in many cases unknown, but residents collectively may act to maintain and protect it. In doing so they become entitled to the support of the law, because they are in possession of the road; but the law also makes them liable in some circumstances to anyone who suffers loss or damage as a result of an accident. In other respects too the law focuses not on the owner of land as such but on the occupier of it*.

1-45

*See for example 10-6.

Licences

Any owner of land can grant permission for others to use it. The law views this as a purely personal matter, between the people concerned, which does not usually give rise to any permanent legal rights. Permission is known legally as a "licence".

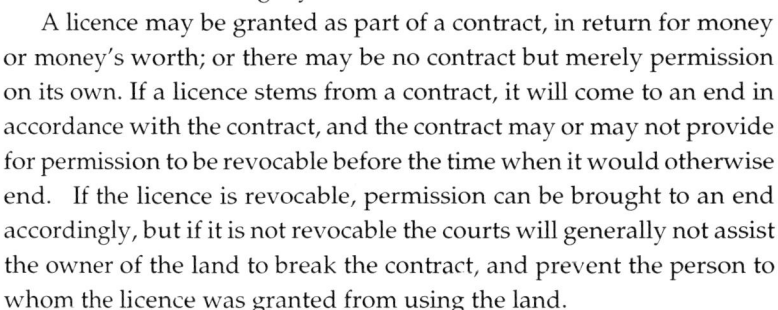

1-46

A licence may be granted as part of a contract, in return for money or money's worth; or there may be no contract but merely permission on its own. If a licence stems from a contract, it will come to an end in accordance with the contract, and the contract may or may not provide for permission to be revocable before the time when it would otherwise end. If the licence is revocable, permission can be brought to an end accordingly, but if it is not revocable the courts will generally not assist the owner of the land to break the contract, and prevent the person to whom the licence was granted from using the land.

1-47

In the absence of a contract, a licence can in principle be ended at any time by the owner of the land. However the courts have power to intervene in certain circumstances, in order to prevent obvious

1-48

for more information see www.barsby.com

unfairness; and this rule applies to (among other things) the termination of licences. Where a resident of a private road had enjoyed the freedom to park in the road for a long time, the courts might insist on notice being given before the licence were terminated. The owner of a private road cannot necessarily, therefore, bring permission to park (or any other sort of licence) to an immediate end if, in granting permission, he has not reserved the right to do this.

Civil and criminal courts

1-49　In England and Wales, civil disputes are dealt with in the County Court or (where the value involved is high) the High Court. Less serious criminal cases are deal with in magistrates' courts, and more serious ones in the Crown Court. Most of the criminal offences mentioned in this text are in the former category (though some can be dealt with in either court) and are usually punishable by a fine.

1-50　The maximum fine which can be imposed in magistrates' courts for a given offence is usually expressed as being a stated "level", the levels being:

Table 1: maximum levels of fines

Level	Maximum
1	£200
2	£500
3	£1,000
4	£2,500
5	£5,000

Administrative law

1-51　Central and local government, and many other public bodies, are subject to the requirements of administrative law. When they take action, and in particular when they exercise the powers they have been given by legislation, they must do so in a way which is rational and reasonable. If they fail to do so, their decisions may be challenged. A challenge may be mounted by bringing proceedings for judicial review in the Administrative Court, which forms part of the High Court.

Conventions

As in previous editions of this book, a number of conventions have been adopted in order to avoid complicating the text unnecessarily. References are to "the local authority" generally, without distinguishing which part of local government is involved. In any given case, enquiries will reveal which body is responsible.

Functions and powers of central government, including the power to make delegated legislation[14], are referred to as though belonging to the relevant government department; though in fact they are usually conferred on the appropriate government minister.

Since the Government of Wales Act 1998, the power to make delegated legislation now rests with the Welsh Assembly. Delegated legislation is thus made separately for England and for Wales. "(England)" may appear in the title, signifying that delegated legislation applies to England, and that a separate piece of delegated legislation, either in the same or different terms, may be made for Wales. This book refers only to English delegated legislation.

Government departments and other public bodies are referred to in the text by their initials, and these include:

Table 2: public bodies

Initials	Body
ODPM	Office of the Deputy Prime Minister (responsible for planning, local government and other matters)
DEFRA	Department of the Environment, Food and Rural Affairs
DfT	Department for Transport

---

14. Also known as statutory instruments, these are "Rules", "Regulations", "Orders", and other pieces of legislation which are made under the authority of an Act of Parliament, usually by the government department responsible for that area of the law. Delegated legislation fills out the details, and performs other tasks such as bringing the Act into force, often in separate stages.

Table 2: public bodies

Initials	Body
DTI	Department of Trade and Industry
OFGEM	Office of the Gas and Electricity Markets
OFWAT	Office of Water Services
OFTEL	Office of Telecommunications

How to use the book

1-56   Lawyers' books tend to deal with legal subjects. Thus there are legal textbooks on real property law (i.e. land law), planning, and so on. This book is intended to be a practical guide to the law, and it contains a mixture of legal subjects, including land law, planning, criminal and civil law and public law, explained in a way relevant to private roads.

1-57   Its arrangement, however, is essentially according to legal subject matter rather than some other scheme. The law on trees, for example, is not dealt with all in one chapter, but in different chapters, since different areas of the law are involved. While chapter 8, on planning law, deals with tree preservation orders, liability for falling trees is dealt with in chapter 6 on civil liability, and the powers which local authorities have in relation to trees are described in chapter 9.

1-58   For this reason, the answer to any particular legal question is unlikely to be found on a single page. Rather, it will be necessary to consider and apply what is said at a number of different points. The Appendix, which contains some sample questions and answers, will serve to illustrate how different parts of the book impact on a given question. The Index and the Table of Contents, together with the marginal cross-references, should enable users to locate the relevant passages.

How to use the website

1-59   While the book is complete in itself, additional material will be found on the Internet, in "Notes and Queries" pages which are cross-referenced to the printed text. These:

- Update the text, when changes in the law occur.

- Provide links to others sites containing information about the law.

- Clarify and expand the printed text, often in response to users of the book who wish to know more about a particular point.

To find the Notes and Queries pages for the book, go to www.barsby.com and click on the Notes and Queries icon underneath *Private Roads: The Legal Framework.* Click on a chapter heading to see the Notes and Queries pages for that chapter or alternatively use the Index, which has hypertext links back to the relevant page. Requests for additions to the Notes and Queries pages can be made by e-mail, to mail@barsby.com, by letter, or telephone.

1-60

Topics not included

Some topics have been regarded as outside the scope of this book. Nothing has been said about conveyancing in relation to private roads, or about the process of litigation. In both cases, if the issue arises, professional assistance is likely to be needed. The compulsory purchase of land is not covered in detail (though it is mentioned in passing in several places). Nor does the book go into questions of taxation, since the tax implications of transactions involving a private road will depend upon the circumstances.

1-61

More generally, the text disregards some parts of the law which seem unlikely to apply to private roads. There is thus no mention in chapter 3, which deals with rights of way and other easements, of the possibility of ancient rights of way existing by custom.

1-62

Chapter 2: ownership

Introduction

2-0 This chapter considers the question of ownership of private roads, and related issues such as how residents may acquire ownership, and how they may register title.

Ownership generally

2-1 Private roads are land, and can be owned, and dealt with and subjected to rights, like other pieces of land. Private roads, or parts of them, can be owned by private individuals, or companies or other bodies*, who may or may not be frontagers or use the road for access.

*See chapter 12 for special rules on the ownership of property by associations and other bodies.

2-2 Like other land, private roads can be sold, or be transferred as part of a person's estate. In practice, some sorts of transaction are likely to be rare—for example, a lease or mortgage of a private road—but there is no legal reason why a private road should not be mortgaged or leased. Other sorts of right will be common; in particular, private rights of way*, and the rights of utility companies to install and maintain pipes, cables and other equipment under and over the road*.

*See chapter 4.
*See chapter 10 on services.

2-3 In any event, the owner of the road is entitled, as owner, to use the road for access or put it to any other use she wishes, subject only to the planning permission and other forms of official regulation, and to the need not to interfere with the right of others. And the owner of land can always grant permission for the land to be used by another, this sort of informal and usually temporary arrangement being known as a licence*. If the owner of neighbouring land needs access via a private road on a temporary basis, permission can be granted by the owner for this without any legal formality.

*See 1-46.

History of ownership

2-4 Private roads can originate in many different ways. But this book is concerned mainly with roads which are used for shared access; and such roads will tend to arise in two main ways:

- The road was constructed in order to provide access to a specific point, or occasionally perhaps as a convenient through-road, and development has since taken place along the road, so that the road has come to be used for access by all those with houses in the road.

- The road was constructed at the same time as the development (or some of it) and so has been from the outset a shared access for houses in the road.

In the first case, the road when constructed will naturally tend to have been in the same ownership as the surrounding land. In the second (and probably more common) case, the road is likely to have been formed from a parcel of land acquired by a developer.

In either case, there will often be no particular reason for the road to change hands, and it may thus simply remain in the same ownership. Indeed, a developer might, for various reasons, wish to retain ownership of the road, for example:

- He had sold the houses in the road on a leasehold basis, so retains an interest in the houses, and hence in the road[1].

- He had retained some land, which he might wish to develop later, and ownership of the road will allow him unfettered access to it.

In some cases, mere inertia may have been the reason why the developer retained ownership of the road, rather than transferring it to residents individually or collectively, inertia being encouraged by the fact that the road itself was considered to have little or no value, and that ownership was unimportant to residents, whose rights of way would allow them access whoever the owner was.

If action has been taken to transfer the ownership of a private road away from the original owner, it may have been transferred to one or more residents individually or collectively, or to some other person[2]. But in practice it is common to find both that there has been no transfer of ownership and that, with the passage of time, the original owner has lost interest in the road and residents in the road have lost contact with he owner. In a few cases it may that the owner can be traced, but has no wish to exercise any rights of ownership over the road.

---

1. Until the early part of the 20th century, land was often sold for development on the basis of a "building lease" of 99 years, the period being chosen to avoid the higher rate of stamp duty for leases of 100 years and more.   a
2. Including in some cases a later developer wishing to carry out development in the road

Presumption of ownership

2-9 The law provides a number of presumptions which can be used by the courts to reach a conclusion on the facts where there is no evidence one way or the other. One of these relates to roads. The presumption is that the road was formed by adjoining landowners, who each agreed to contribute a strip of land along the boundary between them, to form a road which would then give access to the land on either side; and that, as a result, each frontager owns half the width of the road along her frontage.

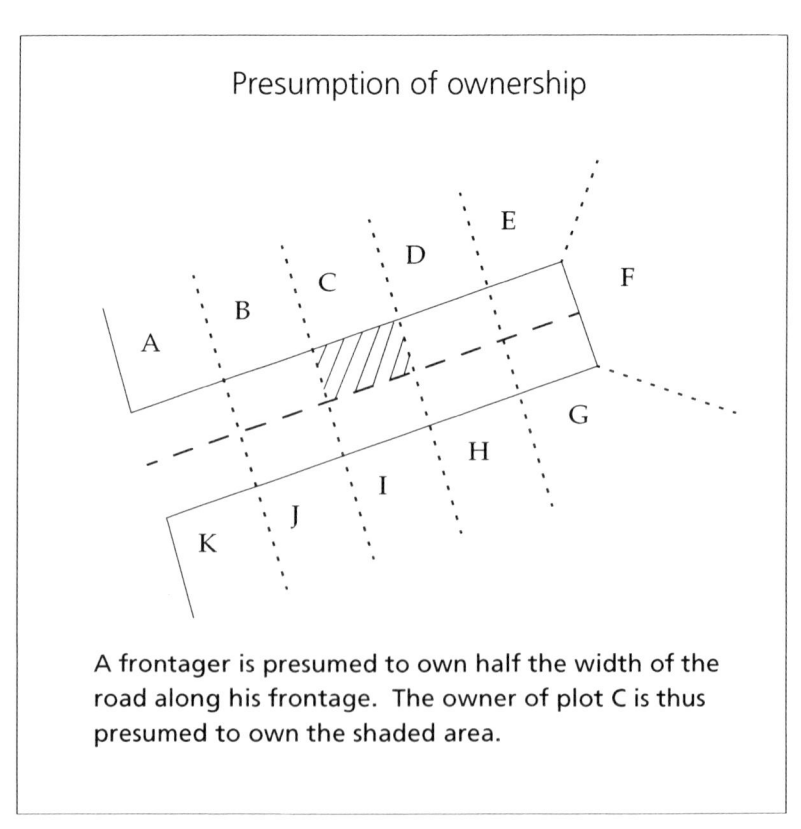

Presumption of ownership

A frontager is presumed to own half the width of the road along his frontage. The owner of plot C is thus presumed to own the shaded area.

2-10 This rule applies to private roads whether or not they are highways[3]. It is, however, only a rule of evidence, and can be applied only if no evidence is put forward which contradicts it[4]. This may in turn depend upon whether a person who owns or has some other interest in the road wishes to come forward and assert his rights.

2-11 One point with which the presumption does not deal in a satisfactory way is the rights of a property owner at the end of a cul-de-

---

3. See *Holmes v Bellingham* (1859) 7 CB (NS) 329.
4. See *Pardoe v Pennington* (1993) 73 P&CR 26.

sac (F in the above diagram) who it seems cannot claim to own any part of the road because, according to the presumption, the part he would claim belongs to E and G.

Adverse possession

Background As a matter of policy, the right to start proceedings to put right legal wrongs does not last indefinitely. The reason is that, if there were no time limit, the law would become very uncertain: a person might, for example, buy property only to find that his ownership was challenged because of some error made generations ago.

The present law For land, the limitation period—the period within which legal action can be taken to evict someone who has taken over the land, and to regain possession—is generally 12 years[5], this being laid down by the Limitation Act 1980. Once this period has expired, the law will no longer help the true owner of the land, but will protect the person who is in adverse possession of it*. The latter is in effect the new owner, and will be able to register title to it on the Land Register*.

*See 1-43 onwards.

*See 2-30 onwards on registration of title.

The rule is a general one, but in practice applies in three rather different sorts of case:

- Where a person goes into possession of a building and excludes others from it, typically by changing the locks.

- Where a person fences off land, and excludes others from it.

- Where a person takes over the maintenance of a boundary marker such as a wall or hedge and treats it as his own[6].

A key question is what action is needed on the part of the person who goes into adverse possession of land, in order to be able to rely on this rule. The law has now been reviewed by the House of Lords in *JA Pye v Graham*[7]. Here the land in dispute was some valuable farmland. The House of Lord confirmed (among other points) that to be in adverse possession a person need not intend to acquire ownership: it is enough that he intended to possess the land. Merely looking after

---

5. Though it is generally 30 years for Crown land.
6. See *Prudential Assurance v Waterloo Real Estate* (1999) 17 EG 131.
7. [2002] 3 WLR 221.

land, however, will not usually amount to a sufficient degree of possession.

2-16 It is also the law that a written and signed acknowledgement of the rights of the true owner will prevent a person claiming title by adverse possession. If, for example, X is in adverse possession, but writes a letter to Y admitting that Y is the true owner of the land, X cannot obtain title by adverse possession (Limitation Act 1980, s. 29(1)).

2-17 Can adverse possession apply to private roads? In some circumstances it can: if a frontager extends his boundary, and fences off part of a private road, excluding others from it, then after 12 years the true owner of the road will no longer be able to re-assert his right to, and the frontager will have obtained a right to the land. The same is true of other situations in which landowners move a fence, or otherwise extend their boundaries so as to take in neighbouring land[8].

2-18 It is very doubtful, however, whether the whole of private road can be acquired by adverse possession. In *Simpson v Fergus*[9] the Court of Appeal was asked to consider a claim to part of a private road. The claimant had marked out parking places in the road, and stopped others using them, but had not actually fenced them off—this would have been impossible in the circumstances. The court was not impressed by the argument that the claimant had done all he could to possess the road, and did not accept that the claimant had acquired title to the road by adverse possession. It is thus unlikely that an application to the Land Registry to register ownership of a private road on the basis of adverse possession would succeed.

2-19 *Changes to the law* While the rule known as adverse possession has a sound logical basis, it is at odds with the thinking behind land registration, which is that the Land Register should be conclusive as to who owns land[*]. The Land Registration Act 2002 accordingly makes some changes to the law designed to reduce the circumstances in which a person may acquire title to land by adverse possession. The law is set out in s. 15 of and Schedule 6 to the Land Registration Act 2002. These new provisions are *not in force* at the time of writing, since this part of the Act has not been commenced. The changes are summarised in the following paragraphs. When in force, they will apply to land which is already registered: if land is not registered, the old law applies as before.

2-20 The meaning of adverse possession is not changed by the new law; but instead of the 12-year period in the Limitation Act 1980 there are new rules. A person who has been in adverse possession of land for 10 years can apply to the Land Registry to be registered as the owner

[*]See 2-30 onwards.

---

8. See *London Borough of Hounslow v Minchinton* (1997) 74 P&CR 221.
9. (1999) 79 P & CR 398

(Sched. 6, para. 1). (If he has been evicted, after 10 years' adverse possession, he must apply within 6 months.)

Once an application has been made, the registered owner of the land must be informed; and she can require that the application be dealt with under paragraph 5 of Schedule 6. This means that the person applying can only succeed if the application falls within one of three very limited categories. Of these the most important is that the land in question is adjacent to land owned by the person applying, and that he has reasonably believed for at least 10 years that the land is his.

Many cases falling within paragraph 5 will be cases in which the land in dispute is merely a narrow strip along the boundary, there being a dispute about where the boundary lies. (But it may be difficult for a person who has moved a fence or other boundary marker to show that he reasonably believed the land was his.) In some cases the area may be larger, and the person applying may nonetheless be able to claim that he has reasonably believed, for at least 10 years, that the land is his.

If the true owner does *not* require that the application be dealt with under paragraph 5, the person applying is entitled to be registered as the new owner of the land. If the true owner successfully opposes an application but does not follow it up by evicting the person in adverse possession, the latter is entitled, after a further two years, to make another application, and this time will be entitled to succeed (Sched. 6, para. 6).

To summarise the law which will apply when the relevant provisions of the Land Registration Act 2002 are in force:

- If land is unregistered, the old law continues to apply.

- If land is registered, and title to it has been established by adverse possession before the relevant parts of the Land Registration Act 2002 are brought into effect, the person in adverse possession has a right to be registered as the owner[10].

- If a person completes 10 years of adverse possession after the start of these provisions, the rules described above apply.

---

10. Meanwhile the land is deemed to be held on trust for him by the person currently registered as owner (Land Registration Act 1925, s. 75(2)).

What land is included in a road?

2-25 The boundaries of a private road will tend to be determined by the boundaries of adjoining property, which will usually have some sort of fence or other boundary marker. Besides the roadway itself, grass verges, pavements and other odd areas of land may be included.

2-26 Frontagers may sometimes encroach on the road, particularly by extending their boundaries so as to include part of a grass verge, and so acquire title by adverse possession, if the land belongs to someone else*. A modest boundary marker, such as low chain-and-post fence may be sufficient for this purpose if it is effective in excluding others from the land. But merely maintaining a grass verge, by mowing the grass and keeping it tidy, will not generally be enough to constitute adverse possession of the land, and so will not allow the frontager to claim that the land is his.

*See 2-12.

2-27 Things attached to the land, such as buildings, trees, shrubs etc, are regarded as forming part of the land. But as an exception to this rule, pipes, cables, and other equipment installed by the utility companies will remain their property. They have special powers enabling them to do this, and to come on to land to maintain their equipment*.

*See chapter 10.

2-28 By contrast, where a road is a highway maintainable at the public expense, there is a presumption that all the land between the boundary markers of adjoining property forms part of the road, and so includes verges, pavements, and other odd areas of land[11]. But this is only a presumption: there may be cases in which a frontager can show that she owns part of the verge[12].

2-29 Ownership of a highway maintainable at the public expense does not include the full depth of the land, but only the top layer or "top two spits", including the surface and a sufficient depth to accommodate the usual pipes and cables.

Land registration

2-30 *The system of land registration* Most land in England and Wales is now registered. Legislation has made it a requirement that land be registered on the occurrence of specified transactions, and the types of transactions triggering the requirement have been increased over the years. Nonetheless, some land remains unregistered, either because it has stayed in the same ownership over a long period, so that the

---

11. *Attorney General v Beynon* [1965] Ch 1.
12. See *Hale v Norfolk County Council, The Times* 19 December 2000.

requirement to register has never been triggered, or because the owner is unknown.

2-31 A private road can be registered like any other land. A road could be the subject of a registered title on its own, if the whole road is owned by one or more individuals or a body such as a company. Different parts of the road might be owned by different people, and thus the subject of different titles. If a frontager owned the part of the road along his frontage, the land as a whole might be shown as one title. As one would expect, pieces of adjoining land can be amalgamated into a single title; and land included in one title can be split into different titles. These processes are carried out by the Land Registry on request.

2-32 If land is owned by a trust, or by an unincorporated association, special rules may apply to the way in which land is shown on the Land Register*.

*See 12-14 and 12-36.

2-33 The underlying principle of land registration is that the Land Register can be relied on to show who is the owner of land and rights over land. Section 5 of the Land Registration Act 1925 thus provides that when a person is shown on the Land Register as owner, they are legally the owner. However, this rule cannot be absolute, and the legislation makes provision for the Land Register to be rectified (i. e. corrected) in certain tightly-controlled circumstances, including fraud (s. 82)[13].

2-34 *Electronic conveyancing* The Land Registration Act 2002 provides the legal basis for an electronic system of land transfer. This will take some years to implement.

2-35 *Registering title to a private road* Since the ownership of a private road is often unknown, residents may wish to take steps to claim and register title. As noted above, an application based on adverse possession is not likely to succeed*. But other options are available:

*See 2-18.

- It may be possible to trace the owner, who may in some cases be a descendant of the original developer of the road, and buy the land from him—at which point there will be a requirement to register title.

- It may be possible to show that the road is *bona vacantia* and has passed to the Crown, because it belonged to a person who has died intestate and without heirs, or to a dissolved company, and to acquire the road from the Crown*.

*See 2-44.

---

13. The Land Register can also be rectified, under the Land Registration Rules 1925, to put right clerical errors.

for more information see www.barsby.com

• It may be possible for the frontagers (or most of them) to rely on the presumption of ownership, and to make a joint application to the Land Registry for the road (or most of it) to be registered in the name of a company or residents association.

2-36 The last option will often be available if the others are not. It may be possible for the majority of frontagers to combine and to register title to most of the road, if not all residents are willing to participate. The Land Registry will generally be supportive and helpful if the original owner of the road is unknown and an application is made based on the presumption of ownership. The appropriate District Land Registry should be approached at an early stage for guidance on how such an application should be made and how it will be handled. Enquiries may have to be made, to see whether the true owner can be found, and if so whether he wishes to oppose the application by the frontagers.

2-37 Subject to that, if the application proceeds and the frontagers obtain registration, it is likely that the former owner will not be able to complain, though may be entitled to be paid compensation.

2-38 *Contents of the Land Register* Besides showing the owner of the land, the Land Register may also show rights affecting land, both in relation to the land which has the benefit of a right and the land which is subject to it. Some rights are "overriding", meaning that they are legally valid even if not shown on the Land Register, and this category includes private rights of way and other easements, as well as the public's right to use a highway*. Such rights may be shown on the Land Register as a matter of convenience; but the absence of an entry does not mean that the land is free of such rights[14].

*See chapter 4 for private rights of way and chapter 3 for highways.

2-39 Other rights depend for their legal validity on being shown on the Land Register, and this includes restrictive covenants*.

*See further 6-44 onwards.

2-40 A "restriction" may be entered on the Land Register to show that the land cannot be disposed of unless certain conditions have been met. And a "caution" may be entered by a person concerned that a disposition of the land may prejudice their rights, as a warning to any person who acquires the land. Entering a caution on the Land Register is a hostile action; whereas entering a restriction is usually non-controversial.

2-41 *Searching the Land Register* The Land Register is open to public inspection, and can be searched by anyone wishing to find out whether a particular piece of land is registered and if so who the owner is and what rights are shown to exist over it.

---

14. The law will be changed by the Land Registration Act 2002, which will restrict the categories of overriding rights.

2-42 The Land Register can be searched by applying by post to the relevant District Land Registry, on the Land Registry's form 96. This process establishes whether land is shown on the "Index Map" as being registered. If it is, form 109 can be used to apply for an "office copy" of the entries on the Land Register, and the "filed plan", showing the land in question. Charges are payable for these searches.

2-43 *Other registers* If land itself is unregistered, certain rights over it may require to be registered in the Land Charges Register, which is a separate register kept by the Land Registry. And, whether or not the land itself is registered land, some rights over it—typically, rights over land which arise under an Act, including tree preservation orders and payments due to the local authority—fall to be registered under the Local Land Charges Act 1972*.

*See also 1-38 for the register of common land.

Bona vacantia

2-44 It is a rule of law that property without an owner—*bona vacantia* is the Latin term—passes to the Crown in certain circumstances. For these purposes the Treasury Solicitor's Department[15] acts for the Crown. This is the case where a person dies without making a will and without relatives who can inherit his property (Administration of Estates Act 1925, s. 46(1)), and also where a company is dissolved and where no members (shareholders or guarantors*) assert a claim to its property. Here the law is to be found in s. 656 of the Companies Act 1985.

*See 12-19 onwards for companies.

2-45 Property which is onerous, i.e. subject to rights or obligations which outweigh its value, can be disclaimed by the Treasury Solicitor's Department, in which case it does not pass to the Crown. Property which is not disclaimed is generally sold. Discretionary payments may sometimes be made to a person who might have benefited under a will if the deceased person had made one; otherwise, money raised goes into the public purse.

2-46 It may thus be possible to show that a private road has passed into Crown ownership, because it belonged to a person who died intestate without heirs, or belonged to company which has been dissolved, and the Treasury Solicitor may be asked to sell the road to residents collectively.

2-47 In many cases, however, it will not be possible to show that a private road whose ownership is unknown has become *bona vacantia*, and this route to acquisition will not be open. But it may be possible to

---

15. Except in the Duchies of Lancaster and Cornwall, where private solicitors, Farrer & Co, act on behalf of the Crown.

register ownership on the basis of the presumption of ownership by frontagers*.

*See 2-9 onwards.

Absence of an owner

2-48 If the ownership of a private road is unknown, residents individually or collectively may wish to exercise control over the road, arranging for any work which needs to be done, such as resurfacing or tree surgery, and regulating the use of the road, for example, its use for parking by residents and non-residents.

2-49 Some of these activities may constitute a trespass or other interference with the rights of:

- The true owner, if they should ever appear; or

- Frontagers, if they wished to rely on the presumption of ownership.

2-50 Residents collectively can address the latter problem by making sure that they act only with the agreement of any frontagers affected, Generally, if they proceed to exercise control over the road, the law will give them a degree of protection, but will also impose responsibilities on them*.

*See 1-43 onwards.

2-51 A rather different situation is where the owner is known, but does not wish to assert his rights—perhaps because he is a remote descendant of the original developer, and has thus inherited the road among other property, but has no interest in or connection with the road. In this situation it may not be possible for frontagers to rely on the presumption of ownership, and a residents' association will be concerned only with the possibility that the true owner, or someone claiming title through him or her, will appear to re-assert ownership.

Assessment

2-52 It will be best for residents collectively, if they can, to acquire and register title to the road, since this strengthens their position both legally and in practice and removes the possibility that some other person may assert ownership.

© A. W. & C. Barsby 2003

2-53 Once the road is registered, rights over it can be shown on the Land Register and the position in relation to rights of way can thus be clarified and made public.

2-54 Even if residents collectively cannot acquire title to the road, they may still assert rights to it; but they will need to be aware of, and to respect, the rights of others over the road, including the presumptive ownership of parts of the road by frontagers*.

2-55 A residents association or management company should be aware of the extent of land which they manage and/or own, and whether this includes verges and other odd areas of land.

*For a fuller consideration of this area, see chapter 12.

Chapter 3: Highways

Introduction

*See 1-6.

*But see also chapter 9 for offences relating to highways.

3-0 A private road can be a highway, or in other words subject to a public right of way (though not, by definition, a highway maintainable at the public expense*) and highway law is thus of importance to many private roads. This chapter deals generally with highways, including their nature, creation and termination ("stopping up")*. Chapter 11 deals separately with Part XI of the Highways Act 1980, a specialised group of provisions concerned with the "making up and adoption" of private roads, i.e. bringing them up to a standard acceptable to the local authority, and then converting them into highways maintainable at the public expense so that they become the local authority's responsibility.

*See 3-49 onwards.

3-1 The chapter also explains the "definitive map and statement" procedure, by which local authorities must record footpaths and other public rights of way which, because they often run across country, are at risk of being lost or obstructed. Roads which became highways before 1836 are necessarily highways maintainable at the public expense, but for other classes of highway the history of the law has been different*.

3-2 Much of the law is contained in the Highways Act 1980, though the common law is also relevant to the creation of highways. In some circumstances the owner of the land can prevent public rights of way from being created. Once a highway has been created, however, the owner of the land has no power to reverse the process himself; this can only be done by means of statutory powers which are in the hands of local and central government. Unless and until such a power is exercised, the highway will continue to exist—the rule is said to be "once a highway always a highway".

Classes of highway

3-3 There are essentially three classes of highway, which differ according to the traffic which may use them:

© A. W. & C. Barsby 2003

- Carriageways* (public rights of way for vehicles, horses, pedestrians and cyclists).

- Bridleways (horses, pedestrians and cyclists[1]).

- Footpaths (pedestrians only)[2].

*See also 3-62 for different types of carriageway.

3-4

The first category includes the second two, and the second includes the third. The typical metalled roads upon which the public drives from place to place are carriageways, and thus open to all classes of traffic. Bridleways and footpaths will also be familiar.

3-5

If a private road becomes a highway (but not one maintainable at the public expense) the public has the right to use it. Ownership, however, is not affected, and responsibility for the highway does not pass to the local authority. The public right of way may be for all the classes of traffic mentioned above, or just some. For example, a private road may be subject to a public footpath, so that the public then has the right to walk along (or, as the case may be, across) the road, but not to drive cars along it. Or part of a private road may be a carriageway. In either case, the public's right of way extends only to the relevant part of the private road*.

*See also 2-28 for ownership of highways maintainable at the public expense.

What land is subject to the public right of way?

3-6

The Highways Act does not answer this question fully, though it provides some assistance, in s. 328, which says that where a highway passes through a tunnel or over a bridge, the tunnel or bridge are to be regarded as part of the highway. Otherwise, the extent of the land subject to the public right of way is a question of fact, related to the way in which the highway has been created. If a defined area of land has been turned into a highway by means of a statutory procedure, the land subject to the right of way will be specified*.

*See 3-35 onwards.

3-7

If, on the other hand, a highway has been created by dedication and acceptance (i.e. use over a period of time*) the physical extent of the highway will depend upon the use which has taken place. Use by pedestrians, for example, may in some circumstances be confined to a

*See further 3-11 onwards.

---

1. The right was added by s. 30 of the Countryside Act 1968. Cyclists must give way to pedestrians and equestrians. Local authorities may make byelaws excluding cyclists from bridleways.
2. These can in some circumstances be used by cyclists under the Cycle Tracks Act 1984.

narrow track; in others it may appear that they have used the full width of a metalled road, and the whole width is therefore subject to the public right of way.

The right to use a highway

3-8 The public's right is essentially a right to "pass and repass"—that is, to go to and fro along the highway. But other, incidental activities, including stopping, are also permitted[3]. A tired pedestrian may thus, for example, sit down and rest by the side of the road, or a motorist may stop to repair a minor breakdown, provided that these activities are reasonably incidental to the right to pass to and fro along the highway[4]. Similarly, vehicles may stop to load and unload.

3-9 The public's right to use a highway is thus quite limited. There is no right to use a highway as, for example, a children's playground, or as a car-park*. Such activities would amount to trespasses, and legal action could be taken by the owner or occupier of the road to obtain compensation and to prevent recurrences. But members of the public do not have to justify their presence: if they wish to use the road to get from one spot to another, they are entitled to do so, whether their journey has a particular object or is merely recreational. The degree of intrusion, and the amount of wear and tear caused to a private road, may be modest if the road is little used. Equally, if the road is well-used by the public it may be considerable. The owner of the road cannot obtain compensation for its lawful use by the public.

*See chapter 5 for parking generally.

3-10 A resident in a private road which is a highway is entitled to make use of the public right of way in order to obtain access to her property*. He may do so at any point along the frontage of his property, though this would probably not entitle a resident to replace a section of grass verge with a crossover (i.e. a short metalled section crossing the verge) without obtaining the permission of the owner of the road.

*But see also 8-15 on planning implications.

Dedication and acceptance

*See also 1-3.

3-11 Dedication and acceptance* is governed mainly by the common law, rather than statute, though the Highways Act 1980 modifies the old

---

3. See *Director of Public Prosecutions v Jones* [1999] 2 WLR 65.
4. See *Hubbard v Pitt* [1975] 3 WLR 201, [1975] 3 All ER 1.

common law rules. Highways have been created by dedication and acceptance for centuries, and may still be so created today.

The process of dedication and acceptance applies to all classes of highway, so that (for example) use by cars or other vehicles[5] will create a carriageway, which pedestrians and other classes of traffic will then be entitled to use. While the principle may sound straightforward, it is in practice more complex since the law applies presumptions about the behaviour of the owner of the land (only the owner of the land can dedicate the land as a highway) and use by the public.

If a landowner makes clear that he wishes a road or path to become a highway, whether by putting up a notice to that effect, or advertising, or any other means, his intention can hardly be in doubt. Such a case, however, is likely to be rare, not least because there are now statutory procedures by which highways can be created*. Any express statement of the landowner's wishes is thus likely to be to the effect that he does *not* intend the land to become a highway. Notices to this effect can be found in cities, often in relation to forecourts, passages or other small areas of land to which pedestrians are allowed access. Signs are often put up at the entrances to private roads for the same purpose.

*See 3-35 onwards.

Often, however, the position may be that the owner of the land has not made his intentions clear, and there is no clear indication of whether he does or does not wish to dedicate the way as a highway, but the way is open to the public and some use by the public has taken place. What construction should be put upon the situation? In these circumstances, the law starts from a different point, and looks at the use which has taken place to see whether it justifies drawing the inference that the owner has intended to dedicate the land.

If it is to give rise to a public right of way, use by the public must be open, as of right, and without interruption. "As of right" means that members of the public must have used the road or path as though they had the right to do so. This will generally be so if the owner has merely tolerated it, and done and said nothing. But if the owner has done or said something to imply that she is giving permission, the use will not be as of right[6], and use by the public will not lead to the creation of a highway.

There is no definition of what constitutes "the public" for these purposes. The requirement is probably that there has been use by a reasonable number of members of the public at large.

Use which is contrary to the criminal law cannot give rise to a public right of way[7]. This is particularly significant in relation to

---

5. Including horse-drawn vehicles.
6. See *R (on the application of Beresford) v Sunderland City Council* [2001] EWCA Civ 1218, [2002] 2 WLR 693.

*See 7-22 onwards.

motorised traffic, since driving over land without permission or other lawful authority has been an offence, under successive Road Traffic Acts, since 1930*. Driving over land will thus in many cases prove to have been criminal, and so incapable of creating a carriageway.

3-18 The use must continue for a certain length of time in order for the inference to arise that the owner intends to dedicate the way as a highway. The common law does not lay down a fixed minimum period. In the case where a landowner positively intends to dedicate a way as a highway, and expressly says so, a modest period, perhaps as short as a few months, might suffice[8]. A relatively short time might also suffice if there were other evidence suggesting an intention to dedicate the way as a highway—in past cases which have come before the courts, periods as short as 18 months have been found sufficient. More usually a number of years' use is required.

3-19 The common law rule has been modified, in that s. 31(1) of the Highways Act now provides that after 20 years' use as of right and without interruption the land is deemed to have been dedicated, unless there is evidence that there was no intention, on the part of the owner, to dedicate the land. The period of 20 years must be measured backwards from the date when the public's right is challenged (s. 31(2)). This means that s. 31(1) has no relevance in considering whether use which has ceased in the past has led to the creation of a highway: this must be determined by the common law rules alone.

3-20 If a landowner's actions demonstrate that he has no intention of dedicating a road or path as a highway, the fact that use by the public has actually taken place is irrelevant. However, once 20 years' use by the public has occurred, and is continuing, then it is for the landowner to prove that he had no intention of dedicating the road or path as a highway; whereas, before 20 years have elapsed, proof of intention rests with whoever is seeking to show that there *is* a highway. The change introduced by s. 31 of the Highways Act is thus a limited but significant one. In practice, 20 years is likely to be regarded by the courts as a sufficient period of use in order to establish a public right of way where there is no specific evidence of an intention on the part of the owner to dedicate a way as a highway; and the courts may be prepared in some circumstances to accept less.

---

7. See *Robinson v Adair*, The Times 2 March 1995, in which use by vehicles was criminal because of s. 34 of the Road Traffic Act 1988.
8. In *Secretary of State for the Environment, Transport and the Regions v Baylis (Gloucester) Ltd.*, The Times 16 May 2000 the court considered that an agreement with the local authority could amount to acceptance on behalf of the public, so that the process of dedication and acceptance could take place very rapidly.

Evidence of use by the public

3-21 In establishing whether sufficient public use has actually taken place, the Highways Act provides that a court or other tribunal must give appropriate weight to "any map, plan or history of the locality or other relevant document which is tendered in evidence" (s. 32)[9]. (This is a general rule—it is not restricted to the circumstances in which s. 31 applies.)

3-22 Apart from the maps and other documents, it may be possible to rely on the word of someone who has known the road or path over a period of many years, and seen the public use it. But if there is no such first-hand evidence, it may still be possible to draw inferences about likely use from the nature of the road or path, or to rely on presumptions which the law makes about use. In practice, this may be the only way in which the necessary use can be established.

3-23 Where a private road is a through-road, joining two highways, there will be a presumption of dedication as a highway: the law presumes, unless evidence to the contrary is produced, that the public have used the way to pass between the two existing highways, and the private road may thus become a highway too. The presumption is rebuttable—in other words, it does not apply if there is evidence to show that the contrary is true[*].

*See 3-27.

3-24 The presumption does not apply to a cul-de-sac. In many cases there will be nothing in the cul-de-sac to attract the public generally, and therefore no reason to suppose that the cul-de-sac has become a highway. Exceptionally, however, there may be a shop, public house or church or some other facility which the public can be assumed to have visited, and there may thus be evidence of sufficient use to create a highway. Because of the "once a highway always a highway" rule, it is possible that a cul-de-sac had in the past some building such as a shop or public house which no longer exists but which attracted the public, and so led to the creation of a highway. A private road may be a dead-end for vehicles, but a through-route for pedestrians. In such a case, use by the public might well establish a footpath.

3-25 Generally, the question of whether there has been sufficient use by the public over the years will tend to be a matter of common sense. If there is a reason for the public to use the road, either to pass from one public road to another, or to reach some specific point, the right conclusion is likely to be that the necessary use by the public has taken place and the road has become a highway through the process of dedication and acceptance. The history of the road may also shed some

---

9. See *Robinson Webster (Holdings) Ltd v Agombar* [2002] 1 P&CR 20, in which the court took into account maps and other evidence in concluding that a road was a highway.

light on the matter. For example, if new houses have been added over the years, the fact that fresh private rights of way were granted for them will tend to show that the road was not at the time regarded as a highway.

*See 1-27.

3-26 The list kept by a local authority under s. 36(6) of the Highways Act 1980* must show all highways in that area which are maintainable at the public expense. There is no obligation to list roads which are highways but which are *not* maintainable at the public expense*. Local authorities may do so, for the sake of completeness; but if they do keep such a list, it will not have any particular significance as evidence of the status of the road.

*But see 3-49 onwards for the definitive map and statement, which applies to all cross-country highways.

Preventing dedication and acceptance

3-27 If the public use a private road, the owner of the road can take action in several different ways to prevent the road becoming a highway through the process of dedication and acceptance. These consist either of interrupting use by the public, or making clear that there is no intention to dedicate.

3-28 The first and perhaps most obvious method is for the owner of the road to put up a notice indicating that the road is not for use by the public, thus demonstrating that there is no intention to dedicate it to the public—indeed, that the reverse is the case. This method has received recognition in s. 31(3) of the Highways Act 1980, which says that the notice has to be "inconsistent with the dedication of the way as a highway". No particular words are laid down in the Act for achieving this result. It may be that a notice which merely says "private", or "private road" will not be enough, since the fact that a road is private is arguably not inconsistent with an intention of dedicating it as a public highway. On the other hand, such phrases as "no highway", "no public access", "residents only", or, perhaps most clearly of all, "this road is not dedicated to the public", make it clear that the public is not intended to use the road. The Highways Act provides that, where a notice of this sort has been put up, it is sufficient evidence, in the absence of proof of a contrary intention, to negative the intention of dedicating a road as a highway.

3-29 Provision is made in s. 31(5) of the Highways Act for situations in which a notice is put up but is subsequently torn down or defaced: the owner of the road can then give notice to the local authority that the way is not dedicated. The giving of such notice is, similarly, sufficient evidence of an intention not to dedicate.

© A. W. & C. Barsby 2003

While a notice is sufficient in itself, it is also possible to rely on closing the road, by means of a barrier or gate of some kind. The existence of a barrier or gate may be significant, even when not closed, as some indication that the road may at times be closed, and hence that there is an intention not to dedicate the road as a highway. But the main point of a gate is to interrupt use by the public, so that no inference of an intention to dedicate can be drawn. The gate should therefore be closed, and preferably locked, for one day a year; for the rest of the year it can stand open.

3-30

Under s. 31(5) of the Highways Act, the owner of land may deposit with the local authority a large-scale map (at least 6 inches to the mile) and a statement setting out what if any public rights of way the owner of the road admits exist over the land. This procedure may be intended for use mainly by the owners of farms and other large areas of land, but it could equally be used by the owner of a private road. Once the map and statement have been deposited, their effect can be continued by the making of statutory declarations[10], at intervals of not more than 6 years, affirming that no further ways have been dedicated. (A statutory declaration is a formal written statement, made before a commissioner for oaths.) These documents, deposited with the local authority, constitute sufficient evidence to negative an intention of dedicating a highway. Strictly speaking, therefore, they render notices and gates unnecessary; but there is an obvious advantage in retaining one or both of the latter.

3-31

It is also possible that the actions of a landowner will in a general sense make clear that there is no intention to dedicate land for use as a highway[11].

3-32

Granting permission to use a private road can also prevent the road becoming a highway, since it cannot then be said that the public has used the road "as of right". However, the owner of the road should be careful to ensure that permission is given specifically to those who wish to use the road, not to the public at large, and that it is clear that the permission may be withdrawn by the owner. Otherwise it may appear that the owner has the positive intention of dedicating the road to the public as a highway*.

3-33

*See 1-46 onwards on licences.

Once the necessary steps have been taken to establish that the owner has no intention of dedicating the road as a highway, use by the public cannot make the road a highway. Members of the public will be

3-34

---

10. A statutory declaration is a formal declaration, signed in the presence of a solicitor, the making of false statements in the declaration being an offence.
11. See *Jacques v Secretary of State for the Environment, The Independent* 8 June 1994. In this case the owner of an estate had put up fences, and gates which were fitted with padlocks and chains, and there were notices saying "Private woods" and "Private".

trespassing in using the road and the owner can take legal action against them if she wishes, to stop the use and to obtain compensation*.

*See 6-34 onwards on compensation for trespass.

Highways Act procedures: highways generally

3-35 The Highways Act 1980 contains three sections (ss. 30, 37 and 38) under which the owner of land may voluntarily dedicate a road or path as a highway. The road or path *may*, in some circumstances, become a highway maintainable at the public expense, but this does not follow automatically in all cases. These sections apply to all classes of highway—carriageways, footpaths and bridleways. The first two sections are unlikely to apply to established private roads; the third is more significant, since developers do often arrange for roads serving new developments to be adopted by the local authority under this provision, and hence to become maintainable at the public expense. Section 38 is often used in preference to the procedure under Part XI of the Highways Act*.

*See chapter 11.

3-36 *Section 30* Under s. 30 a way may be dedicated by a landowner by agreement with a parish or community council. The council may carry out work itself, under the agreement, to maintain or improve the way, or may contribute to any expenses resulting from the agreement. The section might be used, for example, in situations where a person carries out a development intended for public use, to which access will be gained across private land. The section does not provide for the way to become a highway automatically, though this can be expected to follow in due course, when it is used by the public. The way will *not*, under s. 30, become a highway maintainable at the public expense.

3-37 *Section 37* Unlike s. 30, s. 37 does not depend upon agreement, and may lead to the creation of a highway maintainable at the public expense. Under this procedure the owner of the land gives the local authority at least 3 months' notice of his proposal to dedicate a way as a highway. Once the 3 months have elapsed, he must then obtain a certificate from the local authority confirming that the way has been dedicated in accordance with the notice, and that it has been made up in a satisfactory manner. There is a right of appeal to a magistrates' court if a certificate is refused. After that, if (firstly) the way is kept in a satisfactory state for 12 months, and (secondly) it is actually used by the public, it will become maintainable at the public expense.

3-38 Meanwhile, however, the local authority may, if they think the proposed highway will not be of sufficient use to the public to justify the expense of maintaining it, decline to issue the necessary certificate. The local authority may then apply to a magistrates' court for an order that the proposed highway will not be of sufficient use. An order to this effect from the court will prevent the way becoming a highway maintainable at the public expense. If the local authority declines to issue a certificate but does not apply to the magistrates court, the owner of the land may do so. The court may decide that the local authority should have issued a certificate, in which case the position is as though a certificate had been issued. Then, subject to the two conditions mentioned above, the way becomes maintainable at the public expense.

3-39 This procedure is thought to be little used. The reason may be that the owner of the land runs the risk of finding he has dedicated the way to the public as a highway but has not succeeded in making it maintainable at the public expense, because the local authority (and if appropriate the magistrates' court) do not agree that the way will be of sufficient use to the public to justify maintenance at the public expense.

3-40 *Section 38* Subsection (3) of this section provides that:

"A local highway authority may agree with any person to undertake the maintenance of a way—

(a) which that person is willing and has the necessary power to dedicate as a highway, or

(b) which is to be constructed by that person, or by a highway authority on his behalf, and which he proposes to dedicate as a highway;

and where an agreement is made under this subsection the way to which the agreement relates shall, on such date as may be specified in the agreement, become for the purposes of this Act a highway maintainable at the public expense. "

3-41 The section thus applies to existing roads and to roads which are going to be built. On the date specified in the agreement, the way becomes a highway maintainable at the public expense. Where a person wishes to create a highway for the public, adoption by agreement with the local authority under s. 38[12] will generally be a better course than proceeding under s. 37.

3-42 However, the wording of the section suggests that it does not apply to an existing private road which is already a highway[13] but is not maintainable at the public expense, since it provides that the owner must be willing and able to dedicate the road as a highway.

---

12. An agreement made under s. 38 does not bind subsequent owners of the land unless steps are taken to register it: see *Overseas Investment Services Ltd v. Simcobuild Construction Ltd, The Times*, 21 April 1995, [1995] EGCS 63, (1995) 70 P&CR 322, (1995) 94 LGR 408.

Highways Act procedures: bridleways and footpaths

3-43   There are further provisions in the Highways Act 1980 by which footpaths and bridleways can be created, and these procedures can apply to the creation of footpaths and bridleways which run along or across private roads.

3-44   *Section 25*   Under s. 25 a local authority can enter into agreement with a landowner for the dedication of a footpath or bridleway, the agreement being known as a "public path creation agreement". The agreement can contain terms relating to payment and other matters, and may provide for dedication subject to limitations and conditions. Thus an agreement might be made under which the local authority agreed to bear some or all of the costs of construction and maintenance, and limitations may be imposed on the use of the way—for example, it might be closed at certain times of the year. The local authority must, under s. 25, do all it can to ensure that the footpath or bridleway is dedicated in accordance with the agreement, and it must give notice of the dedication in at least one local newspaper. In contrast to s. 30, the dedication of a way under a public path creation agreement automatically makes the way maintainable at the public expense.

3-45   Unless an agreement under s. 25 provides otherwise, the agreement will not apply to subsequent owners of the land; but once a highway has been created the land will be permanently subject to it.

3-46   *Section 26*   While s. 25 is concerned with agreements, s. 26[14] allows a local authority to make an order creating a footpath or bridleway—a "public path creation order". The local authority must have regard to the benefit to the public or to residents in the area, and also to the effect on the owner of the land, taking into account the compensation which may be payable to the landowner under s. 28. An order under s. 26 must be confirmed by the DEFRA before it takes effect. An order may be subject to conditions or limitations, and where a footpath or bridleway is created under s. 26, it becomes a highway maintainable at the public expense for the purposes of s. 36.

---

13. Though perhaps it would apply to a private road which was subject to a footpath or bridleway, and which the owner was able and willing to dedicate as a carriageway.
14. Supplemented by Schedule 6 to the Highways Act.

Footpaths and bridleways created by dedication and acceptance

3-47 Footpaths and bridleways were not affected by the Highway Act 1835*, so continued to be maintainable at the public expense if created by dedication and acceptance. But ss. 47 and 49[15] of the National Parks and Access to the Countryside Act 1949 applied a similar rule to them, after 16 December 1949, when the Act came into force. As explained above, if created by one of the various statutory procedures, a footpath or bridleway will become a highway maintainable at the public expense; but highways created after that date by dedication and acceptance will not: they will merely be highways. Local authorities are subject to an obligation to make up new footpaths and bridleways, whether created by agreement or by order (s. 27 of the Highways Act 1980). The amount of maintenance required in relation to a footpath or bridleway may be modest, however, and many footpaths and bridleways are left unsurfaced.

*See 1-6.

3-48 In accordance with the general rule for highways maintainable at the public expense, footpaths and bridleways which become maintainable at the public expense belong to the local authority*.

*See generally 1-8.

The definitive map and statement

3-49 Some highways—some footpaths, bridleways and carriageways—run across country and are unsurfaced, and are thus in danger of being lost through disuse or through being obstructed by landowners. Since 1949, legislation has been concerned to safeguard these highways by recording them on a "definitive map and statement". Once they are recorded, the map and statement are conclusive evidence that a highway exists. (But not that a highway not shown does *not* exist.) Unsurfaced roads have proved a particular problem, which the legislation has made successive attempts to address.

3-50 *Generally* Under the National Parks and Access to the Countryside Act 1949[16], local authorities were required to prepare a definitive map and statement for their area, and revise it at five-yearly intervals. Work progressed slowly (and is still by no means complete) but the procedure was simplified by the Countryside Act 1968 and is now set out mainly in the Wildlife and Countryside Act 1981, Part III[17]. The

---

15. These sections have since been repealed.
16. Some protection was given to footpaths and bridleways under the Rights of Way Act 1932.

five-year periods have now been abolished: the map and statement must be kept continuously up to date.

3-51 Section 56(1) of the 1981 Act lays down that the definitive map is conclusive evidence that a highway of a particular class exists, and the statement may add details, which are also conclusive, of the position and width of the highway, and any limitations or conditions as to its use. Although the map and statement are conclusive, new highways can be added, and other amendments can be made in the light of new information*.

*See 3-54.

3-52 The 1949 Act introduced the concept of a "road used as a public path" (RUPP)—a highway other than a path, which was used mainly by pedestrians and equestrians. But this concept was unsatisfactory, since it left unclear the question of what precisely the public rights of way were in a given case, and in particular whether there was a public right of way for vehicles. The 1968 and 1981 Acts therefore required local authorities to reclassify RUPPs, according to the right of way which was found to exist, so that they were either footpaths, bridleways, or "byways open to all traffic" (BOATs). According to the definition in s. 66(1) of 1981 Act:

> ""byway open to all traffic" means a highway over which the public have a right of way for vehicular and all other kinds of traffic, but which is used by the public mainly for the purpose for which footpaths and bridleways are so used"

BOATs are sometimes known as "green lanes". Because they are carriageways, they may lawfully be used by off-road enthusiasts in cars and on motorcycles.

3-53 Further changes will be made by the Countryside and Rights of Way Act 2000, when the relevant sections are brought into effect. Any RUPPs which are still shown on definitive maps (because they have not yet been reclassified—the process is still not complete) must be shown instead as "restricted byways", which will mean that there is a right of way for pedestrians, equestrians and vehicles which are not mechanically propelled (ss. 47 and 48). The 2000 Act also lays down a "cut-off date", 1 January 2026, after which no more BOATs can be added to the definitive map and statement (Schedule 5, which adds s. 54A to the 1981 Act); and after which, with some exceptions, footpaths and bridleways created before 1949 but not shown on the definitive map and statement are extinguished (Countryside and Rights of Way Act 2000, ss. 53–56).

3-54 *Modifications* The law allows modifications to be made, so that new highways can be added and amendments made when a highway is

---

17. Supplemented by the Wildlife and Countryside (Definitive Map and Statement) Regulations 1993, SI 1993/12

stopped up or diverted, or when a highway is shown not to exist. The procedure is laid down in the Wildlife and Countryside Act 1981, s. 53 and Schedules 14 and15. A change is carried out by means of a modification order, made by the local authority, which can act on its own initiative or on the application of a member of the public.

3-55 If the local authority takes the initiative, it starts by making an order; but the order cannot take effect until confirmed. Notice must be given in the local press and served on the owners and occupiers of land affected and some other bodies. If there are no objections, the local authority can itself confirm the order, which then takes effect. Where objections have been made (and not withdrawn) the order must go to the DEFRA for confirmation. An Inspector is usually appointed to deal with the matter; and there may be a formal or informal hearing, or the Inspector may act on written representations by those involved (Schedule 15).

3-56 Members of the public may apply for modification orders where a new right of way has been created by dedication and acceptance, or where there is new evidence which shows that:

- There is an unrecorded highway;

- A recorded highway should be shown as being in a different class (e.g. a footpath should be shown as a bridleway)

- A highway is recorded; but there is in fact no public right of way (s. 53(1)(b) and (c)).

3-57 Applications must be made in the form laid down by the 1993 Regulations. Landowners and occupiers must be notified. When the applicant has complied with the necessary formalities and put forward his case, the local authority must decide whether to make the order modifying the definitive map and statement. If it does not do so (or if it fails to act) the applicant may ask the DEFRA to intervene (Schedule 14).

3-58 *Footpaths and bridleways in private roads* Private roads may be carriageways, and so open to public use by all classes of traffic*. But it is also possible for a private road to be subject to a footpath or bridleway, running along or across the road. There are two rather different possibilities.

*See 1-6.

3-59 First, the road may be subject to a footpath or bridleway created by dedication and acceptance since 1949, so that the highway is not maintainable at the public expense and is not owned by the local authority. Such highways should be shown on the definitive map and statement but not the list of highways maintainable at the public expense*. If there is a separate pavement or track running alongside the roadway, use may have been confined to it rather than the roadway, in which case only the pavement or track is subject to the public right of way. In other cases, it may be that the whole of the roadway has been used by pedestrians or equestrians, in which case the whole width will be subject to the public right of way. Typically this will be so where the road is a cul-de-sac for motor vehicles, but there is a way through for pedestrians or equestrians and the public have made use of it for the necessary period.

3-60 Secondly, a footpath or bridleway may have been created by an order or agreement under s. 25 or s. 26 of the Highways Act*. In this case ownership of the highway does pass to the local authority, and there is a public liability to maintain, under s. 41, though if, for example, the footpath runs across or along a metalled road, additional maintenance by the local authority will rarely be required. Such highways should be shown both on the definitive map and statement and the list of highways maintainable at the public expense.

3-61 The owners of the road must be careful not to obstruct the highway*. Disturbing the surface of the highway in such a way as to cause inconvenience to members of the public is also an offence. The local authority have the power to put up signposts to guide members of the public using the highway, under it s. 27 of the Countryside Act 1968. It is an offence for the owner of the land to put up signs intended to discourage use of the highway (National Parks and Access to the Countryside Act 1949, s. 57).

3-62 *Private roads as RUPPs, restricted byways, and BOATs* Can a private road be a RUPP (or, when the Countryside and Rights of Way Act 2000 is fully in force, a restricted byway), or a BOAT? If so, what are the consequences? A RUPP is a road which is used by the public mainly as a footpath or bridleway. It seems possible that a private road might meet this description and be recorded on the definitive map and statement. If so, the coming into effect of the Countryside and Rights of Way Act will convert such a road into a restricted byway, with no public right of way for vehicles (s. 47). Anyone driving a motor vehicle in the road will then be committing an offence under s. 34 of the Road Traffic Act 1988*, unless they have a private right of way or were the owner of the road or part of it[18]. However, s. 49 also provides that such roads will be highways maintainable at the public expense; and since ownership of such highways passes to the local authority under s. 263 of the Highways Act 1980, the road will cease to be private. It will probably be subject to private rights of way allowing residents vehicular access. The local authority are not obliged by s. 48 to provide

---

18. The position of the former owner of the road is protected by s. 50.

a metalled surface; but if the road is already metalled, the local authority may be under an obligation to keep it in repair because of s. 41 of the Highways Act.

A BOAT—a byway open to all traffic—is a highway over which there is a public right of way for vehicles; but which is used by the public mainly as a footpath or bridleway. Again, it seems possible that a private road might be shown on the definitive map and statement as a BOAT, on the basis that, so far as public use was concerned, there was little motorised traffic but many pedestrians and equestrians.

The Countryside and Rights of Way Act 2000 will prevent the addition of new BOATs to the definitive map and statement after 2026. But BOATs are generally not converted into highways maintainable at the public expense in the way that RUPPs are.

Stopping up and diversion of highways

A highway normally lasts indefinitely: "once a highway, always a highway". The owner of the land subject to the highway cannot by herself reverse the process of dedication and acceptance; nor does any later lack of use by the public affect the public right of way. However the Highways Act and other legislation contain procedures by which a highway can be stopped up, i.e. its status as a highway ended. The phrase does not imply that a physical barrier must be erected. A highway can be stopped at both ends, so as to end the public right of way altogether; or it may be stopped up at one end only, thus converting a through-road into a cul-de-sac. These procedures apply both to private roads which are highways and to highways maintainable at the public expense*.

*See 3-66 for the consequences of stopping up a highway.

Procedures Under s. 116[19] of the Highways Act 1980 a local authority can apply to a magistrates' court for an order to stop up a highway. The local authority can make an application to the magistrates' court on the ground that the highway is "unnecessary", or can be diverted so as to make it "nearer or more commodious to the public". The test of whether a highway is necessary is whether it is needed for the purpose of passing and repassing, other matters such as parking being irrelevant[20]. The fact that residents would like their road to be stopped up is not in itself a ground on which the procedure can be used.

---

19. Supplemented by Schedule 12.
20. See *Westley v Hertfordshire County Council* [1995] COD 414.

3-67 If a highway is used by the public, a stopping-up order will generally not be appropriate unless a suitable alternative exists[21]. The application can be made by the local authority on behalf of another person, by virtue of s. 117. A visit may be made to inspect the highway, if the magistrates think fit. In the case of a carriageway, the order may close the highway to all traffic, or may leave a footpath or bridleway. Notice must be served on the owners of property adjoining the road, and on statutory undertakers* with pipes, cables or other equipment under or over the highway.

*That is, the companies supplying water, electricity and other services: see further chapter 10. chapter 9

3-68 The procedure will be particularly appropriate if a private road is a cul-de-sac, but is nonetheless subject to a public right of way, or if it is intended that one end of the road should be closed off so as to turn it into a cul-de-sac. The views of the residents will in practice be of paramount importance: if they wish their road to become private, and if the local authority agree that the public road is unnecessary, the latter may be prepared to make an application to the magistrates' court. Though s. 116 requires that those immediately affected are to be given notice, the local authority may wish to consult more widely before setting in motion the statutory procedure.

3-69 For the sake of completeness, brief mention should be made of ss. 47 and 48 of the Highways Act 1980. Under these provisions, the local authority can apply to a magistrates' court if they consider that a highway maintainable at the public expense is unnecessary, and ought no longer to be maintainable at the public expense. If the magistrates are satisfied that this is so they may make an order to this effect, having considered any objections there may be. The order does *not* bring to an end the public right of way, and the procedure is thus not one which the residents of a public road are likely to urge the local authority to pursue. Where an order has been made under s. 47 it can be reversed, at a later date, if circumstances change and it appears that the highway should be maintainable at the public expense once more.

3-70 There are also provisions in other Acts which deal with the stopping up and diversion of highways. For example, by s. 258 of the Town and Country Planning Act 1990 the ODPM can stop up a highway in order to facilitate development. Local authorities also have power, under the Road Traffic Regulation Act 1984, to restrict the classes of traffic which may use a road*.

*See 9-15.

3-71 *Consequences* The stopping up of a highway means that the public right of way ceases. In a private road, once the public right of way ceases, the public will no longer be entitled to use the road[22]; nor will residents be able to rely on the public right of way to gain access to

---

21. See *Ramblers Association v Kent County Council* (1990) 154 JP 716; (1990) 60 P&CR 464.
22. Unless the private road is a through-road which is merely stopped-up at one end.

their properties. Any private rights of way which existed before the road became a highway will revive, however*.

*See chapter 4 for private rights of way.

Section 116 may equally be used to convert a highway maintainable at the public expense into a private road. In this case, not only does the public right of way cease, and any private rights of way revive, but ownership of the road reverts to the person or persons who owned it before it passed to the local authority.

Assessment

Whether a private road is a highway is a matter of considerable importance to the owners and residents. Public use may be intrusive, to a greater or lesser extent, and the owner and residents may not wish to provide a public facility at their own expense. That said, the position is not entirely straightforward, since the existence of a highway means that there is a public interest in regulating what takes place in the road. Local authorities therefore enjoy greater powers, more criminal offences apply, and there is a greater degree of protection against antisocial behaviour.

In any event, the owners and residents of a private road will wish to be aware of whether public rights of way exist over the road. Any footpaths, bridleways and byways, should be shown on the local authority's definitive map and statement under the Wildlife and Countryside Act 1981 (though absence from the definitive map and statement is no proof that a highway does not exist). A local authority may, in addition to their official s. 36 (6) list, maintain a list of private roads, distinguishing between those which are thought to be carriageways and those which are not; but such lists have no legal force.

It will be rare for a private road to become a highway under one of the procedures laid down in the Highways Act 1980 without also becoming maintainable at public expense. In contrast, the issue of whether a private road has become a highway through dedication and acceptance will often be a live one.

Since motorised trespassing has been an offence since 1930 (and in some situations perhaps earlier), and since criminal activities cannot lead to the creation of a highway, a private road will in general only be a carriageway if the public acquired a right to use it in vehicles (including horse-drawn vehicles) before 1930.

Use by pedestrians and other classes of non-vehicular traffic is another matter; and many private roads may well have become highways by dedication and acceptance. This will be quite likely in the case of through-roads, unless measures have been taken to prevent the creation of a highway, but rare in cul-de-sacs, unless the road has (or had in the past) some feature which would attract the public generally.

3-78 If the position is uncertain, and particularly if it is not clear that 20 years' use by the public, uninterrupted and as of right, has taken place, residents may wish to take measures to prevent further use from leading to the creation of a highway. But it is important to note that the law here is concerned with the ownership of the road: the idea of dedication and acceptance rests on the presumed intention of the owner, and the steps which can be taken to prevent dedication and acceptance are usually for the owner to take. A residents' association which is merely an occupier, not the owner, and does not have the authority of the owner to act—typically, because the owner cannot be traced—will not strictly be in a position to prevent the creation of a highway by (for example) putting up a notice, though if the notice has the effect of stopping public use then it may prevent the creation of a highway.

3-79 On the other hand, a residents' association which is merely an occupier can maintain a gate or other barrier, and close it for one day a year: this will interrupt use by the public and so prevent the creation of a highway. But such action runs the risk of precipitating a dispute and conceivably a prosecution, since obstructing a highway is an offence[*].

[*]See 7-3.

3-80 Stopping-up, so as to end public rights of way, or turn a highway maintainable at the public expense into a private road, may be an attractive aim; and may be worth pursuing, even though the legislation does not encourage stopping-up and the assistance of the local authority will be necessary.

3-81 Legal advice and careful consideration will be required before residents approach the local authority with a proposal of this nature. In the case of a highway maintainable at the public expense, residents will need to be aware of who the former owner of the road was, and consider the implications of ownership reviving. If the owner is unknown, frontagers will be able to rely on the presumption of ownership. In every case, once public rights of way have been extinguished, residents will need to consider what (if any) pre-existing private rights of way there may have been, and if so whether these are adequate for the current use of the land. The question will be particularly relevant to development which has taken place since the road became a highway. If there are no such rights, residents will need to make arrangements with the owner of the road for their creation before the stopping up of the highway takes place.

Chapter 4: Private rights of way and other easements

Introduction

This chapter deals with private rights of way and other some other rights in the same legal class—known as easements*. Much of the law in this area comes from decisions of the courts, though the Prescription Act 1832 is also important. Regulations under the Countryside and Rights of Way Act 2000 have corrected a legal problem concerning rights of way, and have introduced a new procedure for acquiring a private right of way for vehicles.

4-0

*See also chapter 5 for parking.

What is an easement?

An easement is a right to make limited use of someone else's land. Such rights cannot exist independently[1]—the law requires that an easement is attached to one piece of land, and must confer the right to make some use of another, nearby (not necessarily adjoining) piece of land in a particular way. The former land is said to have the benefit of the easement, and the latter to be burdened with it[2].

4-1

The right most commonly forming the subject of an easement is a private right of way: the easement is attached to one piece of land and gives the right to cross another piece of land (whether a road or path or some other land) for access. The use allowed by an easement must not be so great that it prevents the owner of the land making reasonable use of it.

4-2

Easements are classified by the law as land, and the same formalities apply, so that a deed* is generally required in order to grant an easement[3]. Once created, however, an easement is automatically passed on at the same time as the land to which it is attached; and the land subject to the easement remains subject to it despite changes of

4-3

*See 1-34.

---

1. See *Voice v Bell* (1994) 68 P&CR 441.
2. The land with the benefit of the easement is also said to be the "dominant tenement", and the land subject to the easement is said to be the "servient tenement"

owner. An easement is thus the appropriate method for putting in place a long-term right of way.

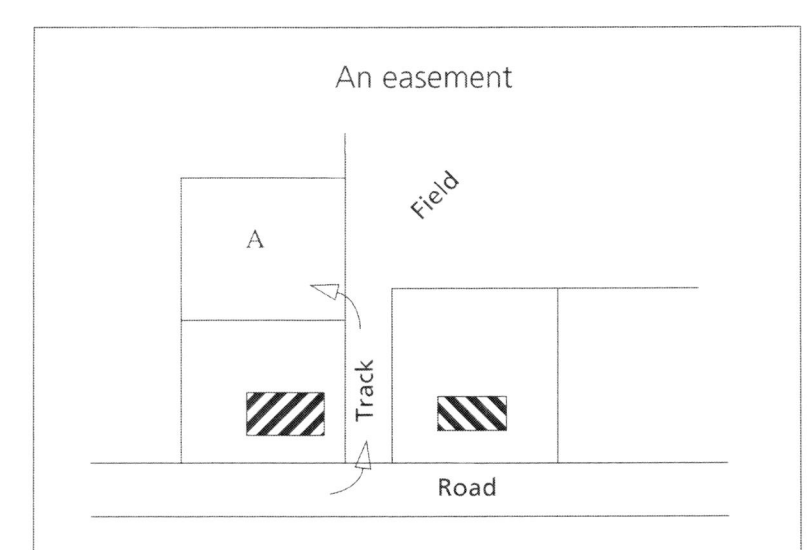

> ### An easement
>
> The field and track belong to a farmer. He grants a right of way (an easement) over the track, for the benefit of the plot marked A, so that development can take place. Plot A has the benefit of the right of way (and is the "dominant tenement"). The track (the "servient tenement") is subject to it.

4-4   Many other sorts of easement are possible, and some examples are considered briefly at the end of this chapter. In each case, the effect of the easement is to allow some specific use of land, for the benefit of nearby land.

Rights of way in a private road

4-5   Most roads are highways maintainable at the public expense, open to all classes of traffic because they are carriageways*. The public right of way is all that is required, and residents in the road do not need

*See 3-3.

---

3. Easements can be "legal" in nature, or "equitable". This chapter is concerned only with the former. Different rules apply to the latter: they can (for example) be created without a deed, or for uncertain periods of time. An equitable easement may be ineffective against a landowner who is not aware of its existence when he acquires the land.

private rights of way in addition. The same is true in a private road which is a carriageway (i.e. a highway for vehicles).

But in a private road which is not a carriageway, each house needs its own arrangements for access. This is accomplished by means of a private right of way in the form of an easement. The easement is attached to the house, and the road is subject to it, and the right of way remains permanently in place when the house and the road change hands. (It is usual to grant an easement on a permanent basis, though easements which last for a fixed period of time are also legally valid.)

4-6

A right of way in the form of an easement must be distinguished from:

4-7

- A public right of way. Public rights of way exist for the benefit of the public generally, and do not belong to anyone in particular. They are not legally a form of property, and cannot be bought and sold. It is principally the role of the local authority, on behalf of the public at large, to safeguard public rights of way. By contrast, an easement is essentially a private matter between the current owners of the two pieces of land concerned.

- Mere permission to use the road. Like any other landowner, the owner of a private road can give permission (a "licence") for use of his property for access, or for other purposes, without granting any permanent rights*. Mere permission is not a satisfactory long-term arrangement, because it is personal in nature and is therefore liable to expire or, depending upon the terms on which it was given, to be revoked.

*See 1-46 onwards for licences.

- A wayleave. The utility companies, which supply water, gas, electricity and other services are given, by statute, the right to install pipes, wires and other equipment under or on the land. Such rights are often known as wayleaves. They are in a class of their own, though in some respects they resemble easements*.

*See generally chapter 10.

- A restrictive covenant*. Restrictive covenants, like easements, can be created by agreement between the owners of two pieces of land, and may bind not only those two owners but later owners of the land. The purpose of a restrictive covenant is to restrict the use of the land subject to the covenant. For example, a restrictive covenant may provide that residential property cannot be used for commercial purposes, or that a plot of land may not be used to build more than one house. An easement may also be granted in terms which limit the use of the property which has the benefit of

*See 6-44 onwards.

for more information see www.barsby.com

*See particularly 6-52.

it, and may thus serve the same purpose of imposing a restriction on the use of the land; but different rules apply*.

4-8 What happens if a private road becomes a highway, that is, subject to a public right of way? If the right of way is for all classes of traffic, private rights of way will in practice lose much of their significance, since the public right of way provides the necessary right of access. However private rights of way do not automatically cease to exist in this situation, and may be significant for some purposes. In particular, a private right of way will usually carry with it the right to repair the road, and may carry the obligation to do so*.

*See 4-48 onwards.

Creation of private rights of way

4-9 Historically, it has been possible for easements to be created in two main ways. They may be granted expressly, by means of a deed, or they may come into existence by "prescription", that is, by virtue of use over a period of time.

4-10 *Creation by grant* The deed creating an easement will make clear that the right is being attached to the land having the benefit of it (either directly, or indirectly by saying that it is to benefit successive owners of the land) and hence that an easement, rather than merely a licence, is being created. It is usual for the deed to include a plan, showing the two pieces of land concerned. In interpreting a deed, the courts' aim is to establish the intentions of the parties at the time when the deed was executed[4]. There is, however, a rule by which ambiguities are generally resolved in favour of the person to whom rights or property are granted by the deed.

4-11 If a right of way is granted in unlimited terms, the result will usually be that the right of way can be used by any classes of traffic visiting the land which has the benefit of the right, and for any purposes. It may happen that the use of the land which has the benefit of the easement changes. Generally, the courts take the view that an unrestricted right of way will continue to exist whatever the use of the land having the benefit of it. In one case[5] a house was turned into an hotel, but the right of way still held good.

4-12 *Creation by prescription* The law recognises that in certain circumstances an easement may arise, without any agreement between

---

4. See *Investors Compensation Scheme v West Bromwich Building Society* [1998] 1 WLR 896.
5. See *White v Grand Hotel, Eastbourne Ltd* [1913] 1 Ch 113.

the owners of land, as a result of use over a period of time. This process is known as prescription. A private right of way may thus arise by prescription when one piece of land is crossed regularly in order to gain access to another, by the owners (or successive owners) of the latter and their visitors. A right of way then attaches to that piece of land, in the same way as an easement which has been granted by deed. In some ways this resembles the process of dedication and acceptance, by which a highway may be created*, but the two areas of the law are distinct and different. For a highway to be created, there must be use by the public at large, and the purpose of use by the public is not to gain access to a particular piece of land, but simply to pass to and fro along the road or path.

*See 3-11 onwards.

(4-13) Prescription consists not merely of one legal rule, but three different rules, each of which can give rise to easements. However the following account will disregard the first, known as a prescription at common law. This depends upon the proposition that use has been taking place since "time immemorial", and is unlikely to be relevant to the creation of rights of way over a private road. The other two sorts of prescription can be taken together[6]. The first is statutory, under the Prescription Act 1832; the second depends upon a legal fiction, which is that an easement has been granted in modern times, but that the deed granting it has been lost—hence the name given to the rule, "lost modern grant". (The fiction is just that: the argument cannot be defeated by showing that there was in fact no deed.)

(4-14) Prescription is regarded by the law as a matter between the owners of the two pieces of land concerned, which is relevant to residents' associations who occupy but do not own a road. Although an easement can be granted for a fixed period, it can only be acquired by prescription on a permanent basis.

(4-15) The law requires that there has been use "as of right"; in other words, that the people using the land have acted as though they had the right to do so. They must not act secretly, or by force, or by permission; nor must they be committing a criminal offence in using the land[7]*. They will in fact be trespassing, and can be stopped from doing so, if the owner or occupier of the land decides to take action. But if she does not take action, an easement will in due course come into being, by prescription, after which there will be a legally enforceable right to go on using the land.

*But see also 4-34 onwards.

---

6. The courts have shown a willingness to take the two together, and a reluctance to emphasise the differences, which are technical. See *Pugh v Savage* [1970] 2 WLR 634, [1970] 2 All ER 353.
7. See *Hanning v Top Deck Travel Group Ltd* (1994) 68 P&CR 14 and *Bakewell Management v Brandwood, The Times* 5 February 2003.

4-16 The use may be begun by one owner of land, and continued by his successor(s). For the creation of a right of way, prescription generally requires a minimum 20 years' use. However, several qualifications must be made to that statement. The 20-year period is that laid down in the Prescription Act 1832, for prescription under the Act. For the purposes of prescription by lost modern grant a 20-year period of use is not a strict requirement. The courts will tend to require the same period, but may in some cases accept a shorter one. Furthermore, the Prescription Act says that the 20 years must run right up to the time when legal proceedings are started to prove the right. If there is a "gap", before proceedings are started, an easement cannot be established under the Prescription Act. This rule does not apply, however, to prescription by means of a lost modern grant.

4-17 The 20 years' use must be uninterrupted. The use will also be interrupted if it is stopped, by legal action or otherwise. But in order to count under the Prescription Act, the interruption must last for at least a year. What is a sufficient interruption for the purposes of a claim by virtue of a claim of lost modern grant will be matter of fact. Permission from the owner of the land will also mean that use as of right is not taking place.

4-18 Permission may be expressly given, or it may be implied—that is, things done or said may lead to the implication that permission is being granted, even though the owner of the land does not grant permission in so many words. Difficulties may arise if use takes place, and the owner of a private road knows about it, but takes no action; but the law generally draws a line between:

- The landowner who is silent, and tolerates use of her land, and who is considered not to be granting implied permission, so that the use is (if other conditions are satisfied) as of right and can lead to the creation of an easement by prescription.

- The landowner who does or says something which positively suggests that the use has her implied permission, in which case there is no use as of right, and hence no basis for the creation of a prescriptive easement[8].

4-19 A related situation is the one in which there is a mistake, and all those concerned wrongly believe that a valid right of way already exists: the persons using it believe that they are already entitled to do so, and the owner of the road takes no action to prevent them because

---

8. See *R (on the application of Beresford) v Sunderland City Council* [2001] EWCA Civ 1218, [2002] 2 WLR 693, [2001] 4 All ER 565, and *Mills v Silver* [1991] 2 WLR 324, [1991] 1 All ER 449.

he imagines that there is already a right enforceable against him. Does this give rise to a right of way? The answer given by the courts is that a prescriptive right can arise in these circumstances[9].

A further complication should be mentioned. Under the Prescription Act 1832, 40 years' use can give rise to a right of way, even though there was *oral* consent to the use before the start of the period. But 40 years' use will *not* give rise to a prescriptive easement if there was *written* consent to it before the start of the period, or *any* consent to it during the period[10]. The complexity of the 40-year rule emerges from the wording of the Prescription Act.

A prescriptive right of way is legally just as valid as one granted expressly. There is no reason why a person who has been expressly granted a right of way in limited terms should not acquire a further right by prescription. There may, however, be a difference of opinion between the owner of the land, and the persons using it, as to whether the necessary uninterrupted use has taken place for a sufficient period to establish the right. In this situation, only the courts or the Land Registry* can give a binding decision as to whether a prescriptive easement has arisen.

*See 4-62 onwards.

It may be thought surprising that the law should reward someone who has trespassed repeatedly, over many years, by giving them a legal right; or that someone who has given oral consent to the use of his land should find, 40 years later, that a legal right, enforceable against him, has arisen. (Similar comments could be made about the creation of public rights of way by dedication and acceptance.) Again, if someone uses a private road in the mistaken belief, shared by the owners of the road, that he already has a right, it may seem odd that the law should be concerned not with correcting the mistake but in giving legal effect to it. The policy of the law is to encourage such results, however, perhaps because creating new rights allows land to be used more fully and effectively.

Scope: rights of way created by grant

What use of the land will be allowed when a right of way is granted by deed? Several questions arise under this heading.

Over what land can a right of way be exercised? Generally, this will depend upon what is said in the deed granting the easement (including

---

9. See *Bridle v Ruby* [1988] 3 WLR 191, [1988] 3 All ER 64.
10. Including a common understanding that the use would take place by permission: see *Jones v Price* (1992) 64 P&CR 404.

any plans) and the physical characteristics of the land at the time when the easement was granted. If the entrance to a road or path is restricted by a gateway, this is likely to be relevant to the extent of the land subject to the right granted, though not necessarily conclusive[11].

4-25 Subject to the terms upon which a right is granted in a particular case, the fact that land is made subject to a right of way does not mean that it must be possible for the right to be exercised over every part of the land. It may be, for example, that rights of way have been granted over the whole of a private road, including verges which contain shrubs or trees. This does not imply that the verges must be cleared so that cars may be driven along them. The rule is that the owner of the land subject to a right of way may exclude users of the right of way from particular parts of the land, provided that reasonable exercise of the right is not prevented[12].

4-26 This principle may be useful to the owners of a private road, since it allows a limited freedom to make changes to the land, for example by narrowing the roadway slightly or excluding users from the verge by means of an ornamental fence. Such steps can be taken by the owners of the road, provided that reasonable use of the road is not denied to those with a right of way.

4-27 *What land has the benefit of the right of way?* Unless the deed granting a right of way provides otherwise, the whole of the land to which a right of way is attached enjoys the benefit of the right. If, therefore, the land is split into separate plots the right of way will apply to each plot separately. A right of way may, however, be granted on terms that it is not "severable", meaning that the land which has the benefit of the right cannot be split into separate plots each enjoying the right. Equally, the deed granting a right of way could make clear that it was for the benefit of only part of the land in question.

4-28 If a landowner enlarges his boundaries by adding more land to his original plot, this may raise the question of whether he can continue to use the right of way which was granted for the benefit of the original plot. If the use of the additional land is merely ancillary to the use of the original land, and especially if the right of way is not being used to gain access direct to the new land, then the existing right of way is likely to be regarded as sufficient[13], and a further right of way, for the benefit of the plot, will not be required.

---

11. See *White v Richards* (1994) 68 P&CR 105.
12. See *Keefe v Amor* [1964] 3 WLR 183, [1964] 2 All ER 517.

> ### Ancillary use 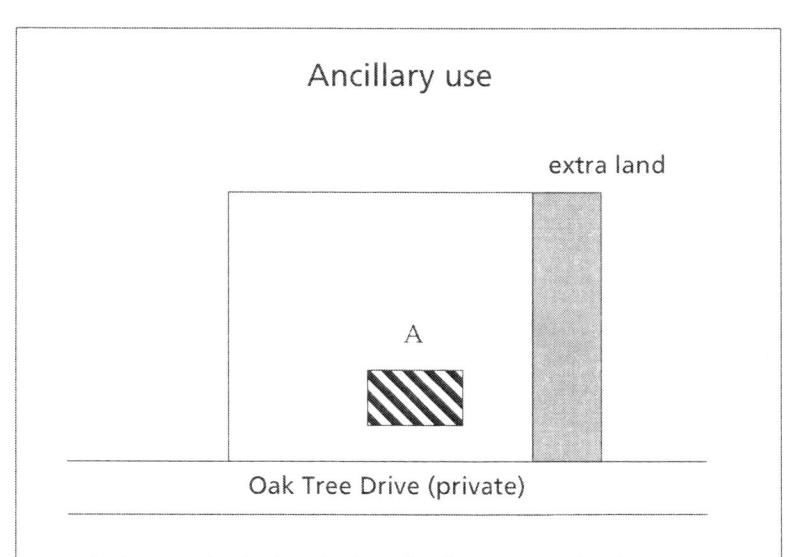
>
> extra land
>
> A
>
> Oak Tree Drive (private)
>
> The land marked A has the benefit of a private right of way over Oak Tree Drive. The owner buys an extra piece of land, to extend her garden. The use of the extra land would probably be regarded as ancillary, so that there would be no breach of the right of way. But if the owner of A wished to use the extra land for some independent purpose, the existing right of way would not suffice.

On the other hand, if the extra land is to be regarded as a separate plot, with access, then the existing right of way is unlikely to be regarded as sufficient and new rights will be required.

What is the extent of the use allowed? A private right of way may be granted in unrestricted terms, or restrictions may be imposed on the use allowed. Restrictions may take various forms. They may, for example, relate directly to the road or path which is subject to the right of way—for example, only vehicles of less than a certain size or weight may be allowed to pass over the land, or access may be permitted only at certain times of day.

Alternatively, limitations may relate to the use of the land which has the benefit of the right. For example, the right of way may be

---

13. See *Massey v Boulden* [2002] EWCA Civ 1634, in which a cottage had been enlarged, so as to include two extra rooms, and the Court of Appeal considered that the existing right of way was adequate. Contrast *Peacock v Custins* [2002] 1 WLR 1815, [2001] 2 All ER 827, *The Times* 21 November 2001, in which a farmer with 15 acres acquired a further 10 acres (existing right of way not adequate) and *Das v Linden Mews* [2002] EWCA Civ 590, *The Independent* 9 May 2002, in which the owners of two mews houses acquired extra land for parking, to which they wanted direct access (existing right not adequate). See also *Sargeant v Macepark (Whittlebury) Ltd*, *The Times* 29 March 2003.

exercisable only so long as the land which has the benefit of it is used for non-commercial purposes, or as a single dwelling. In this case the owner of the land is not absolutely prevented from using his land in other ways, since he may be able to find other means of access. But while he is dependent upon a right of way with this sort of condition, his use of the land is in effect limited. A limitation imposed when a right of way is granted may thus be used—and in practice often is used—to control development in a private road: the right of way will be subject to the limitation that the land having the benefit of it is used only in the specified way, and the owner of the land will have to obtain a further right of way if he wishes to develop the site.

Scope: rights of way arising by prescription

4-32 The scope of a right of way acquired by prescription is generally determined by the use which has actually taken place[14]. If a private road has been used by (say) pedestrians for 20 years, and the use has been by right and without interruption, then a prescriptive right of way for pedestrians will arise. The right will not extend to other classes of traffic. Difficult questions of fact may arise, in any given case, as to what exactly are the classes of traffic for which a prescriptive right has been established. It is for the person asserting the prescriptive right of way to show that the necessary use has taken place.

4-33 The above principle will also apply to the use of the land benefiting from the right of way. The right of way acquired will be for the purposes of the use which took place on the land during the 20-year period; but it will extend to other uses which are reasonable uses of the land in that state. In one case[15] a prescriptive right of way had arisen for two houses, and the court decided that this was sufficient to allow the land to be redeveloped, and used for a block of 6 flats, a bungalow and 7 garages. By analogy with the law relating to expressly-granted easements, it may also be possible in some cases for the plot of land which has the benefit of the right of way to be enlarged to some extent without losing the right.

---

14. There is an exception to this rule: a prescriptive right of way for horse-drawn traffic will extend to motor vehicles. See *Lock v Abercester Ltd* [1939] Ch 861.
15. See *Giles v County Building Constructors (Hertford) Ltd* (1971) 22 P&CR 978. But compare *Guise v Drew* (2001) 82 P&CR DG25 in which the court decided that a prescriptive right of way acquired for one business could not be used for another.

Vehicular Access

4-34 The Vehicular Access Across Common and Other land (England) Regulations 2002[16] provide a new procedure for acquiring a private right of way for vehicles across land—including private roads. Because an easement cannot be acquired by prescription if the use is criminal*, driving over land could not give rise to a right of way for vehicles if this was an offence. Some owners of houses adjoining common land*, who had been driving over the common for many years to get to their houses, found that despite long use no easement had arisen, and that the owner of the common might seek to charge a substantial sum for granting a right of way to regularise the position. In the case of much 4-35 common land, driving on the land without lawful authority was often an offence under s. 193 of the Law of Property Act 1925. A similar offence, but with a much wider application, is s. 34 of the Road Traffic Act 1988—the "motorised trespassing" offence—which applies to private roads*.

*See 4-15.

*See 1-36 onwards.

*See 7-22.

4-36 As a result of publicity about the predicament of landowners, the government decided to change the law. Section 68 of the Countryside and Rights of Way Act 2000 accordingly gave the DEFRA the power to make regulations which allow an easement to be acquired, despite breaches of the criminal law. The Vehicular Access Across Common Land (England) Regulations 2002 have been made by the DEFRA, and came into effect on 4 July 2002.

4-37 The Regulations allow a right of way for vehicles to be acquired on the basis of use, disregarding the fact that use of the land has been criminal. They lay down a procedure by which the landowner wanting a right of way must serve notice on the owner of land over which the right will exist, and must make a payment in return for the right.

4-38 The Regulations apply to any land, not just common land, and so can apply to private roads. The most important offence for these purposes[17] will be s. 34 of the Road Traffic Act 1988. This offence will apply in private roads which are not highways and in which public use is not tolerated*, and where there is no legal authority for the use, such as a private right of way or permission from the owner of the road.

*See 1-20.

4-39 Use which was sufficient to create a prescriptive right of way for vehicles, and which took place at a time when it was not an offence, will have given rise to a valid easement, and this will be unaffected by the Regulations. If, for example, a house in a private road acquired a right of way for vehicular traffic by means of 20 years' use in the late

---

16. SI 2002/1711.
17. Other offences might occasionally be relevant, for example local byelaws.

for more information see www.barsby.com

*See 4-12.

nineteenth century, when it was not an offence to come and go over the road in a horse-drawn vehicle, the prescriptive right will remain valid.

4-40　The Regulations provide that there must be sufficient use to create a prescriptive right—in other words, generally 20 years' uninterrupted use as of right*—ending on or after 5 May 1993[18]. Where there has been the necessary use by vehicles, the landowner wanting the benefit of a right of way may serve notice on the landowner whose land would be subject to it. This must be done within 12 months of the start of the Regulations (i.e. by 4 July 2003) if the use stopped before then; otherwise within 12 months of the date when it stopped. (If the use is continuing, the application may be made at any time.) The notice must contain the information set out in the Schedule to the Regulations, including details of the right of way sought, a map showing the land which is to have the benefit of the right of way, and evidence of the value and age of the premises—the latter being relevant to the amount which must be paid for the right of way.

4-41　For houses and other property in existence on 31 December 1905, the payment is 0.2% of the value of the premises; where they were in existence on 30 November 1930, the payment is 0.5% of the value; and in other cases it is 2% of the value. The payment for a house built since 1930 may thus be substantial.

4-42　A person serving a notice under the Regulations can claim other rights, ancillary to the right of way. It is not clear whether this could include the right to park.

4-43　Once the notice has been served, the landowner whose land will be subject to the right may respond; and can either agree with the notice or can put forward a counter-notice, asserting, for example, that the necessary use has not taken place, that the right claimed is too extensive, or that the valuation given for the premises is too low. Any disputes about the value of the land must be settled by a surveyor; otherwise all disputes go to the Lands Tribunal to resolve.

4-44　The new right of way comes into existence, under the Regulations, when any disputes have been settled and the appropriate payment has been made. Its scope depends upon the use which has taken place, and the Regulations do not change the law of prescription in this respect; though the procedure which has to be followed under the Regulations means that the right should be clearly defined. The Regulations do not prevent the two landowners involved from settling the matter by granting a right of way expressly on agreed terms if they wish. Nor do

---

18. The date on which the case of *Hanning v Top Deck Travel Group Ltd* was decided, this case being regarded as putting landowners on notice that they should take steps to stop vehicles driving across their land if they wanted to prevent a right of way arising.

the Regulations prevent a landowner from obtaining a right of way which is additional to one he already has.

Other ways in which easements can arise

Rights of way, and other easements, can be created in several other ways, besides those mentioned above.

The rule in Wheeldon v Burrows[19] The common law contains a rule which applies where part of an area of land is sold off. The rule is that where one part of the land enjoys "continuous and apparent" rights which would be easements if the land were in separate parts, and if those rights are necessary for the enjoyment of the land, the rights will become easements when part is sold off. If the owner of property in a private road owned property in the road, and one day sold off the road, the law would, under this rule, create a right of way over the road, even if none was expressly created when the road was sold.

Section 62 of the Law of Property Act 1925 This provision also applies when part of an area of land is sold, and has a similar effect, creating an easement; though this provision can apply not just where the right is necessary but where it is merely convenient.

Maintenance and repairs

Neither the owner of a private road, nor the owners of houses which have the benefit of rights of way over the road, are under any automatic *duty* to maintain the road: both parties may generally, if they wish, simply allow the road to deteriorate. The fact that the road is a highway does not change the position, since a private owner of a highway generally does not have an obligation to maintain it*.

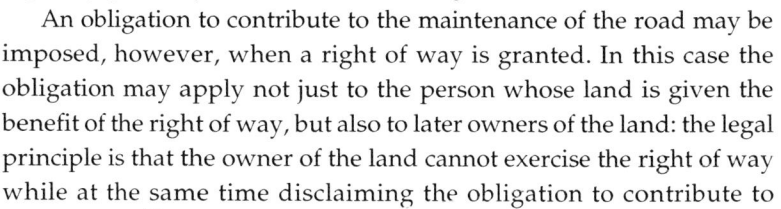

*See 1-8.

An obligation to contribute to the maintenance of the road may be imposed, however, when a right of way is granted. In this case the obligation may apply not just to the person whose land is given the benefit of the right of way, but also to later owners of the land: the legal principle is that the owner of the land cannot exercise the right of way while at the same time disclaiming the obligation to contribute to maintenance[20]. More generally, the residents of a private road may put

---

19. (1879) 12 Ch D 31.
20. See *Halsall v Brizell* [1957] 2 WLR 123, [1957] 1 All ER 371. This is an exception to the general rule that obligations can apply to later owners of land only if they are negative in character.

in place arrangements for managing the road and paying for the necessary maintenance, and these may give rise to continuing obligations*.

*See chapter 12.

4-50 For rights of way created by grant or prescription, the law implies a *right* to make repairs when these are necessary to allow the right to be exercised. This enables the owner of the land with the benefit of the right to keep the surface of a private road in the same condition as it was when the right was acquired, and to make any other necessary repairs. However there is no right to make improvements. An asphalted road could thus be repaired, and ultimately, when it became necessary, resurfaced by the person whose land enjoyed the right of way. In the case of an unsurfaced road, pot-holes could be filled in, but there would (for example) be no right to improve the road by asphalting it or installing up street lighting[21].

4-51 The owner of the road has the right both to maintain and to make improvements to his own property, provided he does not interfere with existing rights of way in doing so*.

*See 2-3 and 4-54 onwards.

Access to the road

4-52 When a right of way is granted, the deed may also deal specifically with the question of access to the road from the land which receives the benefit of the right of way. For example, the deed may give the right to construct a crossover* from the property to the road, at a particular point. If nothing is said, the position and number of crossovers must depend upon the construction of the deed and hence upon the physical state of the land, and the intention of the parties, at the time when the deed was made. In some cases the right interpretation may be that one crossover is allowed, at a point to be chosen by the owner of the land having the benefit of the right of way; in other cases it may appear that two crossovers, an entrance and an exit, are intended. The size of the plot and access arrangements for other houses in the road are likely to be relevant. The proposition that unlimited numbers of crossovers were intended will generally be unlikely[22].

*See 3-10 for the meaning of "crossover".

4-53 In the case of a right of way acquired by prescription, the right of access is at the established point(s): there is no right to construct new crossovers.

---

21. See *Mills v Silver* [1991] 2 WLR 324, [1991] 1 All ER 449
22. See *Pettey v Parsons* [1914] 2 Ch 653.

Breaches of the law

4-54 Chapter 6 deals with the civil law generally, and explains how action can be taken to obtain compensation and uphold legal rights. In relation to private rights of way, it should be noted that the owner or occupier of the land subject to a private right of way, and the owner of the land which has the benefit of the right, are in different positions.

4-55 Using a private road without the right to do so is trespassing. This includes the case where a private (or public) right of way exists but the person concerned is not complying with its terms. If, for example, the owner of a house in a private road has a right of way which excludes commercial vehicles, but nonetheless starts a business which generates commercial traffic, the drivers concerned are trespassing in using the road. The owner or occupier of the road can take legal action to obtain compensation. There is a right to compensation for trespass, though this will be related to the damage actually caused, so that if there is little or no damage the amount will in most cases be modest. More important, however, the owner of the land may ask the court to grant an injunction, requiring the trespassing to stop*.

*See 6-35 onwards.

4-56 Interfering with a right of way is a civil wrong of a different sort, namely a nuisance. A person whose land has the benefit of a right of way may take action against any person interfering with the right, whether that person is the owner of the road, or a person who also enjoys a right of way, or someone entirely unconnected with the road. A right to take action might arise, for example, if the parking of cars in a narrow private road persistently interfered with the exercise of a right of way[23]. Use by others which is within the terms of existing rights of way is unlikely to amount to a legal wrong, even if it causes some degree of interference, since rights of way are usually expressed to be granted for use in common with others having a right of way. But unauthorised use would be a different matter. In the example given above, use by commercial traffic might—in addition to being a trespass from the point of view of the owner of the road—interfere with existing rights of way. In this situation, the persons entitled to complain of a nuisance are the owners of property to which the right of way is attached. (Others visiting the property are not able to take legal action if they are obstructed in the exercise of a private right of way.) Compensation could be obtained, and the court would if necessary grant an injunction in order to restrain further interference with the right of way. Traffic-calming measures such as road humps* will not

*See 9-4 for road humps.

---

23. For a case in which the court had to deal with deliberate obstruction, accompanied by verbal abuse, over a long period see *Horne and Horne v Ball* [1995] CLY 1841.

necessarily amount to a nuisance, provided they do not interfere excessively with rights of way[24].

4-57 What if it is visitors to a particular house in the road who are causing an obstruction? An injunction would not be an effective remedy if the visitors were not always the same people and could not easily be identified and traced. Here the law shows a little ingenuity: an injunction can be granted against the owner of the property with the right of way, to prevent him from inviting visitors unless he makes sure that they do not obstruct the road[25].

Termination and modification of private rights of way

4-58 The current owners of the two pieces of land involved may together, by means of a deed, terminate a right of way, or modify it so as to make the terms narrower or wider, or extend it to other land, or enable the land which has the benefit of it to be split into separate plots. Terminating a right of way is a step which can be taken unilaterally by the owner whose land benefits from the right, by executing a deed to release the other land from the right.

4-59 It is possible—though it would be unusual—for a landowner to take some action which implies that he is abandoning a right of way*. He might (for example) redevelop his land in such a way that it was clear the right of way was never going to be used again. This might be the case if he found some other means of access to the land, and put up a building across the line of the previous access, so as to block it off. But the fact that a right of way has long been disused does not by itself lead to the inference that the right has been abandoned. In one case[26] a right of way had not been used for 175 years, but the court did not consider that this necessarily showed an intention to abandon the right.

*Contrast the rule for public rights of way; "once a highway, always a highway". See 3-2.

---

24. See *Celsteel Ltd v Alton House Holdings Ltd* [1985] 1 WLR 204, [1985] 2 All ER 562
25. See *Jalnarne v Ridewood* (1991) 61 P&CR 143
26. *Benn v Herding* (1993) 66 P&CR 246; *The Times* 13 October 1992.

Other easements

4-60 As noted at the start of this chapter, an easement gives the right to use land in a particular way. There are limits to the sorts of use which may form the subject of an easement: an easement must, for example, be relevant to the use of the land having the benefit of it, and must not interfere too greatly with the land which is burdened with it. But within these limits, many different sorts of easements are possible. Some other examples may be mentioned which, in addition to rights of way, may be relevant to private roads:

- The right to lay, maintain and use pipes, cables and other services under or over the road, which is often granted at the same time as a private right of way. In modern times the suppliers of these services have statutory powers enabling them to lay and maintain pipes, cables etc. and there is generally no need for residents to rely on easements. Sewers and drains, however, may remain private, in which case the right to use and maintain them may remain important[*]. *See chapter 10.

- The right to use land for recreational purposes can exist as an easement. It is probably rare for such a right to be granted in relation to a private road. But a prescriptive easement might arise, if, for example, the owners of a house in or near a private road get into the habit of using it for walking dogs, or as a play area for children, subject to the rules explained above for the creation of prescriptive easements.

- The right to enter on to a neighbour's land in order to obtain access for maintenance of a wall or other structure may be an easement.

- Parking may be the subject of an easement[*]. *See chapter 5.

4-61 The rules which apply to rights of way, including those relating to the creation of easements by prescription and their entry on the Land Register, apply to easements generally.

Registered and unregistered land

4-62 If a private road is unregistered, a private right of way over it, whether granted by deed or acquired by prescription, will normally be valid

*See 2-30 onwards for land registration generally.

without any further formalities. Many private roads are not registered, either because the owner is unknown, or because it has remained in the same ownership for a lengthy period and no transaction has occurred to trigger the requirement to register*.

If, on the other hand, ownership of land in England and Wales is shown on the Land Register, which is operated in accordance with the Land Registration Acts. A private right of way may also be shown on the Land Register, both in the entry for the land which has the benefit of the right, and the entry for the land which is subject to it.

4-63   The fact that a private right of way is not shown on the Land Register does not generally affect its validity, because the law classifies such interests as "overriding" rights[27]. If, however, a right of way is shown, it forms part of the land to which it is legally attached, and its presence on the register acts in effect as a guarantee of its validity. Before adding a right of way to the register the Land Registry, in accordance with the Land Registration Rules,[28] must make sure that the right is genuinely an easement, attached to some piece of land, failing which the right cannot be shown on the Land Register. Before making an entry, the Land Registry should inform the owner of the land which is said to be subject to the right, so that he has an opportunity to comment. If the right was granted by a deed, the Land Registry should normally insist on seeing the deed in question.

4-64   A private right of way arising by prescription can equally be shown on the register. In this case it is doubly important that the owner of land said to be subject to the right has an opportunity to comment, since there may be a dispute about whether a right has indeed arisen, and if so what its extent is. Statutory declarations by the person claiming the right, and others with knowledge of the use that has taken place, will normally be required.

Assessment

4-65   Though other possible easements should not be overlooked, the owners or occupiers of a private road will be concerned primarily with private rights of way.

4-66   In a private road which is not a highway, the ability to grant or refuse new private rights of way is valuable because it may permit a degree of control over development: existing rights of way may be

---

27. The law will change under the Land Registration Act 2002.
28. The Land Registration Rules 1925, SI 1925 No. 1093, since amended on many occasions, supplement the Land Registration Act 1925.

limited, and further rights may therefore be needed in order for development to take place. Conversely, private rights of way lose much of their practical significance if a private road becomes a highway. The grant of fresh rights of way calls for careful consideration in the light of legal advice. An unrestricted right of way may be a hostage to fortune, since it will allow the land in question to be used for any purpose, whether or not the owner of the road, or residents, approve of it or foresaw it. It will usually be desirable for the grant of a right of way to be subject to carefully-framed limitations and conditions. An obligation to contribute to the cost of maintenance will usually be imposed in the deed granting the right of way.

Prescription may lead to the creation of new rights of way, and other easements. The owners or occupiers of a private road thus need to be alert to any unauthorised use of the road to gain access to property. It is difficult to see any advantage in allowing easements to arise by prescription, in view of the possible uncertainty about whether a right has arisen, and if so what its scope is. The better course, if unauthorised use of the road is taking place, is for the owner to take action to regularise the position by:

- Granting permission, if the intention is to create a temporary right. This should be done in writing, and should make clear that the permission is personal to the person concerned and may be withdrawn at any time without notice.

- Granting an easement, if the intention is to create a permanent right for the benefit of land, taking care to impose suitable limitations on the use of the road and/or on the use of the land having the benefit of the easement.

4-67

The latter option will not be available to a person or organisation which is merely an occupier but not an owner of the road*. But occupiers and owners can take action to halt unauthorised use, and this will prevent a right being acquired by prescription. (those in possession of land, as well as owners, can take action for trespass*.)

4-68

*See 4-14.

*See 6-5.

The regulations made under s. 68 of the Countryside and Rights of Way Act 2000 will be important if the road has been used for vehicular access to houses in the road but the road is not a highway and there is no expressly-granted private right of way for vehicles. Such use cannot give rise to a prescriptive right of way for vehicles unless it pre-dated the Road Traffic Act 1930 and was not criminal for any other reason. But owners of houses are now able to obtain a right of way by following the procedure in the regulations and serving notice on the owner. If the true owner is unknown, it appears that notice can be

4-69

served separately on each of the frontagers, and a right of way thereby obtained, though the regulations contain no guidance on how the sum payable is to be shared between them.

4-70 If the owner of the road is a residents association or management company, a right can be granted. There is every advantage in pre-empting the procedure under the regulations and reaching agreement for the grant of a vehicular right of way, on whatever terms appear appropriate. Indeed, the same can be said of alleged prescriptive rights: if their scope is uncertain, there may be advantage in replacing the prescriptive right by one granted by deed, so that its terms are clear.

4-71 In the event of a dispute about rights of way, whether granted by deed or acquired prescription, legal advice is likely to be needed. If it is decided to apply to the court for an injunction, to halt unauthorised use of the road, the application should be made promptly, since the court may refuse an injunction if the delay has been unfair to the person concerned—for example, someone who, in the belief that he enjoys the necessary rights of way, is well advanced with a development by the time the court is asked to intervene.

Chapter 5: Parking

Introduction

The parking of motor vehicles is likely to be of importance in most private roads. This chapter is devoted to parking—whether a right to park exists, and what action can be taken if parking causes problems.

Contrary, perhaps, to popular perception, there is no general right to park in highways maintainable at the public expense; though parking is often tolerated by local authorities, as the owners of these roads, except where parking restrictions are in force. In a private road there is equally no automatic right to park, whether for owners of property fronting the road, or for residents and their visitors, or indeed for the public at large. Only the owner of the road can claim that right*. But parking may be permitted; and in certain circumstances a legal right to park may exist as an easement.

*See 2-1 onwards for the right of an owner of land.

The following paragraphs deal first with private roads which are not highways; then those which are highways are considered separately.

Licences

The owners of a private road may choose to say specifically who does and does not have their permission to park in the road. If so, they may either give permission under a contract, in return for a payment of some kind, in money or money's worth; or they may give permission without asking anything in return. In both cases there is a licence to park*.

*See 1-46 onwards for licences generally.

Perhaps more common is the situation in which the owner of the road has neither expressly granted nor expressly refused permission, but the road has been freely used by residents (and perhaps others) for parking. What construction should be put upon this state of affairs— is it that those parking on the road have no permission and are trespassing in doing so, or that the owner of the road is impliedly agreeing to the parking, so that there is permission? This is in effect the same question considered in chapter 4 in relation to prescriptive rights of way*. The accepted answer is that where nothing is said by the

*See 1-48 on the revocation of licences.

owner of the road about parking there is no implied consent[1]; and the person concerned is therefore trespassing.

Parking as an expressly-granted easement

5-5 While a licence may be a satisfactory way of permitting parking in a private road on a temporary basis, it will not be a satisfactory long-term arrangement, which will survive changes of ownership of the road and of the house with the benefit of the right. A permanent right can in principle be granted in the form of an easement—a right by which the owner of one piece of land can make some use of nearby land*.

*See 4-1 onwards.

5-6 To be valid, however, an easement must not interfere too greatly with the use of the land by its owner. This is an important issue in relation to parking, since parking a car generally means monopolising, for the time being, the land on which the car is parked, leaving little use of the land to the owner[2]. But there is a difference between parking always on the same spot, whether or not this is marked out as a parking place, and parking in different places within a larger area—for example, a stretch of road—since the latter interferes much less with the owner's use of the land.

5-7 For many years it was uncertain whether the courts would regard a right to park in a particular spot as a valid easement, though there was less doubt about a right to park somewhere within a defined area[3]. But the better view is now that both sorts of right would generally be recognised by the court as valid easements, if granted by the owner of the land[4]. One relevant argument is that if a deed is unclear, it is generally interpreted in the way less favourable to the person granting rights under the deed[5]. So if a doubt is raised about whether a right to park leaves the owner of the land with sufficient use of his land, the doubt is likely to be resolved against the landowner, who has in effect, in granting the right, said that he is content with the use of the land left to him.

5-8 However, this is not to say that a right to park will be a valid easement in all circumstances. In particular, it may be that where what

---

1. See *R (Beresford) v Sunderland City Council* [2001] EWCA Civ 1218, [2002] 2 WLR 693, [2001] 4 All ER 565
2. The same legal problem arises in relation to storing other things on land.
3. See *London & Blenheim Estates Ltd v Ladbroke Retail Parks Ltd* [1994] 1 WLR 31, [1993] 4 All ER 157, *Handel v St Stephen's Close Ltd* [1994] 1 EGLR 70.
4. *Stonebridge v Bygrave* [2001] All ER (D) 376.
5. Sometimes known as the "contra proferentem" rule.

© A. W. & C. Barsby 2003

is contemplated is that a vehicle will remain stationary in the same spot for long periods, rather than coming and going from time to time, the right granted will be regarded not as a valid easement but as some other form of arrangement—perhaps even a lease of the land.

Parking as a prescriptive easement

5-9 A resident in a private road—or the owner of nearby property—may have parked regularly in the road for 20 years or more. Can this lead to the creation of a prescriptive easement, in the same way that use of land for access can give rise to a prescriptive right of way, in accordance with the rules explained in chapter 4[*]?

*See 4-12 onwards.

5-10 Assuming that there has been use "as of right" for the necessary period, the answer is not necessarily the same as that given above for an easement expressly granted. The reason is that the rule of interpretation which works against a person granting a right expressly does not apply, and in its absence the courts are more likely to insist that the pre-conditions for the existence of an easement are observed strictly. In many cases, the courts have said that the right to store goods on land cannot exist as a prescriptive easement, so that, even if there has been use of the appropriate kind for 20 years (or 40 years, if oral permission has been given) no prescriptive easement will result.

5-11 It is certainly clear that where parking monopolises the use of the land in question, it is unlikely to lead to a prescriptive easement. In one important case[6], the right claimed was the right to park six cars in a stretch of private road long enough to contain just six cars, during office hours. The Court of Appeal decided that this was too great an interference with the rights of the owner of the road for it to be a valid prescriptive easement.

5-12 Where, however, the right claimed is the right to park one or more cars over a larger area, the court might well reach the conclusion that the right did not interfere excessively with the use of the land by the owner, and could constitute a valid easement. But there are many unresolved questions. What is the relationship between the vehicles and the land over which the right is claimed. Must the latter be at least twice the size of the former? Or ten times as big? And what about the periods during which vehicles are parked—is this relevant to the question of whether a right to park can be a valid easement? The

---

6. *Batchelor v Marlow* [2001] EWCA Civ 1051. And see also *Central Midland Estates Ltd v Leicester Dyers Ltd, The Times* 18 February 2003.

decisions of the courts provide no clear answers to such questions, and the law is therefore uncertain.

Parking in connection with a right of way

5-13 A right to park may be granted on its own, or as a right additional to a right of way[7]. A separate, and more important question, is whether a right of way by implication carries with it a right to park.

5-14 When an easement is granted, the right granted is considered to extend to anything which needs to be done in order for the right granted to be exercised. "Necessary" in this context means actually necessary, not merely convenient. This rule applies to rights of way, and is the reason why there is an implied right to repair a road over which there is a private right of way[*]. Depending upon the physical layout of the property which has the right of way, a right of way may often bring with it a right to stop vehicles in the road, for the purposes of loading or unloading, or to use the road for turning round. In one case[8] involving commercial premises with a right of way over a private road, the court considered whether there was an ancillary right to park in the road, for loading and unloading, but decided that there was not, because the premises included a forecourt which could be used for this purpose.

[*]See 4-50.

5-15 Here the law is perhaps only reflecting common sense. It is likely that in many cases a right of way over a private road would bring with it the right to park for brief periods so that people could get into or out of cars and goods could be loaded and unloaded. But this is rather different from parking which has no immediate connection with arrivals at, or departures from, houses in a private road, but which amounts to using the road as storage space for cars. Could the latter ever be upheld, as being necessary for the exercise of a right of way?

5-16 In one case[9], the courts found that it could. Here, however, the right of way had been granted for the benefit of land which had already been built on—a coach-house, at the back of a large house—and where there was apparently no room for parking on the land which had the benefit of the right of way. The court concluded that it was reasonably necessary to park on the private driveway, which

---

7. See *Patel v WH Smith (Eziot) Ltd* [1987] 1 WLR 853, [1987] 2 All ER 569, where a right to load and unload vehicles in a yard had been expressly granted, and *Warmhaze Ltd v Soterios Aspris* [2001] All ER (D) 196.
8. See *London and Suburban Land and Building Co (Holdings) Ltd v Carey* (1991) 62 P&CR 480
9. *Graham v. Philcox* [1984] QB 747.

belonged to the owners of the large house, in order to enjoy the right of way which had been granted.

This reasoning is unlikely to have a very wide application. Generally, in relation to a house in a private road, the position is likely to fall into one of the following two categories:

5-17

- The house was built, and the right of way granted, at a date (perhaps from the 1920s or 1930s onwards) when the owners would expect to own cars, and parking or garaging space was accordingly provided within the curtilage of the house[10].

- The house was built at an earlier date, when the owners would not expect to own cars, and no parking space was provided—and it therefore cannot be said that in the circumstances a right to park was, when the right of way was granted, necessary in order for the right of way to be exercised.

A right to park in a private road might possibly be acquired as a right additional to a right of way, under the Vehicular Access Across Common and Other Land (England) Regulations 2002*.

5-18

*See 4-42.

Remedies for unlawful parking

Civil law Parking in a private road without permission or a legal right to do so is trespassing, and legal action can thus be taken against the person concerned. The wrong is done not just to the owner of the road, but (if different) to the person in possession of it*. That person can bring legal proceedings to obtain compensation, though the amount of harm done would typically be small, and the compensation therefore very modest. More important, perhaps, they can insist that trespassing ceases, and could if need be obtain an injunction against the person concerned.

5-19

*See 1-44 and 6-5.

Whether or not someone is trespassing by parking in a private road, if they obstruct the road and so interfere with its use by those with private rights of way, a different civil wrong (nuisance) is committed —in this case, against the person whose land has the benefit of the right of way. The same would be true if a parked car obstructed access to a private road, and prevented residents from entering it. As in the case

5-20

---

10. In modern times, it may be a condition of planning permission that parking spaces be provided.

of a trespass, legal action could be taken to obtain compensation, and if necessary an injunction to prevent a recurrence of the obstruction.

Criminal law If a private road is not a highway, nor a road in which public use takes place and is tolerated, driving into the road for more than 15 yards in order to park is an offence, under s. 34 of the Road Traffic Act 1988. If parking caused damage, for example to a grass verge or a pavement, it would in principle be possible to prosecute for the offence of criminal damage, under the Criminal Damage Act 1971.

Self-help One particular form of self-help which is now often used in relation to unauthorised parking is wheel clamping, so that a vehicle is immobilised, and a fee can be demanded for its release. Interfering with someone else's property can itself be a trespass (that is, a trespass to goods). But within strictly-defined limits it is lawful. The courts have emphasised that a landowner must show that a person whose car has been wheel-clamped was made aware by a notice or otherwise of the risk that this would happen[11]. In addition[12]:

• The fee for releasing the clamp must be reasonable.

• The vehicle must released without delay when the fee is tendered. And

• Arrangements must be in place so that the motorist can contact the owner of the land and pay the fee.

In these circumstances, wheelclamping as a response to a trespassing motorist is lawful. Wheelclamping may be a particularly effective way of responding to unauthorised parking when the culprits are not the same people on each occasion but many different members of the public. It should be remembered, however, that taking this course is a substitute for, not an addition to, obtaining redress from the courts; also that the courts do not encourage such action.

Wheel-clamping and other activities which tend to be carried out by private security workers will be regulated under the Private Security Industry Act 2001. This Act is *not yet fully in force*. A body known as the Security Industry Authority will license security staff. Among the activities which will be regulated is immobilising vehicles, "...by the immobilisation of a motor vehicle by the attachment to the vehicle, or to a part of it, of an immobilising device", where this is "....for the purpose of preventing or inhibiting the removal of a vehicle

---

11. *Vine v Waltham Forest London Borough Council, The Times* 12 April 2000.
12. See *Arthur v Anker, The Times* 1 December 1995, [1996] 2 WLR 602, [1996] 3 All ER 783

by a person otherwise entitled to remove it" (paragraph 3 of Schedule 2 to the Act).

5-24 The requirement does not apply, however, to "...any activities carried out in relation to a vehicle while it is on a road within the meaning of the Road Traffic Act 1988". As a result, it appears that residents in a private road which is a road within the meaning of the 1988 Act* will be able to carry out wheel-clamping without authorisation under the Act, but that residents in other private roads will require authorisation.

*See 1-20.

Private roads which are highways

5-25 The fact that a private road is a highway does not affect the ownership of the road. Private rights over the land may still exist, in the same way as if the road was not a highway. But, in relation to parking, the fact that the road is a highway introduces several other considerations.

5-26 First, members of the public will have the right to use the road. The public's right to use the road will include stopping briefly for purposes incidental to the use of the highway, but not the use of the road for parking in the sense of storing a motor vehicle for a period of hours or days: this will be a trespass against which the owner or occupier of the road may take legal action.

5-28 Secondly, parking which unreasonably obstructs a private road which is a highway is an offence*, quite apart from any civil liability which flows from interfering with private rights of way. There are also specific offences, applying to "roads" within the meaning of the Road Traffic Act 1988, of:

*See further 7-3.

- Leaving a vehicle in position which involves the danger of injury to other road users (s. 22).

- Parking a heavy commercial vehicle (i.e. one weighing more than 7.5 tonnes) on the verge of a road (s. 19).

5-29 Local authorities also have powers to regulate traffic, whether by prohibiting waiting, or by marking out parking places and charging for parking*.

*See chapter 9.

for more information see www.barsby.com

Assessment

5-30 Depending on the physical characteristics of a private road, there may be ample space for parking, and so no particular reason for disputes to arise. If space is limited, however, the question of who has a right to park, and where, may become relevant. Parking which consists merely of stopping in the normal course of arrivals and departures is unlikely to constitute a civil wrong, and should not generally cause problems, unless the driver of the vehicle is trespassing in coming into the road.

5-31 Parking for longer periods is a different matter. Few residents are likely to have an expressly-granted right to park in the road. The central question therefore is whether residents who have used the road for parking—typically, perhaps, the part of the road outside their own house—may be able to claim a permanent right to do so, by prescription. For the reasons explained above, the law on this point is not entirely clear, and no simple answer can be given to the question until the courts reach a conclusive view. However, the owners or managers of the road may in practice be able to deal with disputes, by indicating who may park and where, if those concerned will refrain from asserting the right to park and accept his decision. If a licence to park is granted, this should be done in writing and should make clear whether the licence can be revoked by the owner of the land.

5-32 The law concerning parking which obstructs the road, or access to it, is not subject to the same uncertainty: in the event of a dispute, the person whose right of way is being obstructed may take legal action against the person causing the obstruction.

Chapter 6: Civil law

Introduction

Parts of the civil law have been considered in other chapters*. This chapter deals more generally with civil law. It concentrates on the potential liability of a residents association or company for torts (civil wrongs), but also explains the Access to Neighbouring Land Act 1992 and restrictive covenants. The latter are unlikely to affect residents associations directly, since a private road itself is unlikely to be subject to a restrictive covenant, but this topic is included because it may indirectly be of relevance, particularly in relation to development in a private road.

*See particularly chapter 5 on parking.

Torts

The law of torts defines circumstances in which one person can take legal action against another in the civil courts to obtain redress. Torts overlap to some extent, but do not cover every situation in which one person causes injury or loss to another. Each tort has its own rules about such matters as what must be proved, and what sorts of injury or loss are covered. Some of the law comes from legislation; much is to be found in the decisions of the courts.

Trespass

Trespass consists of going on to land unlawfully. It may take the form of any direct entry on to land, for example walking or driving along a private road, or parking or dumping rubbish in the road. Different classes of people may be legally entitled to use a private road, so that what they do will not be a trespass. These include:

- The owner, and others using it with his permission, for access, parking any other purposes*.

*See 2-3.

- Those using it for access, by virtue of a private right of way*.

- Officials and others with legal powers enabling them to enter on to land.

- The utility companies, who will be entitled to enter to install, inspect and repair, pipes, cables and other equipment under and over the road*.

- If the road is a highway, members of the public exercising their rights of way, who will be entitled to use the road for access*.

*See chapter 4.

*See chapter 10.

*And other ancillary purposes: see chapter 3.

6-3   As to the third category, many local government and other officials are given power to enter land, inspect it, and in some cases carry work. Some examples are mentioned elsewhere in the text*. A general power—which is not limited to officials—is that contained in s. 324 of the Town and Country Planning Act 1990. Any person authorised in writing by the local authority may enter land for the purpose of surveying it in connection with a planning application, or for other planning purposes.

*See e.g. 10-20.

6-4   A person who goes on to land without being entitled to do so is trespassing, and this includes a person who has some right or permission which he exceeds; for example, a person with a right of way for non-commercial traffic who drives down a private road in a commercial vehicle is trespassing, as is an official who has a right of entry for a particular purpose but goes on to land for some other purpose.

6-5   Legal action for trespass can be taken by any person in possession of land, whether or not they are the owner of it, since the policy of the law is to protect a person in that position against anyone other than the true owner of the land. Compensation is payable, and the courts may grant an injunction to prevent further trespassing*.

*See 6-35.

6-6   The owners of dogs, cats and other animals can be liable for the trespassing of their pets, but only if it can be shown that they were negligent, or intended the trespass. In practice, then, there is usually no remedy for straying dogs and cats—unless they cause damage, in which case it may be possible to take action under the Animals Act 1971.

6-7   Some trespasses are criminal in nature, in recognition of the fact that they are particularly serious and that punishment should ensue for a breach of the law*.

*See 7-27.

Nuisance

Legally, a "nuisance" is anything which causes annoyance to others, typically by threatening their health or comfort or by interfering with their right to enjoy land. The law recognises that in certain circumstances a nuisance which affects the public at large—a public nuisance—is a criminal offence*. To the extent, however, that a nuisance (whether or not it is also a public nuisance) affects one or more occupiers of land, it is a civil matter, and the civil courts can award compensation and grant other remedies.

*See 7-4.

Interference with a right of way or any other easement is a nuisance for legal purposes, because an easement is a right in the nature of land*. There are also some special rules which apply to highways, and these are considered below*.

*See 4-56.
*See 6-13.

Land generally Nuisances may take many different forms; but they fall into several rather different categories. Encroachments on to land by trees or other vegetation which overhangs a boundary, or whose roots grow across a boundary, are a nuisance. (Because they are indirect rather than direct entries on to land, the law regards them as nuisances rather than trespasses.) Damage caused by water often falls within this category[1]. Finally, anything such as noise, fumes, smells, smoke or vibration may be a nuisance to an occupier of land, because they may interfere with his health or comfort. This latter class differs in that here the law is concerned only with interferences which are unreasonable. What is reasonable depends to a large extent on the nature of the neighbourhood[2]. The noise and fumes which may be acceptable in an industrial estate, for example, are likely to be unreasonable in a quiet residential area. Minor interferences with the enjoyment of land are expected to be tolerated; and temporary disturbances, for example those caused by building work, are unlikely to constitute a nuisance if the person carrying out the works is using reasonable care and skill to avoid causing an annoyance to neighbours.

The right to take action in relation to a nuisance belongs to the person occupying the land in question, who will be the person suffering from the nuisance. The proceedings will be against the person causing the nuisance, who may or may not be the owner or occupier of the land from which the nuisance is coming.

---

1. But the natural drainage of water from one piece of land to another does not amount to a nuisance: see *Palmer v Bowman, The Times* 10 November 1999.
2. It may be asked whether a grant of planning permission can change the character of the neighbourhood, and so affect liability for nuisance. The answer appears generally to be in the negative: see *Wheeler v JJ Saunders* Ltd [1995] 3 WLR 466, [1995] 2 All ER 697. However, large-scale development may change the character of an area and so affect the legal position.

6-12 In most respects, a private road is unlikely either to be a source of nuisances from the point of view of the owners of neighbouring land, or to be affected by nuisances from neighbouring land. Traffic using a private road may cause a certain amount of noise and fumes, but provided the use of the road is not out of keeping with the area in question, the court would be unlikely to regard the noise and fumes as unreasonable, and hence as a nuisance to neighbouring land. The sort of nuisance most likely to apply to a private road is perhaps overhanging vegetation: trees in the road might overhang adjoining land, or roots might encroach on to it, and vice versa. A residents association or management company could be liable for damage caused by roots or overhanging vegetation, even if they were not the owners of the road, on the ground that they were exercising control over the tree[3].

6-13 *Highways* Anything which obstructs a highway, or causes a danger to users of it (or both) may be a public nuisance. The person responsible for the nuisance may therefore find both that he has committed an offence, and that he is liable to compensate any person who suffers particularly as a result of the nuisance. Leaving an unlit car in a dangerous position in a highway at night may thus be an offence; and if a user of the highway collides with the car and is injured he may be entitled to compensation from the person who left the car there. These principles apply to many different sorts of obstructions and dangers, including things left in a highway, excavations and building works in a highway.

6-14 A person responsible for a tree or an artificial structure adjoining the highway may be liable if injury or damage is caused to a user of the highway. Though the law is not entirely clear, it seems that there will be no liability to users of the highway for trees in respect of a danger which is not apparent; but the law may be stricter for artificial structures, and there may be liability for them even if there is no fault on the part of the person responsible.

Occupiers' liability

*See 1-43 for occupation of land.

6-15 The law imposes duties of care on an occupier of land to have regard to the safety of those who come on to the land*. If the occupier breaches the duty by failing to take sufficient care, and injury or damage is caused, she may be liable to pay compensation. Different duties of care apply, according to the status of the person who comes on to the land:

---

3. See *Jones v Portsmouth City Council* [2003] 1 WLR 427.

in particular, a higher standard applies to those who have been invited on to the land, and a lower one to trespassers. There are other differences in the law, apart from the different standards. The resulting pattern of liability in a private road is perhaps more complex than might be expected.

6-16   For most practical purposes, the duties of care are imposed by the Occupiers' Liability Acts 1957 and 1984. (There are some situations which are not covered by these duties, but which are covered by the general duty of care imposed by the law of negligence, this latter duty being otherwise comparable to the duty under the 1957 Act.)

6-17   *Who is an occupier?* In a private road, the occupier may be the owner of the road, or a committee or some other body which is exercising control—or there conceivably may be no occupier at all, since the owner is unknown and nobody is exercising control over the road.   Residents who have private rights of way over a private road will not be occupiers of the road by virtue of that fact alone, since they will not have a sufficient degree of control over the road to make them occupiers for the purposes of the Occupiers' Liability Acts.

6-18   *The Occupiers' Liability Act 1957: "visitors"* This Act imposes a general duty of care towards all "visitors" to land, that is, to all who are on the land as a result of an invitation, express or implied. People who are specifically invited to come to a private road by the occupiers—typically, a residents association—are likely to be few in number, but may include people such as contractors who are asked to come to mow the grass verges or carry out work on trees. Implied permission might also include such people as non-residents who use the road for parking, without objection from the owner of the road, and children playing in the road.

6-19   The law sometimes goes a long way to imply permission, particularly where children are concerned. If the occupier of land knows that children come on to the land, but does nothing to stop them, he may well be treated as inviting them, especially if there is some attraction which causes them to come, with the result that they are visitors for the purposes of the 1957 Act and hence owed the higher duty of care.

6-20   "Visitors" is also deemed to include (this being laid down by the 1957 Act) those who have a right of entry on to land conferred by the law (s. 2(6)). Such rights are often needed to enable officials to discharge their responsibilities in relation to planning, public health, and so on. Many different statutes confer such rights, giving officials and others the right to come on to land in specific circumstances and for specific purposes, for example to inspect premises or carry out work. Such visitors must stay within the terms of the permission they enjoy, and not start doing other things on the land, or going on to parts of it where they have no need to go, otherwise they will cease to be visitors so far as the law is concerned and become trespassers, and owed only the lesser duty of care under the 1984 Act.

6-21 The class of "visitors" thus excludes trespassers and, importantly, those exercising private rights of way. The latter category will include the owners of property in a road, who have a private right of way, and people visiting them; but such people will *not* be "visitors", from the point of the occupiers of the road, for the purposes of the 1957 Act[4]. They have a right to use the road for access; but their rights are not rights conferred by law (they are conferred by the owner of the road) and they are thus in a different position from officials with statutory rights of entry.

6-22 The extent of the occupier's duty of care under the 1957 Act is defined by s. 2(2) as follows:

> "The common duty of care is a duty to take such care as in all the circumstances of the case is reasonable to see that the visitor will be reasonably safe in using the premises for the purposes for which he is invited or permitted by the occupier to be there."

6-23 It is not possible to say precisely what an occupier must do in order to fulfil his duty. If a visitor is injured, or his property is damaged (the 1957 Act covers both possibilities) it is necessary to look at all the circumstances to see whether the accident was the result of a failure by the occupier to discharge the duty of care. The Act does provide some further help about the care required, however, since it says that an occupier has to take into account the degree of care to be expected of a visitor of that sort. The Act gives two examples, which are as follows (s. 2(3)):

> "(a) an occupier must be prepared for children to be less careful than adults; and
>
> (b) an occupier may expect that a person, in the exercise of his calling, will appreciate and guard against any special risks ordinarily incident to it, so far as the occupier leaves him free to do so."

6-24 The first paragraph is self-explanatory, and requires the occupier to do more in order to make the land safe for children. The second paragraph is relevant where a person has some special expertise. A tree-surgeon, for example, may be expected to appreciate and guard against the risks inherent in his work. The occupier of the land would not normally be liable for an accident which occurred while work was being carried out. But if there were some unusual danger, which a tree-

---

4. See *Holden v White* [1982] QB 679.

surgeon could not be expected to foresee, the occupier might be liable for failing to protect the tree-surgeon against it.

A warning of some specific danger may absolve the occupier from liability, but only if it enables the visitor to be reasonably safe (s. 2(4)(a)). Some things will not be the responsibility of the occupier, because he has no right, and hence no ability, to take action in respect of them. If, for example, a private road has street lighting installed by the local authority, the residents association would not normally be liable for any accidents caused by the inadequacy of the lighting*.

6-25

*See 9-5 on street lighting.

If an occupier of land engages a contractor, to carry out work, does the occupier incur liability if the contractor's work is faulty, and a visitor is injured? The 1957 Act provides in s. 2(4)(b) that the occupier is not liable if he has acted reasonably in entrusting the work to a contractor and has taken reasonable steps to satisfy himself that the contractor is competent and the work properly done[5].

6-26

The Occupiers' Liability Act 1984: trespassers, private rights of way
The 1984 Act imposes a lighter duty, which applies to people other than those covered by the 1957 Act. It thus covers trespassers, and those coming on to the land in pursuance of a private right of way (s. 1(3). The 1984 Act does *not* apply to members of the public exercising their right of way in a highway (s. 1(7)). The duty arises only where the occupier knows, or has reasonable grounds to know, of a danger on his premises, and of the presence of the person who is injured, and:

6-27

"...the risk is one against which, in all the circumstances of the case, he may reasonably be expected to offer the other some protection" (s. 1(3)(c)).

If these conditions are not satisfied, there is no duty on the occupier. The sort of dangers which the 1984 Act is intended to cover are those which are real and serious—for example, unlit excavations in the road which pose an obvious risk—so that if the occupier knows or ought to know that there is such a danger, and that someone may come on to the land, she should as a matter of common decency take steps to protect that person against the danger, even if the person is a trespasser. The duty is a duty:

6-28

"....to take such care as is reasonable in all the circumstances of the case to see that [the person] does not suffer injury on the premises by reason of the danger concerned" (s. 1(4)).

The 1984 Act does not cover damage to property suffered by a trespasser or the user of a private right of way: it covers only physical injury. In some circumstances, however, a trespasser may be able to

6-29

---

5. An occupier should check that a contractor has public liability insurance, but is not under a duty to check the terms of the policy: see *Gwilliam v West Hertfordshire Hospital NHS Trust* [2002] EWCA Civ 1041, 24 July 2002.

obtain compensation for damage to his property, on similar principles, in accordance with the general law.

6-30 *Highways* Neither the 1957 Act nor the 1984 Act applies to those who, as members of the public, use a highway; and there is no legal duty on the owner of a private road to maintain the surface so that it is safe[6]. But, as explained above under the heading of "Nuisance", a person who suffers injury or damage in a highway may in some circumstances be able to take legal action against a person responsible for an obstruction or danger*.

*See 6-13.

6-31 The pattern of liability towards different classes of person who come into a private road may be summarised as follows:

Table 3: Occupiers' liability

Class	Examples	Law	Duty
People with express or implied permission; officials exercising statutory rights.	Contractors asked to carry out work by residents association; children playing in road, whose presence is tolerated.	Occupiers' Liability Act 1957	Duty to make sure that visitors will be reasonably safe, for the purposes for which they are permitted to be on the land
Trespassers	Drivers from nearby roads parking without permission; children who have been told they are not to play in the road.	Occupiers' Liability Act 1984	Duty to take reasonable care to protect people from dangers
People exercising private right of way	Residents and their visitors	Occupiers' Liability Act 1984	Duty to take reasonable care to protect people from dangers
People exercising public right to use highway	Members of public driving or walking along road	Common law	No duty to maintain surface, but occupiers of road may be liable for dangers and obstructions

---

6. See *McGeown v Northern Ireland Housing Executive* (1995) 70 P&CR 10.

Negligence

The law recognises that a person is under a broad duty of care to those who are closely affected by his conduct. (Duties owed under the Occupiers' Liability Acts are essentially just instances of this general idea.) The civil wrong which imposes this general duty is known as negligence. Whether a duty of care exists in a given situation is a matter of law: not every situation is regarded as giving rise to a duty of care. Whether the person concerned has broken the duty of care depends upon several factors, including the nature of the risks being run and whether it is reasonable for the person to run those risks. Negligence has a wide application, overlapping with nuisance and occupiers' liability.

The courts can award compensation for injury or damage to property caused by negligence. It is a defence to a claim that no duty was owed to the person concerned, or that there was no breach of the duty of care; that the person making the claim consented to run the risk, or that the person making the claim was himself careless, and so partly to blame (in which case, he receives only part of the compensation he would otherwise be entitled to).

Remedies

Compensation Monetary awards ("damages") are the primary remedy for civil wrongs, and their main purpose is to compensate for the injury or loss sustained. Where no actual injury or loss has been suffered but a person's rights have been infringed, for example by a trespass which causes no damage, the amount is likely to be small; though the courts may in some cases award larger amounts as compensation for behaviour which is particularly flagrant or designed to make a profit.

Injunctions The courts have power to grant an injunction, in order to restrain further wrongdoing, where that appears to be necessary. Breach of an injunction is a contempt of court, and is punishable with up to two years' imprisonment. This remedy may be applied, for example, against a person who trespasses, or who causes a nuisance by interfering with a right of way or otherwise.

An injunction is a discretionary remedy: the courts are not obliged to grant an injunction but will do so if they feel that it is appropriate. As a general rule, the courts will grant an injunction to protect an occupier of land from trespassers or from a nuisance. But an injunction may be refused if the wrong was trivial, or if there is no need for one, because the person concerned has apologised and undertaken not to repeat what he has done, or if an injunction would be unfair and oppressive in the circumstances. The courts may be particularly reluctant to grant an injunction if there has been delay and an injunction would therefore be unfair to the person concerned. In one case[7], the court declined to grant an injunction to a resident in a private road who owned part of the roadway. The injunction was sought against another resident, who was in the course of building a new house on land he had bought. The existing rights of way were insufficient, so using the road for access meant trespassing on it. The court decided not to grant an injunction, because the application was made only when building work was well-advanced, so that an injunction would be oppressive, and because a (modest) sum would provide adequate compensation—under s. 50 of the Supreme Court Act 1981, the court may award compensation instead of a granting an injunction.

6-37 An injunction can be granted on an interim basis, pending trial of the dispute; and the court may grant an injunction where a trespass or other civil wrong is threatened, but has not actually taken place.

6-38 *Self-help* The law recognises that a person affected by a civil wrong may in some circumstances take action himself to put a stop to the wrong. This is so in the case of a nuisance. It is well-established that the occupier of land is entitled to deal with overhanging branches by cutting them off at the boundary of his land, and roots crossing the boundary may be dealt with in the same way. Vegetation removed in this way remains the property of the owner of the land on which it grew.

6-39 The right of self-help extends to going on to the land from which the nuisance comes, and "abating" it (putting a stop to it). But the courts do not encourage action of this sort, and great circumspection is required by the person who decides to do so. Action should only be attempted if it can be taken peacefully and without causing disproportionate damage, and notice should be given. The courts have expressed the view[8] that the right is limited to cases where life or property is threatened.

6-40 Self-help action can also be taken to deal with trespassers*. Again, great care is required. It is an alternative to legal proceedings, not an additional remedy. Nor can it be used after legal proceedings: if the court has considered the dispute and has refused to grant an injunction, or awarded compensation instead of an injunction, the right of self-help no longer applies[9].

*See also 5-21 onwards for wheelclamping as a way of taking action against unlawful parking.

---

7. See *Jaggard v Sawyer* [1995] 1 WLR 269, [1995] 2 AER 189.
8. See *Co-operative Wholesale Society Ltd v British Railways Board, The Times*, 20 December 1995.

Similarly, an obstruction in a highway can be removed by someone who is actually obstructed by it and wishes to pass.

Access to neighbouring land

For many years there was no general right enabling a landowner to go on to someone else's land in order to maintain or repair her own land (though it was possible for such a right to exist as an easement)*. Landowners were therefore often dependent upon getting permission from their neighbours if they needed access from neighbouring land in order to carry out work. Now, however, that gap in the law has been filled by the Access to Neighbouring Land Act 1992. The Act does not depend upon the commission of any civil wrong, but it is convenient to mention it at this point. It allows a landowner to obtain a court order, if necessary, allowing her access via neighbouring land, in order to carry out maintenance or repairs to her own land. In a private road, residents will have private rights of way, or, if the road is a highway, will be able to rely on the public right of way. But property may back on to a private road, without enjoying any right of access over the road. In such a case the 1992 Act may be relevant, because it will allow the road to be used temporarily for access. The owners or occupiers of a private road might, occasionally need to take advantage of the Act, for example if the road had a boundary wall which needed repair and which was accessible only from neighbouring land.

*See 4-60.

If permission to use land for access is refused, the landowner in question can apply to the County Court for an access order. An order can be made if the work is reasonably necessary and it would be impossible or substantially more difficult without access to neighbouring land. The order will carefully specify the terms upon which access is allowed. If the work is to be done to benefit land which is not residential land, compensation can be ordered, and this will take into account the benefit to the person who gets access, and the inconvenience to the person who has to give access. The existence of this statutory scheme gives neighbours an obvious incentive to make sensible arrangements voluntarily, thus avoiding the need for an application to the court.

---

9. See *Burton v Winters* [1993] 1 WLR, 1077 [1993] 3 All ER 847.

Restrictive covenants

6-44 Although a private road itself is unlikely to be subject to a restrictive covenant, the properties in the road may well be, and may be relevant to the use of the road and development within it. Residents associations and others concerned with private roads may therefore need to be aware of the law.

6-45 *Generally* A restrictive covenant is an undertaking in a deed which restricts the use of one piece of land and is enforceable by the owners of one or more other pieces of land.

6-46 While it is easy to set up such an arrangement between two or more current landowners, there will in many cases be a desire to impose a restriction which endures despite changes in the ownership of the land.

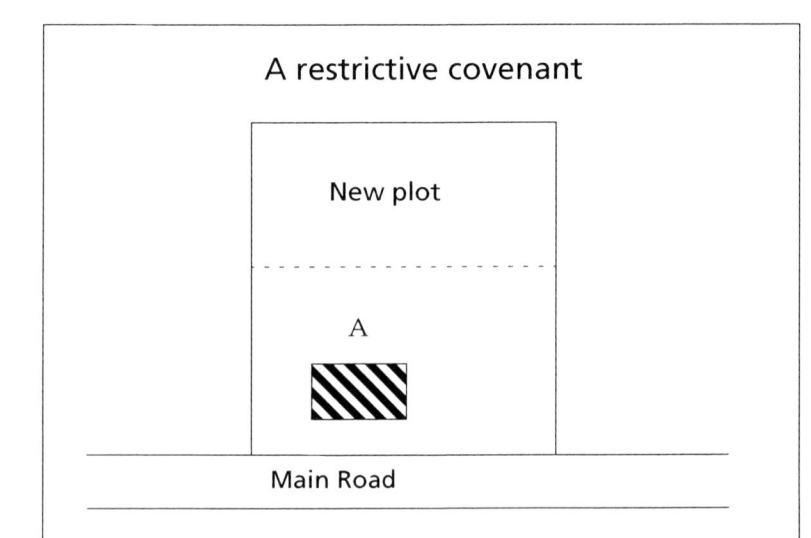

A restrictive covenant

New plot

A

Main Road

The owner of land marked A sells off the rear part of the garden, so that new development can take place. To protect the amenity of A, he imposes restrictive covenants which confine the use of the new plot to a single dwelling and forbid the parking of caravans and boats. The new plot is burdened with the restrictive covenant, and land A has the benefit of it.

6-47 The law allows such an arrangement to endure, and to apply to successive owners of the two pieces of land, provided that[10]:

---

10. These rules do not apply to covenants in leases, which continue to bind successive landlords and tenants.

- The undertaking is negative—an undertaking *not* to do something. (Hence the term "restrictive covenant".)

- It is relevant to the land which has the benefit of it, and not merely personal in nature.

- There is an intention that the restrictive covenant should be binding on future owners of the land subject to it.

- Later owners are aware of the existence of the restrictive covenant when they buy the land.

6-48 A restrictive covenant will be shown on the Land Register in relation to the land affected by it; and a purchaser of the land will thus be aware of it and bound by it when he acquires the land.

6-49 Many different restrictions on the use of land may be imposed by means of restrictive covenants. Common are covenants which forbid the use of land for purposes other than residential use, or limit the number of houses which may be built on the land, or prevent the landowner from putting caravans on the land, putting up fences, keeping pets, and so on.

6-50 A restrictive covenant is a private arrangement between the landowners in question, and is thus for them to enforce*. If they wish, the current owners of the land can agree to alter or remove the restrictive covenant, on whatever terms they think fit. These might include the making of a payment, or some other form of quid pro quo.

*See 6-55 on enforcement.

6-51 *Building schemes*   Estates of houses and other sorts of property are common; and in this situation the law has a special rule, whereby restrictive covenants can be imposed on each property as it is sold off, and can benefit all the other properties. Restrictive covenants are often applied to houses in a housing estate in order to preserve the amenity of the whole estate, for example by restricting fences at the front of properties, colours and styles which may be used on the outside of houses, and so on.

6-52 *The role of the Lands Tribunal*   The Lands Tribunal, which was set up in 1949, has a specialised jurisdiction under which it deals with various forms of property dispute. One task it performs is to deal with applications to discharge or modify restrictive covenants (i.e. cancel them, or alter them so that they are less restrictive). This power was given to the Lands Tribunal by s. 84 of the Law of Property Act 1925[11].

---

11. The Law of Property Act 1969 enlarged the power. The legislation applies to certain other restrictions, but not to restrictions which are imposed as part of the planning process. Restrictions written into private rights of way are also generally considered to be outside the jurisdiction of the Lands Tribunal.

6-53 Since restrictive covenants may last for a very long time, they may become obsolete; and, even if recent, may unreasonably impede development. Hence the procedure by which restrictive covenants may be discharged or modified. The planning background will always be relevant, though not conclusive, to the Land Tribunal's approach: if planning permission has been granted for development, this will be taken into account in considering whether a restrictive covenant which prevents that development should be discharged or modified.

6-54 The legislation allows the Lands Tribunal to act in four different situations:

- The restriction is obsolete (s. 84(1)(a)).

- The restriction impedes reasonable use of the land and *either* (a) it gives no practical benefit, *or* (b) it is contrary to the public interest (s. 84(1)(aa) and (1A)).

- Everyone who has the benefit of the restriction agrees that it should be discharged or modified (s. 84(1)(b)).

- Discharging or modifying the restriction will not harm the people who have the benefit of it (s. 84(1)(c)).

6-55 *Enforcement* A landowner whose land has the benefit of a restrictive covenant does not have to enforce it. If he wishes to do so, he will generally want to obtain an injunction, to stop a particular use of the land subject to the restrictive covenant, rather than compensation. In principle, the courts will generally grant an injunction in such circumstances. But they may decline to do so if there has been a delay, and it would be unfair or oppressive to do so[*].

*See 6-35 on injunctions generally.

6-56 A restrictive covenant may also prove to be unenforceable if:

- The landowner with the benefit of the restrictive covenant has in the past disregarded breaches, and thus given the impression that he does not intend to enforce the covenant.

- There are legal difficulties in proving that the land has the benefit of the restrictive covenant. This will tend to be so if the covenant is an old one and there have been many dealings with the land over the years.

- The Lands Tribunal discharge or modify the restrictive covenant.

Assessment

6-57 Trespass has a special significance for the owner or occupier of a private road: if anyone is using the road unlawfully, legal action can be taken against him for trespassing. The courts will generally be prepared to grant an injunction if that is necessary to ensure that the trespassing ceases. But, as explained above, prompt action may in some circumstances be vital if an injunction is to be obtained, failing which the only remedy may be compensation.

6-58 The right to trim overhanging vegetation is long-established and well understood, and is one example of the right to take physical action to remedy a civil wrong. The owner or occupier of a private road can thus trim vegetation overhanging the road, and the owner or occupier of adjoining land would equally be entitled to trim vegetation from the road overhanging that land. A person with a private right of way which was obstructed by vegetation could, on the same basis, cut it back. With this exception, do-it-yourself action to deal with civil wrongs is often unwise, and if undertaken needs to be undertaken with great care.

6-59 The occupier of a private road may be liable to compensate a person who suffers injury or damage while using the road. While private roads may not be thought of as inherently dangerous places, they do not necessarily have the safety features, such as lighting, pavements, and sight-lines across bends and junctions, which are taken for granted on public roads; and there has been a noticeable increase in litigiousness in recent years, perhaps due partly to the availability of "no win, no fee" agreements with solicitors. The risk of accidents must thus be taken seriously.

6-60 If the road is not a highway, duties of care are owed to people who come into the road. The less onerous duty under the 1984 Act will tend to be the more important, since this is the duty owed to those exercising private rights of way, and to trespassers. If an obvious danger arises, such as a large hole in the road or a fallen tree, action will be required to prevent injury to users of the road, for example putting up warning notices and temporary fencing, until such time as the danger can be dealt with.

6-61 The more extensive duty under the 1957 Act will be owed only to those who, like maintenance contractors, visit the road as such (rather than houses in the road). This class is likely to be quite small. But it needs to be remembered that anyone who is in the habit of using the road without permission may, if the owner of the road knows about it and tacitly allows such use, be regarded not as a trespasser but as a "visitor", and so within the 1957 Act. This is particularly relevant to children, since there may be a natural and understandable tendency for a quiet private road to be used as a playground by children, whether the children of residents or of families living nearby. If the owner of a private road tolerates such use, the children are likely to be regarded as "visitors", and so owed the duty of care laid down by the 1957 Act, which is a duty to see that they are reasonably safe in using the road for the purpose for which they are invited or permitted to be there. If the road cannot be rendered safe for those purposes, in view of the traffic using it and other matters, it will be prudent to make clear that such use is not permitted. The duty then owed will be the lighter duty, under the 1984 Act.

6-62 If the road is a highway, it is likely that users will be regarded as exercising the public right of way, even though they might otherwise have been entitled to make use of a private right of way. As explained above, the duties of care under the 1957 and 1984 Acts do not apply to users of a highway; however, any person responsible for an obstruction or danger in the road (which may or may not be the occupier of the road) may be liable to compensate a person who suffers injury or damage. Since it may be unclear whether a public right of way has arisen, it may also be unclear whether the duty under the 1984 Act is owed to users of a private road. In any event, a person not covered by the public right of way would be a trespasser, and the duty under the 1984 Act would apply.

6-63 The legal position concerning the duties of care owed to different sorts of persons who come on to land is thus quite involved. In practice, a residents association or company should be able to protect itself from liability by:

- Making sure that action is always taken in respect of serious dangers.

- Seeing that anyone within the limited class of "visitors" for the purposes of the 1957 Act is reasonably safe.

- Making sure that things are not placed in or near to the road, especially if it is a highway, so as to cause an obstruction or a danger.

6-64 Though these measures should minimise the risks, it will always be prudent for a residents association or company to maintain public liability insurance in respect of the road. This will be especially so in the case of a residents association, since the persons responsible for looking after the road may then be personally liable[*].

[*]See 12-13.

Chapter 7: Offences

Introduction

The following paragraphs deal with a range of offences, under the Highways Act 1980 and other Acts, which are concerned with misbehaviour in relation to roads. Some offences apply only to highways, some more widely. In most cases the maximum punishment is a fine*.

7-0

*See 1-50 for maximum levels of fines.

Highways Act offences

Most of the offences mentioned below are designed to punish those who endanger or interfere with the users of a highway, or who damage or obstruct a highway. These are of relevance only to private roads which are highways. Some offences go further, however, and apply to all roads which are "streets", as defined in the Highways Act 1980, and thus apply to all private roads*.

7-1

*See, for the meaning of "street", 1-19.

If, for example, an accident occurs, in the course of building operations in or near a street, and the accident gives rise to the risk of serious injury to any person in the street, the owner of the land commits an offence (s. 168). A person proposing to erect or take down a building in a "street or court", or repair the outside of a building, must erect a close-boarded hoarding or fence so as to separate the building from the street (s. 172). A hoarding in or adjoining a street must be "securely fixed to the satisfaction of the [local authority]" (s. 173). A person executing works in a street must take proper precautions in relation to any danger to traffic, including the erection of barriers and warning signs and the lighting of works during the hours of darkness (s. 174). In each case, failure to do so is an offence. It is also an offence to construct a "vault, arch or cellar" or other building works under a street without the consent of the local authority (s. 179).

7-2

Offences in relation to highways include (in addition to the above) the following:

7-3

- Damaging the highway. It is an offence to make ditches or excavations in a highway which is a carriageway*; or to remove any soil or turf except for the purpose of improving the highway

*See 3-3 for the meaning of "carriageway".

[*] See 1-25 for the meaning of "made-up".

[*] See 9-18 for power to remove signs.

[*] See also 9-27 onwards for naming of roads, and 9-17 for road signs.

and with the consent of the local authority; or to deposit anything on the highway so as to damage it; or to damage it by means of any fire or firework or firearm, or to damage any official traffic sign, milestone or signpost (s. 131).

● Disturbing the surface of a footpath or bridleway or a carriageway which is not made-up, so as to make it inconvenient for the exercise of the public right of way (s. 131A)[*].

● Making any mark on, or affixing any sign to the highway, or any tree or structure on or in the highway[*] (s. 132). (It is, however, a defence that the person concerned had a "reasonable excuse", and this would seem to cover a sign giving the name of a private road[*], and any other sign erected for a good reason, for example to warn of some danger.)

● Obstructing the highway without lawful authority or excuse. Whether the offence has been committed is essentially a question of what is a reasonable use of the highway. Minor and momentary obstructions may be regarded as excusable. It is not necessary, however, that any person should actually have been obstructed or inconvenienced, nor that the whole of the highway should have been blocked[1] (s. 137).

● Erecting a building or planting a hedge in a highway which contains a carriageway, without lawful authority or excuse (s. 138). (This would not prevent the owner of a private road from planting a hedge along the verge, for example, provided he did not thereby commit some other offence, such as obstructing the highway: as owner of the land, he would have the necessary authority to plant a hedge on it.)

● Depositing a builder's skip in a highway without the permission of the local authority. The Highways Act contains detailed provisions in relation to skips. The local authority, in granting permission for a skip to be placed in a highway, may impose conditions; for example conditions as to its siting, and the way in which it is to be lit. Provided that any conditions are observed, it is a defence to any charge of obstructing the highway that the skip was placed there with permission. The local authority, or a constable in uniform, may require the skip to be

---

1. See *Torbay Borough Council v Cross* (1995) 159 JP 682, in which the court decided that a shop display was an obstruction, though it covered only about 5% of a wide pedestrianised street.

removed or repositioned, even though it was placed on the highway with permission, and failure to do this is an offence. The local authority or the police may themselves remove or reposition a skip, and may recover the cost from the owner of the skip (ss. 139 and 140)[2]. Skips deposited on a highway must be marked in accordance with regulations[3].

● Planting a tree or shrub in a made-up carriageway, or within 15 feet of the centre of a made-up carriageway, and failing to remove it when served by the local authority with notice to do so (s. 141; compare s. 138, mentioned above). If the carriageway is less than 30 feet wide, the section will extend to part or all of the verge. The reason why planting is prohibited may be that trees and shrubs growing on or too close to the carriageway are dangerous, or may interfere with the use of the highway, or damage it. But local authorities have a special power to grant permission to the occupier or owner of any premises adjoining the highway[4] to plant and maintain trees, shrubs, plants or grass in any part of a highway (s. 142). A person who plants in accordance with permission does not commit an offence. (But if he breaches any conditions, he is deemed to have committed an offence under s. 141.) In most cases, the road will be a highway maintainable at public expense, and the owner will necessarily be the local authority, which is thus in a position to agree in its capacity as owner, as well as giving permission under s. 142. It is not entirely clear how this provision is to work for private roads which are highways, but which are not maintainable at the public expense, and so do not belong to the local authority—presumably the permission of the owner of the road is required as well, so that his wishes cannot be overridden by the grant of permission by the local authority. Section 142 may be intended mainly for verges and other small pieces of land which form part of a highway, and which an adjoining owner may wish to maintain. Conditions can be attached to the permission granted, and the permission can be expressed as applying to subsequent owners of the land adjoining the highway. The person to whom permission is given must

---

2. A charge may be made, under the Local Authorities (Transport Charges) Regulations 1998, SI 1998/948, only if the highway is maintainable at the public expense. So in private roads which are highways, the consent of the local authority is required to deposit a skip, but no charge can be made by the local authority.
3. The Builders' Skips (Markings) Regulations 1988, SI 1988/1933.
4. Oddly, perhaps, it seems that permission cannot be granted to the person who actually owns the highway if he is not also the owner of adjoining land.

indemnify the local authority against a claim for compensation not due to the local authority's negligence.

- Depositing things on a highway without lawful authority or reasonable excuse (s. 148). This embraces several different prohibitions. No "dung, compost or other material for dressing land, or any rubbish" may be deposited on a made-up carriage way or within 15 feet from the centre of the carriageway. Nor may "any thing whatsoever" be deposited on a highway so as to interrupt its use. The section also extends to a hawker or itinerant trader who pitches a booth, stall or stand on a highway.

- Causing various kinds of danger or annoyance to users of the highway. This is also a multifarious offence, covering the deposit of anything on a highway so as to cause danger or injury; lighting fires on a highway which is a carriageway, or discharging a firework or firearm within 50 feet of the centre of a carriageway, so as to cause interruption, injury or danger; playing football or any other game so as to cause annoyance to users of the highway; allowing filth or other offensive matter to flow on to a highway from adjoining premises (s. 161).

- Causing injury, interruption or danger to a user of a carriageway by lighting a fire on adjoining land (s. 161A).

- Mixing mortar on the highway in such a way that it may stick to the surface of the highway, or enter drains (s. 170).

Public nuisance

7-4   Most sorts of interference with the use of a highway by the public are now dealt with by statute, but the courts retain the ability to punish any other sort of interference as the common law offence of public nuisance. Any behaviour which endangers the health or comfort of the public may be a public nuisance[5], but it must be such as to affect people in the immediate neighbourhood generally, not merely a small number of specific householders. If the effects are confined to one or more residents, but do not affect the public in the area generally, those

---

5. For an example involving a "rave" party see *R v Shorrock* [1994] QB 279, [1993] 3 WLR 698, [1993] 3 All ER 917.

affected may have a civil remedy for the nuisance*, but the nuisance will not be an offence.

*See 6-8.

Theft and criminal damage

Land, including things attached to it or growing in it, can be stolen by being removed by a person who is not in possession of the land*. A person who dishonestly removed soil or turf, or a fixture such as fencing or a signboard, could thus be guilty of theft, under the Theft Act 1968. But an exception is made for the taking of mushrooms or the flowers, fruit or foliage of any plant growing wild on land, provided this is not done for a commercial purpose.

7-5

*See 1-43 for possession of land.

Just as land can, in the above sense, be stolen, so it is also an offence to damage it, under the Criminal Damage Act 1971, though an exception is again made for mushrooms and the flowers, fruit or foliage of any plant growing wild on land. Defacing signs with graffiti, or destroying cultivated plants, would amount to criminal damage. Depositing refuse on land could also constitute criminal damage, though here the law provides more specific offences*.

7-6

*See 7-10 onwards.

Environmental matters

Litter Under s. 87 of the Environmental Protection Act 1990 it is an offence to drop litter in any place in the open air to which the public is entitled or permitted to have access without payment. The offence applies to (among other places) private roads which are highways or where public use is tolerated.

7-7

Dumping cars and other things By s. 2 of the Refuse Disposal (Amenity) Act 1978:

7-8

"(1) Any person who, without lawful authority—

(a) abandons on any land in the open air, or on any other land forming part of a highway, a motor vehicle or anything which formed part of a motor vehicle and was removed from it in the course of dismantling the vehicle on the land; or

(b) abandons on any such land any thing other than a motor vehicle, being a thing which he has brought on to the land for the purpose of abandoning it there

shall be guilty of an offence....."

7-9 Whether a motor vehicle has been abandoned is something to be deduced from all the circumstances of the case, but the provision seems to be concerned with permanent rather than temporary abandonment: unauthorised parking in a private road would not amount to the offence of abandoning a motor vehicle, since the owner would no doubt intend to retrieve the vehicle in due course. Abandoned motor vehicles (but not other things) are subject to sections 3 and 4 of the Act. These impose a *duty* on the local authority to remove and dispose of vehicles which appear to have been abandoned. Notice must first be given to the occupier of the land; and if it appears that the vehicle which is to be removed should be destroyed, the local authority must first fix a notice to that effect to the vehicle.

7-10 This offence now overlaps with a wide prohibition on the "depositing" of "controlled waste" on any land, contained in s. 33 of the Environmental Protection Act 1990[6]. "Waste" means any object or substance which the person holding it intends to discard (s. 75); and "controlled waste" is waste falling into one of the categories defined in the Act. The categories are "household waste", "commercial waste" and "industrial waste", according to the sorts of premises from which the waste has come. Depositing a pile of grass cuttings or leaves by the side of a private road would not generally be an offence, since waste from the gardens of houses, or from a private road, is not within the definition of "household waste". By contrast, builder's rubble from a house would be "household waste", and depositing it would be an offence.

7-11 *Hedgerows Regulations 1997* A power in the Environment Act 1995, s. 97(8), allows regulations to be made to provide special protection for hedgerows. The Hedgerows Regulations 1997[7] have duly been made, and these regulate the removal of hedgerows. The Regulations do not define what a hedgerow is, so that this is left to common sense. The Hedgerows Regulations are free-standing, rather than being an offshoot of planning like the law on tree preservation orders[*].

[*]See 8-22 onwards for tree preservation orders.

7-12 The Regulations do not apply to all hedgerows, but only to those which are at least 20 metres long (or which are shorter than that but join other hedgerows) and which are in, or adjacent to:

- Common land[*].

[*]See 1-36 onwards for common land.

- "Protected land".

---

6. As amended by the Environment Act 1995.
7. SI 1997/1160.

- Land used for agriculture or forestry, or the breeding of horses, ponies or donkeys.

7-13 "Protected land" means land which is a nature reserve, under s. 21 of the National Parks and Access to the Countryside Act 1949, or a Site of Special Scientific Interest ("SSSI") under s. 28 of the Wildlife and Countryside Act 1981. The Hedgerows Regulations do not apply to a hedge which is part of the boundary of the curtilage of a dwelling, or which is within the curtilage.

7-14 If the Regulations do apply to a hedgerow, the owner of the land is free to carry out some sorts of work, such as removing a part of the hedge to form an access, or to carry out work for which planning permission has been granted. However, most of the provisions of the GPDO do not apply, so that development permitted by the GPDO cannot usually include the removal of a hedgerow. Work can be done for the "proper management" of a hedgerow, so that a hedge can be relaid or trimmed as necessary.

7-15 If a landowner wishes to remove a hedgerow, she must give notice (a "hedgerow removal notice") to the local authority, who are responsible for administering the Regulations. The local authority may either grant permission, in which case the hedgerow can be removed, or serve a "hedgerow retention notice". They can do so if the hedgerow is "important", meaning that it has existed for at least 30 years and that it satisfies detailed criteria set out in Schedule 1 to the Regulations. These focus on two sorts of test:

- Archaeology and history: whether, for example, the hedgerow marks the boundary of a parish or township which existed before 1850, or includes an archaeological feature or is within an archaeological site.

- Wildlife and landscape: whether the hedgerow contains certain numbers of various species of plants and trees.

7-16 A landowner can appeal to the DEFRA against the giving of a hedgerow retention notice. The landowner and the local authority must be given the opportunity to be heard if they wish (otherwise the appeal can be dealt with on the papers) and the DEFRA can decide to hold a local enquiry if they wish (reg. 9).

7-17 Removing a hedgerow in breach of the Regulations is an offence for which the maximum fine is £5,000 if the offence is dealt with in the magistrates' court or an unlimited fine if the offence is dealt with in the Crown Court. In deciding what the fine should be, the court must take into account any financial benefit which the landowner has obtained by removing it (reg. 7). The local authority may require the landowner to replace the hedgerow, and if he does not do so they may do the work themselves and recover the cost from the landowner (reg. 8). Local authorities also have the power to obtain an injunction to prevent a hedgerow from being removed (reg. 11)*. They must keep records, open to the public, of notices received and issued and the results of any appeals (reg. 10).

*See 6-35 for injunctions generally.

7-18 If a private road is fully built-up and contains only residential property, the Hedgerows Regulations will not apply. But in some roads the Regulations may be significant, for example because part of the road runs alongside agricultural land, or common land.

Noise

7-19 By s. 62 of the Control of Pollution Act 1974[8], it is an offence to operate a loudspeaker in a street between 9 p.m. and 8 a.m., subject to exceptions for the emergency services and certain others. "Street" is given a special meaning in this Act, and applies to highways and other roads which are for the time being open to the public*.

*See generally 1-22.

7-20 The maximum punishment for the offence is a level 5 fine; and an additional £50 for each day on which the offence continues after conviction (s. 74).

Motoring offences

*See 1-20 onwards.

7-21 The Road Traffic Act 1988[9] applies to private roads which are highways and those where public use takes place and is tolerated*. This definition governs a range of common motoring offences, which can therefore be committed on a private road which is a highway or where public use is tolerated. The following examples may be mentioned:

- Dangerous driving (s. 2).

- Careless and inconsiderate driving (s. 3).

- Driving with excess alcohol (s. 5).

---

8. As amended by the Noise and Statutory Nuisances Act 1993.
9. As amended by the Road Traffic Act 1991

- Leaving a vehicle in a dangerous position (s. 22).

- Dangerous and careless cycling (ss. 28 and 29).

- Failing to have third party insurance (s. 143).

- Failing to stop after an accident and (if required to do so) give name and address (s.170).

One further offence under this Act—the "motorised trespassing" offence—merits special attention. By s. 34 of the Road Traffic Act 1988[10]:

> "(1) Subject to the provisions of this section, if without lawful authority a person drives a mechanically propelled vehicle—
>
> (a) on to or upon any common land, moorland or land of any other description, not being land forming part of a road, or
>
> (b) on any road being a footpath, bridleway or restricted byway*,
>
> he is guilty of an offence."

*See 3-53 for the meaning of "restricted byway".

The section goes on to provide that:

> "(3) It is not an offence under this section to drive a mechanically propelled vehicle on any land within fifteen yards of a road, being a road on which a motor vehicle may lawfully be driven, for the purpose only of parking that vehicle on that land."

There is also an exception for driving on land in an emergency (subs. (4)). Furthermore, s. 34A provides that it is a defence for a person to prove that they drove on land over a footpath, bridleway or restricted byway in order to gain access to land belonging to them, and the driving was reasonably necessary for the purposes of a business, trade or profession.

The meaning of "common land, moorland or land of any other description" was considered in the case of *Massey v Boulden*[11]. As a rule of statutory construction, words such as "any other description" may be interpreted in the light of the preceding words, if these have something in common. Here that did not appear to be so. "Common land" is a legal concept*, while "moorland" is merely a physical description of land. The Court of Appeal therefore concluded—though not without some concern about the wide scope of the provision—that

*See 1-36 onwards.

---

10. As re-enacted, with some amendments, by the Countryside and Rights of Way Act 2000, s. 67 and Schedule 7. The offence has been incorporated in the road traffic legislation since 1930.
11. Court of Appeal, 14 November 2002; EWCA Civ 1634.

7-25 Section 34 is thus a very important provision for private roads which are not highways and which are not subject to public use. Motorised trespassers commit an offence, unless they drive no more than 15 yards into the road and do so in order to park (lawfully or otherwise). The maximum punishment for the offence is a level 3 fine.

7-26 In contrast to the position under the Road Traffic Act, a car without a tax disc may be left in a private road, since an offence is committed only if the car is used on a "public road", which means a highway repairable at the public expense (see the Vehicles Excise and Registration Act 1994, s. 62.)

Criminal trespasses

7-27 Besides the "motorised trespassing" offence in s. 34 of the Road Traffic Act 1988, some other sorts of trespass are criminal in nature, and so can be the subject of a prosecution; for example:

- Trespasses which are designed to cause disruption to activity taking place on land, under s. 68 of the Criminal Justice and Public Order Act 1994. The maximum sentence is 3 months' imprisonment or a level 4 fine.

- Using or threatening violence to gain entry to premises, contrary to s. 6 of the Criminal Law Act 1977. By s. 12 of this Act, "premises" includes the site of a building or buildings, and land ancillary thereto, so could apply to a private road. The maximum sentence is 6 months' imprisonment or a level 5 fine.

Unauthorised camping and caravanning

7-28 The Criminal Justice and Public Order Act 1994, in ss. 61 and 77, contains provisions under which people coming on to land in motor vehicles, with the intention of taking up residence, can be directed to leave. The directions can be given by (respectively) the police and the local authority, and failure to leave when requested is an offence.

Old statutes

7-29 Several old statutes are still in force and may affect private roads in particular areas. The Town Police Clauses Act 1847 applies only where its provisions have been incorporated into a special local Act, passed for a particular town. The point of the Act was to provide model provisions for use by local government. It affects "any road, square, court, alley and thoroughfare"; but it is thought not to include a road from which the public could be excluded, and thus to apply only to those private roads which are highways.

7-30 Section 28 of the Act lays down a long list of things which are prohibited when they cause obstruction, annoyance or danger to residents. The forbidden activities include flying kites, making slides in the snow, maliciously ringing door bells, putting lines across the street, shaking or beating mats or carpets in the street (except that door mats may be shaken before 8 a.m.) and many other minor nuisances.

7-31 There is a similar list in s. 54 of the Metropolitan Police Act 1839 for "any thoroughfare or public place". This applies to the Metropolitan Police District, which takes in Greater London and small parts of the surrounding counties.

7-32 The Highway Act 1835 contains several offences which apply to highways. It is an offence to ride a horse (and to drive horses and other animals) on a footpath by the side of a road (s. 72); and it is an offence for the driver of a carriage to cause any hurt or damage to other users of the highway (s. 78).

Dogs

7-33 Some offences relating to dogs may be mentioned briefly. It is an offence for a person in charge of a dog to allow it to be "dangerously out of control in a public place", under s. 3 of the Dangerous Dogs Act 1991[12]. A "public place" for these purposes is "any street, road or other place...to which the public have or are permitted to have access...", thus including private roads which are highways or where public use is tolerated (s. 10)[*].

*See 1-20 onwards.

7-34 Under the Dogs (Fouling of Land) Act 1996, the local authority can designate the Act as applying to any specified area of land which is open to the air and to which the public is entitled or permitted to have access—thus bringing in private roads which are highways and those where public use takes place. If the dog defecates, the person in charge

---

12. As amended by the Dangerous Dogs (Amendment) Act 1997.

of it must remove the mess, failure to do so being an offence. This Act supersedes any local byelaws in force which are to the same effect.

7-35 While on a highway or other "place of public resort", a dog must wear a collar marked with the name and address of its owner. Packs of hounds and other working dogs are exempt from this requirement, however. Any person who allows a dog to be on a highway or in a place of public resort in breach of this requirement commits an offence, and a dog not wearing a collar may be seized by the local authority, as a stray[13].

Assessment

7-36 The offences mentioned above restrict what can be done in a private road, but also provide protection against antisocial behaviour. Their effect in relation to highways is far-reaching: most sorts of interference with the road and its use are dealt with. In highways and in roads to which the public has access, many common motoring offences also apply. Roads which are not highways, and to which the public does not have access, enjoy little in the way of special protection; but one offence which is important for such roads is s. 34 of the Road Traffic Act 1988[*], which criminalises motorised trespassing in the circumstances explained above. The general criminal law applies to all private roads, as it does to other land, so that offences such as theft and criminal damage are relevant.

[*]See 7-22.

7-37 Once a private road has become a highway, its status cannot be changed by the owner or occupier. But if the road is not a highway, its use by the public is within the control of the owner or occupier, who can thus exert some influence over whether the offences apply in the road.

7-38 The criminal offences exist, in some cases, alongside the remedies provided by the civil law. Vandalism, for example, is both an offence (criminal damage) and a civil wrong. Prosecution is normally a matter for public bodies such as the local authority or the police. A private prosecution may be brought if, as is sometimes the case, these bodies are unwilling to take action, but this is not a step to be taken lightly.

---

13. See the Control of Dogs Order 1992, SI 1992/901.

© A. W. & C. Barsby 2003

Chapter 8: Planning

Introduction

Private roads are land, and therefore subject to the system of planning control. Planning law is a large and complicated subject; but this chapter is concerned only with the different ways in which planning control affects a private road itself, rather than the houses or other properties in the road. Besides the different rules which determine which particular activities require planning consent, the planning legislation also contains rules dealing with the related subjects of trees and advertisements. Much of the law is contained in the Town and Country Planning Act 1990, as amended by the Planning and Compensation Act 1991. The Planning (Listed Buildings and Conservation Areas) Act 1990 is also relevant. As in other areas of the law, these Acts are supplemented by delegated legislation.

Development

Central to planning law is the principle that planning permission is generally required for "development", this term being defined in s. 55(1) of the Town and Country Planning Act 1990 as:

> "the carrying out of building, engineering, mining or other operations in, on, over or under land, or the making of any material change in the use of any buildings or other land".

This principle is extended and elaborated elsewhere, both in the Town and Country Planning Act 1990 and other legislation. Some activities which would otherwise amount to development are deemed not to be, including, under s. 55(2), the carrying out by local authorities of works required for the maintenance or improvement of a road, and the carrying out, by a local authority or a statutory undertaker, of work for the purpose of inspecting or repairing sewers, water mains, pipes, cables and other apparatus, in a street or other land. "Road" is not defined in the 1990 Act, so it is a question of fact what is a road, and private roads will be within the scope of the provision; though the effect of the provision is not to give local authorities the power to carry out works in a road where they do not otherwise have the power to do so. "Street" is not defined by the 1990 Act either; but "street or other place" is wide enough to include all private roads.

8-3 For many minor classes of development, planning permission is granted by the General Permitted Development Order 1995[1], thus removing the need to apply to the local authority. The classes of permitted development are set out in the Schedules to the Order.

8-4 The meaning of "building", and hence "building operation", is wider than might be supposed, since it is defined by s. 336 of the Town and Country Planning Act as including:

> "any structure or erection, and any part of a building, as so defined, but does not include plant or machinery comprised in a building".

8-5 Fences and walls and other structures can thus be, and often will be, "buildings". There is no simple way of telling whether a structure is a "building" for the purposes of planning law, but the courts, in interpreting the planning legislation, have put forward four relevant criteria:

- Size, and the question of whether the thing in question was built *in situ* or brought on to the site ready made.

- Whether it is physically attached to the land.

- Its degree of permanence. And—

- Whether it can be moved (though something may be a "building" even though it can be moved to a certain extent)[2].

8-6 The term "building operations" is also defined in s. 55, and includes (apart from any other work which would be regarded as building):

> "(a) demolition of buildings;
>
> (b) rebuilding;
>
> (c) structural alterations of or additions to buildings; and
>
> (d) other operations normally undertaken by a person carrying on business as a builder".

8-7 It was for a long while unclear whether demolition constituted development, but the 1990 Act now makes clear that it is. But this is

---

1. Its full title is the Town and Country Planning (General Permitted Development) Order 1995, SI 1995/418. It has since been amended on various occasions. Another order, made at the same time, the Town and Country Planning (General Development Procedure) Order 1995, SI 1995/419, deals with procedural matters.
2. See *Barvis Ltd v Secretary of State for the Environment* (1971) 22 P&CR 710.

balanced by provisions in the General Permitted Development Order which say that demolition of buildings is generally permitted.

Specific provisions affecting private roads

8-8 The General Permitted Development Order contains provisions on several sorts of development which are particularly relevant to private roads.

8-9 *Maintenance of private roads* First, and perhaps most important, permission is automatically granted by Part 9 of Schedule 2 for:

"The carrying out on land within the boundaries of an unadopted street or private way of works required for the maintenance or improvement of the street or way."

8-10 An "unadopted street", for the purposes of the Order, is one which is not a highway maintainable at the public expense, and a "private way" is "a highway not maintainable at the public expense and any other way other than a highway". The two terms (which overlap to some extent) thus include all private roads, whether or not they are highways. It will be a question of fact what are the boundaries of a road[3].

8-11 The scope of this provision was considered in the case of *Cowen v Peak District National Park Authority*[4]. The court felt that the provision related only to the surface and foundations of a road. Resurfacing would generally be included, either as an "improvement" or an "alteration" (it was not easy to say what the distinction was). Given the court's view, work which does not relate to the surface will probably not be within the exemption, and a planning application will be needed if the work involves "building operations". But the provision probably includes work such as the replacement of kerbstones or repair of surface water drains, and may include the installation of road humps*.

*See also 9-4 on road humps.

8-12 *Gates, fences, walls, etc.* Secondly, permission is granted by Class A of Part 2 of Schedule 2 for:

"The erection, construction, maintenance, improvement or alteration of a gate, fence, wall or other means of enclosure".

8-13 In order for a gate, fence, wall etc. to be within this provision it must be functional rather than decorative; that is, it must to some extent serve the purpose of enclosing an area of land[5], rather than being

---

3. See *Ministerial Planning Decision* [1996] 1 JPL 70.
4. [1999] 3 PLR 108.

purely ornamental. It seems likely that, in the context of a private road, a wall or fence erected in order to serve as a barrier between the road and an adjoining property would be permitted, as would a wall or other barrier at the entrance to a private road, but that walls and fences which were purely ornamental would not be permitted by the General Permitted Development Order and would therefore require an application for planning permission.

8-14 Some sorts of development are not permitted under this heading, and will thus need to be the subject of an application for planning permission in the ordinary way. In particular new gates, fences, walls etc must not be more than 2 metres high, or 1 metre if adjacent to a highway used by vehicular traffic*. "Adjacent" means that the 1-metre limit applies even if the fence, wall etc is not right next to the highway, but is separated from it by (for example) a narrow strip of verge. Where gates, fences or walls etc are altered they must not exceed their former height, or 1 or 2 metres (depending on whether adjacent to a highway) whichever is the greater. The demolition of the whole or any part of a gate, fence, wall or other means of enclosure is also permitted by Part 31 of Schedule 2.

*See 3-3 onwards for highways.

8-15 *Access to a highway* Thirdly, permission is granted by Class B of Part 2 of Schedule 2 for the formation of an access to a highway in some circumstances. The definition of "engineering operation" in s. 336 of the Act includes "the formation or laying out of means of access to a highway", so that planning permission will be required for this work. In granting permission, the General Permitted Development Order applies only where the access is required in connection with development permitted by the Order, apart from Class A of Part 2*. Permission is thus automatically granted for the formation of an access to a highway where, for example, it is required in connection with hardstanding which is ancillary to the use of a house, or an extension to a house, or for the demolition of a building, these being types of development for which planning permission is granted by the General Permitted Development Order. The permission for an access does not apply to a highway which is a trunk road or classified road[6], nor where the access would obstruct the view of people using a highway open to vehicular traffic, so as to cause danger, and is only for the formation of an access required in connection with development permitted under the General Permitted Development Order.

*I.e. the construction of gates, fences, walls, etc: see 8-12.

8-16 Permission is not granted by the General Permitted Development Order for making an access to a private road which is not a highway.

---

5. See *Wycombe District Council v Secretary of State for the Environment* [1994] EGCS 61.
6. That is, classified as an "A" or "B" road.

An application for planning permission will thus be necessary if building or engineering operations are involved.

8-17 Where an application for planning permission involves the formation or alteration of access to a highway, permission cannot be granted until local authority staff concerned with highways have been consulted. The authority thus has the opportunity to express a view on safety and other aspects of the proposal[7].

8-18 *Services* The General Permitted Development Order grants planning permission for development which consists of the repair or renewal of pipes, drains, cables, etc (Part 10 of Schedule 2). For local authorities and statutory undertakers, such work does not constitute "development"[*]. For others, the work does constitute development, but permission is granted automatically. Permission is also granted for some development by sewerage undertakers (Part 16); and for some development by companies supplying electricity and gas and by the Post Office, in installing post boxes (Part 17).

*See 8-2.

8-19 *Security cameras* Part 33 of Schedule 2 to the General Permitted Development Order grants permission automatically for closed circuit television cameras on buildings, installed for security purposes, subject to various conditions. The building on which the camera is installed must not be a listed building[8], and the camera, with any associated mounting brackets and other equipment, must be no more than 75 x 25 x 25 centimetres in overall dimensions, and not less than 250 centimetres above the ground.

Disapplying the General Permitted Development Order Local authorities[9] can decide that the automatic grants of planning permission under the General Permitted Development Order should not apply in their area (article 4(1)).

Enforcement of planning control

8-20 Local authorities have a range of powers enabling them to ensure that planning law is complied with. Their main weapon is the enforcement notice, under s. 172 of the 1990 Act, which calls on the owner or occupier of land to remedy the specified breach of planning control. An appeal is possible on various grounds, including the ground that planning permission ought to be granted; but, subject to the possibility

---

7. By article 10 of the General Development Procedure Order 1995.
8. That is, a building listed under the Planning (Listed Buildings and Conservation Areas) Act 1990.
9. Central government also has this power.

of an appeal, failure to comply with an enforcement notice is an offence. If the matter is dealt with in the magistrates' court, the maximum is £20,000, while in the Crown Court there is no limit.

8-21 In urgent cases, the local authority can serve a stop notice, under s. 183 of the Act, which accompanies or follows an enforcement notice and requires the immediate cessation of the breach of planning control. Other procedures are the breach of condition notice, to address breaches of conditions imposed when planning permission was granted, and the planning contravention notice; and local authorities have a special power to seek an injunction to enforce planning control.

Tree preservation orders

8-22 Trees have their own special form of protection, known as tree preservation orders. The law is set out in the Town and Country Planning Act 1990, ss. 198–214D, and some regulations, the Town and Country Planning (Trees) Regulations 1999[10].

8-23 Under s. 198 of the 1990 Act, a local authority can make a tree preservation order if they consider that it is "expedient in the interests of amenity". A tree preservation order can be made in relation to a single tree, a group of trees, or an area of woodland. Tree preservation orders cannot be made in relation to hedgerows, which now have their own form of protection*, and do not apply to bushes and shrubs; though there is no precise definition of what a "tree" is for these purposes—common sense must no doubt be applied.

*See 7-11 onwards for the Hedgerows Regulations.

8-24 The 1999 Regulations lay down a model form for a tree preservation order, which local authorities can adapt to suit the needs of particular cases. The order must specify the trees or woodland in question and there must be a map showing their position. The order will generally forbid the "cutting down, topping, lopping[11], uprooting, wilful damage or wilful destruction" of the trees. An order generally comes into effect only when it has been confirmed, thus allowing the landowner a certain period in which to make comments about the need for the order. The order is served on the landowner, and a copy is made available for public inspection. The local authority order can decide not to confirm the order; or they can confirm it with or without modifications (s. 198 of the 1990 Act).

---

10. SI 1999/1892.
11. To "lop" means to remove lateral branches, not the top of the tree: see *Unwin v Hanson* [1981] 2 QB 115.

8-25 Alternatively, if the local authority feel that immediate protection is necessary, they can make a tree preservation order on the basis that the order comes into effect at once, but on a provisional basis. The order will then either be confirmed or not, as explained above (s. 201).

8-26 Tree preservation orders (which should appear on the register of local land charges)* can be altered or cancelled at a later date. There is a procedure for appealing against the making of an order, appeals being dealt with by the ODPM. Normally the landowner and the local authority send in their cases in writing, and a site visit is made.

*See 2-43 for the Local Land Charges Register.

8-27 When a tree preservation order is in force, the activities forbidden by the order (cutting down, topping etc.) are an offence unless they are covered by an exception. These include:

- Trees which are "dying or dead or have become dangerous" (s. 198(6)(a)).

- Trees which must be cut down, topped or lopped in order to prevent a nuisance (s. 198(6)(b))*.

*See 6-12.

- Trees which must be cut down in order to implement a planning permission (but not outline planning permission) (para. 5 of the model order, in the 1999 Regulations).

- Fruit trees cultivated for the production of fruit, which are cut down or pruned etc for the purposes of the business (para. 5, ditto).

- Trees cut down, topped, etc in accordance with consent given by the local authority (para. 6, ditto).

8-28 Where the local authority give consent for a tree to be cut down, they may as a condition require a replacement tree to be planted. If the local authority refuse consent, or grant it subject to conditions, the landowner may appeal to the ODPM.

8-29 Breach of a tree preservation order is an offence:

"If any person, in contravention of a tree preservation order—

(a) cuts down, uproots or wilfully destroys a tree, or

(b) wilfully damages, tops or lops a tree in such a manner as to be likely to destroy it,

he shall be guilty of an offence" (s. 210(1) of the 1990 Act).

8-30 The maximum punishment is a fine of £20,000 in the magistrates' court or an unlimited fine in the Crown Court (s. 210(2)). The court must take into account, in determining the size of the fine, any financial benefit resulting from the offence. If a tree protected by a tree preservation order has been removed in order to allow some profitable use of land, this will be taken into account by the court. There is also a less serious offence which consists of breaches which are not likely to lead to the loss of the protected tree, for which the maximum punishment is a level 4 fine (s. 210(4))*.

*See 1-50 for maximum levels of fines.

8-31 Additionally, where a tree is removed in breach of a tree preservation order, the landowner is under a duty to plant another. The same duty applies where a tree has been cut down because it is dying or dead, or has become dangerous*. If he does not do so, the local authority may serve notice requiring a landowner to plant replacement trees (s. 207). There is a right of appeal (s. 208). But subject to that the local authority may come on to the land and plant a new tree themselves, at the landowner's expense (s. 209). The new tree becomes subject to the tree preservation order. Local authorities can also apply for an injunction if this is necessary to prevent damage to a protected tree (s. 214A).

*See 8-27.

*See 8-42.

8-32 Trees within conservation areas are subject to special rules*.

Control of outdoor advertisements

8-33 Advertising control comes within the general framework of planning law, though it is the subject of a largely separate system of rules. The law comes mainly from the Town and Country Planning (Control of Advertisements) Regulations 1992[12], which have been made under s. 220 of the Town and Country Planning Act 1990.

8-34 Advertisements which are in accordance with the system of advertisement control are deemed to have planning permission for any development which may be involved, whether operational development (such as the erection of a hoarding) or a change of use (s. 222)*. So a separate application for planning permission is not required. On the other hand, if there is a breach of advertising control, action can be taken in relation to any breaches of planning control.

*See 8-1 onwards for operational development.

8-35 A wide range of advertisements is covered by the Regulations, including signs, placards, boards, notices, awnings and blinds with writing or graphics on them, and other devices which are used to advertise something or to make an announcement or give a direction ("this way to the car boot sale").

8-36 Some advertisements are exempted by the Regulations (reg. 3(2) and Schedule 2). The Regulations do not apply at all to these

---

12. SI 1992/666. These regulations have since been amended on several occasions.

advertisements, provided that certain conditions are complied with. The conditions are in some cases specific to a particular sort of advertisement, but there are also standard conditions applying to all exempt advertisements—the site must be kept clean and tidy, the advertisement must be safe, the owner of the site must consent, and traffic must not be obstructed. Schedule 2 includes, among other sorts of advertisement:

- Advertisements on enclosed land, provided that they are not readily visible from outside.

- Advertisements inside buildings, provided that they are not illuminated.

- Notices relating to public elections.

- Official traffic signs.

Schedule 3 lists a further class of advertisement, for which the local authority's consent is deemed to be granted, so that there is no need to apply for it. The consent is deemed to be subject to the standard conditions which apply to exempt advertisements, and various detailed conditions set out in Schedule 3 itself. Within this class are:

- Signs identifying buildings or giving warnings or directions about land or buildings[13].

- Nameplates and other signs relating to persons carrying on business at an address.

- Temporary signs relating to the sale or letting of property.

- Signs for neighbourhood watch schemes.

An application for consent to the display of an advertisement can be granted or refused by the local authority, or granted subject to conditions (including, usually, a condition that the consent lasts only for five years, after which it must be renewed) (reg. 13). The local authority must decide applications on the basis of "amenity and public

---

13. Private roads will almost always have a sign giving the name of the road and adding other information ("Private", "No public access", cul-de-sac", etc). To be exempt from advertising control such signs must be no more than 0.3 square metres in area, and unilluminated. They must be no more than 4.6 metres above ground level.

safety"—it cannot refuse on the grounds that it does not agree with the message being conveyed by the advertisement (reg. 4). If consent is refused, or granted on unacceptable conditions, there is a right of appeal to the ODPM. The procedure follows the procedure for appeals against a refusal of planning permission (reg. 15). Local authorities must keep a register (which must be indexed) in which applications and planning decisions are recorded, so that members of the public can check the position concerning advertisements.

8-39 Displaying an advertisement in breach of the Regulations is an offence for which the maximum punishment is a level 3 fine; and if the offence continues after conviction there is an additional fine of one-tenth of that amount for each day on which it continues (s. 224(3))*. Under s. 225, local authorities have a special power which enables them to remove or obliterate fly-posted advertisements which are displayed in breach of the legislation.

*See 1-50 for maximum levels of fines.

Special areas

8-40 *Conservation areas* By s. 69 of the Planning (Listed Buildings and Conservation Areas) Act 1990 local authorities have a duty to designate as conservation areas "areas of special architectural or historic interest the character or appearance of which it is desirable to preserve or enhance". In a conservation area, some special controls apply, with the aim of providing extra protection against inappropriate development[14]. A conservation area could include a private road. (There are other forms of protection, such as the listing of buildings, which are not directly relevant to private roads.)

8-41 In a conservation area, the local authority is under a duty in exercising its powers—including the power to grant planning permission—to pay "special attention" to the "desirability of preserving or enhancing the character or appearance of that area" (s. 72 of the Act). What this provision actually means has been the subject of consideration by the courts. Does it mean that permission can be granted provided that the proposed development does not actually harm the conservation area, or that it can only be granted if it makes a positive contribution towards "preserving or enhancing" the area? The latter interpretation would make the provision more effective; but the courts incline towards the former view: development which does not

---

14. See generally the ODPMS Circular PPG/15, *Planning and the Historic Environment*.

harm a conservation area can be regarded as helping to preserve the character or appearance of the area[15].

8-42 Trees within a conservation area enjoy special protection even if not protected by tree preservation orders. A landowner wishing to remove a tree or do work on it must first give the local authority notice (s. 211 of the 1990 Act). This allows the local authority the opportunity to make a tree preservation order if they feel this is necessary. If the local authority give consent, or if six weeks pass without a tree preservation order being made, the work can proceed. Damaging a tree in a conservation area in breach of these provisions is an offence with the same penalties as breach of a tree preservation order.

8-43 *Other areas* Advertising control may also be stricter within a conservation area, and local authorities can also designate areas which are subject to special control in relation to advertisements[16]. An area of special control may cover the same area as a conservation area, or may be separate from it.

Planning decisions and rights of way

8-44 In a private road which is not a highway, a would-be developer may be precluded from carrying out development, even if he obtains planning permission, because he is not able to obtain the necessary rights of way from the owners of the road. Should a local authority take this into account in considering whether to grant planning permission? There is no requirement that they should do so; but it is possible, and perhaps desirable, for planning permission to be granted conditionally upon the developer obtaining the necessary rights of way.

8-45 If the use of a private road changes, can this be a "material change of use" and so require planning permission? For a road which is a carriageway, and so subject to a public right of way for vehicles, it could be argued that there is no change in use, even if the amount of traffic increases. For a road which has only private rights of way, it seems that in principle a sufficiently major change—from, say limited amounts of residential traffic to large amounts of commercial traffic— might in principle amount to a development and so require planning permission.

---

15. See *South Lakeland DC v. Secretary of State for the Environment* [1992] 2 AC 141; [1992] 2 WLR 204; [1992] 1 All ER 573.
16. In an area of special control, a road sign must be no more than 3.6 metres above the ground.

Assessment

8-46   The owner or managers of a private road will often be concerned with such matters as walls and fences, and trees; and may sometimes wish to carry out minor operations, such as the erection of signs, which might amount to building or other operations, and hence be development. Development also includes a "material change of use". It must be rare for there to be material change of use of a private road; but any proposal with a radical impact on the amount or type of traffic using the road should be considered from this point of view.

8-47   Often, it will prove to be the case that no application for planning permission is necessary, since permission is granted by the General Permitted Development Order. But the position should always be checked with the local authority, not least because there are areas of uncertainty. Local authorities have a special power, by s. 192 of the Town and Country Planning Act, to issue a certificate as to the lawfulness of proposed operations on land, and this procedure can be used in cases of doubt about whether proposed work would amount to development, or, if it would amount to development, whether permission is deemed to be granted for it by the legislation. More important, perhaps, where planning issues arise, is for the managers of a private road to make contact informally with the planning staff of the local authority and discuss the matter with them. Invaluable guidance can be obtained in this way, and problems can often be averted if a flexible approach is adopted.

8-48   It will always be wise for the owners of a private road to examine development plans and other proposals put forward by local authorities for the future development of an area, because these may affect private roads indirectly if not directly. The opportunity to comment should be taken when a proposal affects a private road, as for example where a new scheme to restrict parking in public roads might lead to pressure from the public to use the private road for parking.

Chapter 9: Powers of local authorities

Introduction

Local authorities are given, by legislation, a wide range of legal powers. Some are specific to roads, and some apply to land more generally. Occasionally a *duty* is imposed, so that the local authority is under an obligation to take the action in question.

Local authorities stand in a special position in relation to highways. They are under a general duty to maintain highways maintainable at the public expense (s. 41 of the Highways Act 1980) and also to assert and protect the rights of the public over all highways, preventing obstruction and other interferences with the public's rights so far as possible (s. 130). The Highways Act also contains many more specific powers.

Some of the powers available to local authorities are considered elsewhere in this book*. This chapter deals with a selection of other powers. Many of them are contained in the Highways Act 1980; but other Acts also confer powers which apply to private roads.

*See particularly chapter 8 on planning, and chapter 10 on the making up and adoption of private streets.

The Highways Act 1980

Powers under the Highways Act may be said to fall into four categories.

Powers relating only to highways maintainable at the public expense
These powers do not apply to any private roads, and therefore need not be set out here; but one power which should nonetheless be mentioned is the power to construct road humps (sometimes known as "sleeping policemen") and other measures for traffic calming (see ss. 90A to 90I of the Highways Act, and delegated legislation[1]). Because the power applies only to highways maintainable at public expense, local authorities have no power to construct road humps, or take other traffic-calming measures, in private roads.

---

1. The Highways (Road Humps) Regulations 1999, SI 1999/1025. See also the Highways (Traffic Calming Regulations) 1999, SI 1999/2056.

9-5 *Powers relating to highways* This is the largest category, which applies both to highways maintainable at the public expense and also to private roads which are highways. The following powers may be noted:

- To widen any highway, and for that purpose to reach agreement with the owners of adjoining land for the use of that land (s. 72 et seq).

- To install lighting (s. 97).

- To drain a highway, and to fill in dangerous ditches (ss. 100 and 100).

- To apply to a magistrates' court for an order stopping up or diverting a highway (s. 116)*.

*See 3-65 onwards.

- To stop up a private access to a highway, if it is dangerous (s. 124).

- To require anyone responsible for a "structure" on the highway to remove it. "Structure" includes any "machine, pump, post or other object of such a nature as to be capable of causing an obstruction" (s. 143).

- To require the owner of land which is a highway to widen a gate if it is less than the minimum width. The minimum width is 10 feet for a carriageway and 5 feet for a bridleway (s. 145). If the owner does not comply within 21 days he commits an offence and may be fined 50p for each day on which the failure continues.

- To require the owner of land to maintain any stile, gate or similar structure across a footpath or bridleway in safe condition (s. 146).

- To authorise the erection of stiles and gates on footpaths and bridleways (s. 147).

*See 6-13 onwards for nuisances generally.

- To serve a notice requiring the removal of things on a highway which constitute a nuisance* (s. 149). This provision applies not merely to things such as piles of soil or refuse, but to objects[2]. The

---

2. See *Scott v Westminster County Council* [1995] RTR 327, 93 LGR 370 which concerned braziers on barrows, from which chestnuts were being sold.

nuisance may be an obstruction[3] or some other form of interference. If the local authority's notice is disregarded, they may apply to a magistrates' court for an order for the removal of the nuisance*.

*See 7-3 for the offence under s. 148 of depositing things on a highway without lawful authority.

- To remove snow, or banks which have fallen down, or other similar obstructions[4] from a highway (s. 150). It should be noted that this is a *duty*, not just a power.

- To carry out works to repair highways, other than made-up carriageways*, of which the surface has been disturbed so as to make it inconvenient for the exercise of the public right of way (s. 160A and Schedule 12A). This provision may be aimed particularly at footpaths and other unmetalled highways which are damaged by use.

*See 1-25 for the meaning of "made up carriageway".

- To require the removal of barbed wire from a fence on land adjoining a highway (s. 164).

9-6

Where there is a power to require someone to do something—for example, to require a person to remove a "structure" from the highway—the local authority is generally given also the power to carry out the work itself and recover some or all of the cost from the person concerned.

9-7

Powers relating to roads to which the public has access Two powers should be mentioned which apply in relation to a road to which the public has access*. The phrase is likely to have the same meaning in the Highways Act, and therefore to extend to all private roads which are highways, and some private roads which are not highways but to which the public do in fact have access. The powers are:

*See 1-21 for roads subject to public access.

- In relation to hedges, trees and shrubs, the local authority may require the occupier of land to take action in two circumstances. First, it can do so where a hedge, tree or shrub overhangs a road to which the public has access, "so as to endanger or obstruct the passage of vehicles or pedestrians, or obstruct or interfere with the view of drivers of vehicles or the light from a public lamp". Secondly, it can do so if a tree or shrub is dead, diseased or damaged and is likely to cause damage by falling on a road or

---

3. For an example, see *Cornwall County Council v Blewett* [1994] COD 46, in which the court decided that an obstruction covering about one third of a pavement was a sufficient obstruction to amount to a nuisance.
4. See *Worcestershire County Council v Newman* [1974] 1 WLR 938, [1974] 2 All ER 867, 72 LGR 616.

footpath to which the public has access. "Hedge, tree or shrub" is defined to include vegetation of any description, thus eliminating any argument, in this context, about what is a tree or a shrub. A notice has to be served, specifying the work to be done. The recipient can appeal to a magistrates' court. If he does not do the work, the local authority can do it, and recover the cost from him (s. 154).

• The local authority may require fences, shrubs, trees and other things to be removed if they obstruct the view of users of a highway maintainable at public expense at a junction with a road to which the public has access. The authority must serve notice on the owner or occupier of the land, who commits an offence if he fails to comply, but who, once he has done the work, can recover reasonable costs from the authority (s. 79).

9-8 *Powers relating to all "streets"* "Street" has a wide definition in the Highways Act, s. 329(1)[*]. The term thus includes all private roads, whether or not they are highways, as well as highways maintainable at the public expense. A smaller range of powers applies to all streets (there being less need to regulate places to which the public has no right to go). These include the following.

[*]See 1-19.

• The local authority can construct guard-rails for safety reasons (s. 67)

• The local authority can require the removal of any projection from a building which obstructs "safe or convenient passage along a street" (s. 152).

• Notice may be served by the local authority on the occupier of any premises adjoining a street, where a door or gate opens outwards on to the street, requiring him to alter it. Failure to comply with the requirement is an offence (s. 153)[5].

• The local authority can require the owner or occupier of land adjoining a street to take action if that land contains a source of danger. If he does not do so, the authority can carry out the necessary work at his expense (s. 165).

---

5. The section applies to all doors, whether or not they pre-date the section: *Wandsworth London Borough Council v Lloyd* 96 LGR 607.

- The construction of certain retaining walls is subject to the approval by the local authority of the plans and specifications (s. 167). This requirement applies to any retaining wall which is not part of a permanent building and which is intended to serve as a support for earth or other material on one side of the wall only, if all or part of the retaining wall is to be within 4 yards of the street and at any point more than 4' 6" above the level of the ground at the boundary of the street nearest to the wall. (The provision thus applies to walls which may be in danger of collapsing on to the street, but not those which support the street.)

- The local authority can install refuse or storage bins (s. 185).

- In cases of emergency, or where it is likely that a street will be crowded, the local authority may put up barriers (s. 287).

Marking of footpaths, etc

9-9 Under s. 27 of the Countryside Act 1968, local authorities have a general power, after consultation with the owner of the land in question, to put up and maintain signposts along any footpath, bridleway or byway open to all traffic (or "BOAT")* (s. 27(1)).

*See 3-52 for BOATs.

9-10 They also have a duty to put up signposts at the point where any footpath, bridleway or byway joins a metalled road, unless the parish council agrees that in any particular case no sign is needed. The signs should, so far as the local authority considers appropriate, show the class of highway, its destination, and the distance involved (s. 27(2) and (3)).

Dangerous trees

9-11 Local authorities have a further power, additional to the power in s. 154 of the Highways Act, in relation to trees. The power is conferred by the Local Government (Miscellaneous Provisions) Act 1976, s. 23, and is essentially a power to make a tree safe if it appears likely to cause damage to persons or property. The power applies to trees on "any land", thus including all private roads, whether or not highways, and highways maintainable at the public expense.

9-12 The local authority can act in three different situations. The first is where it receives a request to make a tree safe from someone who is the owner or occupier of the land on which the tree is growing. The authority can carry out the work and recover the cost from the person in question. The second situation is where a request to make a tree safe comes from a person who is the owner or occupier of some other land. If the owner of the land on which the tree is growing cannot be found, the authority can proceed with the work and recover the cost from the person who made the request. But if the owner of the land can be found, the authority must (if it decides to take any action) proceed by serving a notice on that person requiring him to do the necessary work. The person concerned is entitled to appeal to the County Court against the notice, on one of four different grounds set out in s. 23. If he fails to carry out the work, the authority can do so and recover the cost from him.

9-13   The final situation is where there is no request to make a tree safe, but a tree is likely to damage persons or property on land owned by the local authority itself.

Traffic regulation

9-14   The Road Traffic Regulation Act 1984 gives powers to local authorities to regulate traffic. The powers are generally exercisable in relation to "roads", the word "road" being defined in s. 142 in a way which includes all private roads which are highways, and also those which are subject to public use*.

*See 1-20.

9-15   Under the Road Traffic Regulation Act, a local authority may make "traffic regulation orders" for roads to which the Act applies. The power may be exercised for a variety of purposes, including:

- Avoiding danger to users of the road (s. 1(1)(a)).

- Facilitating the passage of any class of traffic (s. 1(1)(c)).

- Preserving or improving the amenities of the area (s. 1(1)(f)).

9-16   A road traffic regulation order may restrict or regulate the traffic, for any of the purposes mentioned in s. 1. Common examples are orders making a road one-way, or restricting the classes of traffic which may use it, or prohibiting waiting, unloading, or overtaking (s. 2).

9-17   Speed limits apply to "roads", in the sense defined in the Road Traffic Regulation Act. There is a general speed limit of 30 m.p.h. for "restricted roads", and a road is a restricted road if it has a system of street lighting with lights less than 200 yards apart[6]. Private roads can thus be "restricted" if they have street lighting. However the local authority can include or exclude roads from the category of "restricted roads" as it thinks fit (ss. 81 and 82). The 200-yard rule is thus not absolute. Apart from this general limit, there is power to impose higher speed limits on roads which are not restricted (s. 84). A private road to which the public has access thus may or may not have a speed limit, but if it has street lights less than 200 yards apart the 30 mph limit is likely to apply. Local authorities have a general power to put up traffic signs (s. 65). If a private road is a "restricted road" because of its lighting, a speeding offence may be committed even if there are no signs indicating the speed limit; but if the road is restricted by virtue of a decision by the local authority, no speeding offence can be committed in the absence of signs (s. 85).

9-18 In addition to the general power to put up traffic signs, local authorities have power to require the owner or occupier of any land to remove a sign (s. 69). This applies to any:

"object or device (whether fixed or portable) for the guidance or direction of persons using the road".

9-19 The provision appears to be aimed essentially at unofficial traffic signs. (It is not clear whether a roadside sign advertising fruit or vegetables for sale would be regarded as "for the guidance or direction of persons using the road".) Section 69 applies to any sign which can be seen by users of a road, in the sense explained above; the sign itself may be on the road, or on some other land. The Road Traffic Regulation Act offers no guidance as to how a local authority should exercise this power, but it would probably be entitled to require the removal of a sign which was misleading or distracting. If the owner or occupier of the land does not take down the sign as required, the local authority may do so, causing as little damage as possible, and recover the cost from him[*].

[*]See also 7-3 the offence under s. 132 of the Road Traffic Act 1984.

9-20 There is power to remove vehicles which are parked on a road in various circumstances, under ss. 99–103 of the Road Traffic Regulation Act[7]. By s. 99, a vehicle may be removed by the local authority if it:

- Is contravening a statutory prohibition, for example a prohibition on parking (s. 99(1)(a));

---

6. But see *Spittle v Kent County Constabulary* [1985] Crim LR 744, in which the court said that a slightly greater gap between two lamps in a long line did not matter. Nor did it matter that one lamp did not work.
7. Supplemented by the Removal and Disposal of Vehicles Regulations 1986, SI 1986/183, as amended by later regulations.

- Is causing an obstruction or danger (s. 99(1)(b)). Or—

- Appears to have been abandoned (s. 99(1)(c)).

9-21 The power again applies to highways and other roads to which the public has access. Depending upon the circumstances, a vehicle may be removed by the local authority, or by a police constable, or a traffic warden. Steps must first be taken to find and notify the owner of the vehicle (s. 101). The Road Traffic Regulation Act goes on to provide for the disposal of vehicles which have been removed*.

*See also 7-8 for the Refuse Disposal (Amenity) Act 1978.

9-22 Some other powers also apply to highways and other roads to which the public has access. For example, in such private roads the local authority may establish pedestrian crossings, or authorise the use of part of the road for parking (ss. 23 and 32). But in some cases, a power applies only to a road which is a highway. Examples include ss. 45 and 46 of the Road Traffic Regulation Act, by which a local authority may make charges for parking. A charge could thus be imposed by a local authority for parking in a private road only if it was a highway; though the road or part of it could be designated as a parking place if the road was one to which the public had access.

Amenity

9-23 Local authorities have several powers which relate to the amenity of land. By s. 215 of the Town and Country Planning Act 1990:

> "(1) If it appears to the local planning authority that the amenity of a part of their area, or of an adjoining area, is adversely affected by the condition of land in their area, they may serve on the owner and occupier of the land a notice under this section."

9-24 This provision applies to all land. The authority's notice must set out the steps which are to be taken to remedy matters. There is a right of appeal against the notice, to the courts. But subject to that, failure to comply with the notice is an offence. The local authority can if necessary enter the land, and carry out the work themselves, and the expense then falls on the owner.

9-25 There is similar power in s. 89 of the National Parks and Access to the Countryside Act 1949. This applies to land which appears to the local authority to be "derelict, neglected or unsightly". With the consent of anyone interested in the land the local authority may carry out whatever work they consider to be expedient for the purpose of reclaiming or improving the land. In this case, the expense falls on the local authority.

Either power could be exercised in relation to a private road if it was in a sufficiently poor state, though the use of these powers in relation to private roads is likely to be uncommon.

Names and numbers of roads and houses

Even for a private road which is not a highway, the law regulates the naming of roads and the numbering of houses. This is perhaps not unreasonable, since it is in the public interest that they should be clear. Different Acts, however, deal with different areas. Outside Greater London, some areas are covered by the provisions of the Towns Improvement Clauses Act 1847, and some by the Public Health Act 1925—enquiries will reveal which Act applies in any given area.

Under the 1847 Act, local authorities are under a duty to put up street names, and it is an offence for a person to deface or destroy a street name (s. 64). "Street" has a wide definition for these purposes, and is likely to include all private roads. Local authorities must also "cause houses and buildings in all or any of the streets to be marked with numbers as they think fit". This leaves them free not to require buildings to be numbered if, for example, there are so few that it is not thought to be necessary. The occupiers of houses and other buildings must mark them with the appropriate numbers, and must renew the numbers when they become obliterated. A person who fails to number a house or building, or to renew a number, within a week of being given notice to do so by the local authority, commits an offence (s. 65).

Local authorities have power to alter the name of a street, under s. 21 of the Public Health Acts Amendment Act 1907. The consent of two-thirds in number and value of the ratepayers in the street is required. Any person who defaces or destroys the new name commits an offence.

In areas covered by the Public Health Act 1925, there are rules governing the names of streets, but none on the numbering of individual buildings. "Street" again has a wide definition, similar to the definition in the 1847 Act. Any person proposing to name a street—for example, a developer who has just built a new private road—must give notice to the local authority, which may within one month object to the name. The person concerned may then appeal against the objection to a magistrates' court. It is an offence to put up a street name until the matter has been settled in this way (s. 17). The local authority may name a new street, or alter the name of an existing street. First it must put up a notice at both ends of the street giving notice of the proposed new name; and any person "aggrieved" (which would seem to include any person living in the street and who objects to the name) may appeal to a magistrates' court (s. 18). The name of every street must be put up or marked in a conspicuous position, and it is an offence to deface or destroy the name, or to put up any notice or advertisement within 12 inches of the street name (s. 19).

9-31 Within Greater London, the legislation (the London Building Acts, and regulations made under them) is different again, though the result is broadly the same in that local authorities have the final say about street names.

9-32 Generally, there seems no legal reason why a house should not be given a name by the owner or occupier, provided the name is in addition to any number which the house may be given by the local authority.

Public entertainments

9-33 A licence from the local authority may be required in order to hold a public entertainment. The law is contained in s. 1 of and Schedule 1 to the Local Government (Miscellaneous Provisions) Act 1982. A licence is required for "public dancing or music or any other public entertainment of a like kind", but there are exceptions for an entertainment which takes place wholly or mainly in the open air, and an entertainment held in a "pleasure fair" (paragraphs 1 and 2 of Schedule 1). A pleasure fair is, by s. 75 of the Public Health Act 1961, essentially any place used for providing entertainments such as circuses, exhibitions of humans or performing animals, merry-go-rounds, and so on.

9-34 A licence *may* be required, depending upon whether the local authority has adopted the relevant part of the Schedule, for a public musical entertainment held wholly or mainly in the open air, or on private land, but here again there are exceptions since the requirement does not apply if the music is incidental to a "garden fête, bazaar, sale of work, sporting or athletic event, exhibition, display or other function or event of a similar character" (paragraphs 3 and 4).

9-35 In most cases, therefore, an entertainments licence will not be required in order for a fête, street party or similar event to be held in a private road[8].

---

8. But such events may be unlawful for other reasons, especially if they interfere with the use of a private road which is a highway—see chapter 8.

An event at which alcoholic drinks are to be sold is likely to require a licence or permission from the licensing justices, in accordance with the Licensing Act 1964.

9-36

Other powers

The above remarks are not exhaustive, and omit, for example, the various powers which local authorities have to acquire land compulsorily.

9-37

Assessment

Of the powers considered above, some apply to all roads, or simply to all land, and so can be exercised by the local authority in relation to any private road. More powers apply to all highways, whether or not they are maintainable at the public expense, and no doubt many private roads fall into this category. In some cases the legislation goes further and allows local authorities to exercise powers where there is no highway, and hence no public right of way, but where the public does in fact have access to the road.

9-38

Intervention by the local authority may in some cases be seen as helpful. A highway enjoys a much greater degree of legal protection from obstruction and interference. Another benefit is the local authority's ability to carry out work in the road, as for example installing street lighting; though it is a matter for the local authority whether it wishes to use these powers in a given case. In other instances action by the local authority might be less welcome, for example when the local authority considers it necessary to widen a highway, or to stop up a private access to a highway.

9-39

The owner of the road can in some circumstances determine the extent of the powers exercisable. Once a road has, through public use, become a highway, the process cannot be reversed by the owner of the road; but until then, if the public are using the road, the owner can choose whether to allow the use to continue, or whether to stop it[*]. Legally, it is possible for the owner of a private road both (a) to make clear that the road is not dedicated to the public (so that it will never become a highway), but (b) to allow the public to use the road, so that it is a road to which the public has access. If the use continues, the road will be one to which the public has access, and the local authority's powers relating to roads of this sort will be exercisable. In

9-40

[*]See 3-11 onwards on dedication and acceptance.

particular, there will be power to regulate the traffic. This may be something which residents of a private road would wish to have, and in one case[9] an application was made to the court (unsuccessfully) for a declaration that the public had access and that the local authority's powers were exercisable. It is not clear what the position would be if the public had access to a private road, and the local authority exercised their powers accordingly, but public access was then discontinued.

9-41 Decisions about whether to allow use of a private road by the public require careful consideration of these factors.

---

9. See *Adams v Commissioner of Police of the Metropolis* [1980] RTR 289.

Chapter 10: Services

Introduction

Most of the services enjoyed by houses depend upon cables, pipes and other apparatus, which is usually installed under or over roads. The suppliers of these services are now privatised, and are companies operating on a commercial basis. Legislation provides for their regulation and gives them the legal powers to fulfill their functions, and they also, in some circumstances, have obligations to provide services. Each has its own Act or Acts: electricity companies, for example, are governed mainly by the Electricity Act 1989. The regulatory body concerned with the industry is OFGEM, which also regulates the supply of gas. The DTI has overall responsibility for the industry. Companies carrying out work in accordance with legislation are sometimes known as "undertakers" or "statutory undertakers" (because they undertake activities in accordance with a statute) and the Acts governing the companies supplying services often use these terms.

This chapter is concerned mainly with the law relating to the pipes, cables and other apparatus running under and over a private road itself, not with the those running under and over land adjoining the road. As a general rule, the legislation provides that the apparatus belongs to the company concerned: it belonged to the public body which supplied the service before privatisation, and ownership passed on privatisation to the company. Any new apparatus installed by the undertaker similarly belongs to the undertaker. Sewers and drains under a private road form an exception, however, since they may be in private ownership.

The service companies are equipped by the legislation with a range of powers, for example the power to acquire land compulsorily, or to disturb pipes and cables belonging to other companies, or to disconnect the service for non-payment. For the purposes of this book, the most important powers are those which give the companies the right to install their apparatus under and over private roads, including the right to maintain, inspect and repair it. The companies have powers to install apparatus in other land as well, however, and these powers are also referred to—they may be relevant to private roads where land other than the road itself is collectively owned and managed, for example, where a private road forms a loop enclosing a central area of land.

10-3 Street works are subject to the New Roads and Street Works Act 1991. Part III of the Act is concerned with co-ordinating the activities of those who carry out works in the street, particularly statutory undertakers installing and maintaining their apparatus. The following paragraphs consider the New Roads and Street Works Act, then deal with the legal position of the service companies, first generally then individually—there are significant differences in the legislation, and separate treatment is therefore necessary. The text concentrates on powers to enter land and carry out work, but some other relevant powers are also mentioned.

The New Roads and Street Works Act 1991

10-4 Part III of the New Roads and Street Works Act 1991 (ss. 48 to 106), supplemented by regulations[1], contains provisions designed to see that street works are carried out as efficiently as possible, with minimum disruption, and that streets are not dug up and repaired repeatedly. The expression "street works" is defined in s. 48(3) and includes placing apparatus on or under a street, and inspecting, maintaining, adjusting, altering or renewing apparatus. It thus covers all kinds of work on water and gas pipes, sewers, telephone and electricity cables and other apparatus, but it does not include alterations or improvements to the street as such. Another sort of work is also covered—though to lesser extent—by the Act, namely "works for road purposes". This expression is defined in s. 86(2). It is confined to highways and includes works for maintenance and improvement, the erection of traffic signs, and the making of crossways over footpaths or grass verges.

10-5 The Act as a whole applies not only to highways maintainable at the public expense but to other streets as well, though in the latter case is subject to exceptions and adaptations set out in the regulations (s. 48(2)). The definition of "street" in the Act is the same wide definition already explained*. All private roads are thus likely to be covered by the Act.

*See 1-19.

10-6 The New Roads and Street Works Act refers to the person or body responsible for the street as the "street authority". In a street which is a highway maintainable at the public expense, the street authority is

---

1. The Street Works (Registers, Notices, Directions and Designations) Regulations 1992, SI 1992/2985, as amended by SIs 1995/990, 1995/2128, and 1999/1049.

the local authority (or, for trunk roads and motorways, the DfT). But in a private road, including one which is a highway, the street authority consists of the "street managers", which in turn means "any authority, body or person having control of the street" (s. 49). In a private road, then, the street authority will be whoever manages or has control of the road, whether or not that person is the owner of the street. If nobody is exercising control over the street, there will be no street authority. The 1992 Regulations modify the way in which the Act works if the street authority is not the local authority.

10-7 The working of the Act in relation to highways maintainable at the public expense should first be explained. Persons carrying out street works—including companies supplying services and others—are referred to in the Act as "undertakers". Street works may be carried out either by virtue of statutory powers or permission granted by the street authority—a "street works licence". In the absence of statutory power, or a street works licence, it is an offence to carry out street works, and street managers may direct an offending undertaker to remove any apparatus installed and to re-instate the street (ss. 50 and 51).

10-8 Undertakers must give advance notice to the street authority of their intention to carry out street works (ss. 54 and 55). More detailed provisions are supplied by the 1992 regulations: the undertaker must give one month's advance notice of street works relating to "major projects", which includes projects identified specifically in the undertaker's annual operating programme, or which would normally be planned at least 6 months in advance; and (a separate requirement) 7 days' notice of the starting date of street works, unless they are minor or urgent. For urgent street works, notice must be given as soon as practicable, and for minor street works no notice is required[2] (regulations 6 and 7). "Minor works" means:

"works (not being emergency works or urgent works) whether in the footway, verge or carriageway, which are of a planned duration of not more than 3 days, do not form part of a rolling programme and do not involve at any one time more than 30 metres of works or leave less than 3 metres width of carriageway available for traffic or less than 2.5 metres width of carriageway where the traffic is expected to consist only of motor cars and light locomotives within the meaning of the section 185(1) of the Road Traffic Act 1988 (regulation 2(1))".

10-9 The regulations contain a form which must be used for giving notice.

---

2. The requirements differ if a street has been designated as "traffic-sensitive" by the local authority, but this will be rare in the case of private roads.

10-10 A street authority may give directions as to the timing of street works if it appears that they are likely to cause serious disruption to traffic and that the disruption could be reduced if the works were to be carried out only at certain times (s. 56). However, the requirement to obtain a street works licence, and the provisions of ss. 54, 55 and 56 do not affect emergency repairs (s. 57). The street authority has a general duty to co-ordinate street works and other works (including works for road purposes)(s. 59); and undertakers have a general duty to co-operate with the street authority and with each other, failure to co-operate being an offence (s. 60). Street authorities and undertakers must have regard, in relation to these three sections, to codes of practice issued by the DfT[3], and under s. 59 the DfT can give directions to street authorities which do not appear to be discharging their duties properly. Schedule 3 to the Act supplements s. 50, and lays down the powers and duties of a street authority in granting a street works licence. Before granting a licence, the street authority must give notice to undertakers who may have pipes, cables or other equipment in the street. The street authority may require the payment of a reasonable fee to cover expenses, it may attach conditions to a street works licence, and it may withdraw the licence in certain circumstances.

[*]See 10-4.

10-11 In addition to the above rules, street authorities have a particular function in relation to works for road purposes[*]. Where these are "substantial"—which in brief means, by regulation 9 of the 1992 regulations, reconstruction or resurfacing which extends for more than 30 metres and which temporarily reduces the width of the street by more than one-third—the street authority may restrict the carrying out of street works during the next 12 months (s. 58). But some street works may still be carried out, including urgent work, works for the supply of services to new customers, and some minor work.

10-12 Once work has been carried out, an undertaker must reinstate the street. The street authority may carry out "investigatory works", to check that the street has been properly reinstated. If it has not, the undertaker must bear the cost of the investigatory works. The street authority may then serve a notice on the undertaker, requiring the street to be reinstated within a specified period of at least 7 days, and if the undertakers fails to comply the street authority may carry out the work and recover its reasonable costs from the undertaker (s. 72).

10-13 A street authority must keep a register showing the work which has been carried out, and the work planned for the street, including street works and works for road purposes (s. 53(1) and regulation 3). Undertakers are responsible for sending the street authority copies of

---

3. See particularly *Safety at Street Works and Road Works - A Code of Practice* (ISBN 0-11-551144-X) and *Code of Practice for the Co-ordination of Street Works and Works for Road Purposes and Related Matters* (ISBN 0-11-551162-8).

notices relating to street works, and informing the street authority of street works carried out. The street authority is responsible for recording information about works for road purposes which the authority itself carries out, and about street works licences granted (regulation 3 of the 1992 regulations).

10-14 Further provisions of the Act deal with special controls in particular sorts of street, and the Act also deals with safety measures, the avoidance of delay and obstruction, the duty to re-instate the street, and other matters (ss. 61–73). Under s. 80, undertakers must report to the street authority any pipes, cables and other equipment they find in the course of carrying out street works.

10-15 For streets which are *not* highways maintainable at the public expense, the main differences are as follows, as a result of amendment of the Act by the 1992 Regulations. First, the obligation to keep a register of street works under s. 53(1) falls on the local authority rather than on the street managers, and reports under s. 80* go to the local authority. The street authority, however, remains responsible for seeing that the appropriate information is recorded (see above) and advance notice of street works must still be given to the person who is the street manager for a private street. Section s. 61 of the Act (on "protected streets") does not apply to streets which are not highways maintainable at the public expense (regulation 10). Subject to these modifications, the street managers in a private street fulfill the functions of the street authority: it is for them to co-ordinate the activities of undertakers, having regard to the code of practice under s. 59, to give directions as to the timing of street works, to grant street works licences to those who do not have statutory powers to carry out street works, and to take decisions under s. 58.

*See 10-14.

Exercise of powers by statutory undertakers

10-16 The principles governing the exercise of powers by statutory undertakers were worked out by the courts during the nineteenth century, when such powers were often granted by Parliament so that canals, railways and other works of public benefit could be carried out by commercial enterprises. The courts are careful to see that powers of this sort are not abused.

10-17 An undertaker must exercise his powers in good faith, and with strict regard to the terms of the legislation, which will define the purposes for which the powers may be used and the procedures which must be followed. He must proceed promptly, with due care and skill, and must cause as little damage and inconvenience as possible to those affected by the work carried out. The onus is on the undertaker to show that it has acted lawfully. Provided the powers are exercised in this way, the courts will regard the legislation as authorising what might otherwise be a crime or a civil wrong. Conversely, however, the undertaker who fails to meet the standards expected by the courts is likely to find that his activities are not regarded as authorised by the legislation, and that he is liable under the civil or criminal law in the same way as any other person not protected by legislation.

10-18   Such powers are a great advantage to an undertaker; but they require from the undertaker a real sense of responsibility and a high standard of competence and care. Legislation conferring powers is often complex, and in order to exercise the powers an undertaker must devote time and effort to understanding the purposes for which particular powers are intended to be used, and the ways in which the legislation seeks to balance the interests of undertakers against the interests of those whose interests will be affected by the exercise of the powers[4].

Nature of statutory powers

10-19   In some respects the powers granted to statutory undertakers may appear to be very broad, and the wording of the Acts in question may give the impression that they are designed to cover every eventuality. But in reality powers are conferred sparingly by the legislation, and do not necessarily cover all that an undertaker might wish to do.

10-20   Undertakers are usually given the power to carry out work on land, and, in most but not all cases, the power to enter on to land in order to carry out work. These are different powers because an undertaker may not need a power to enter—this is true particularly of work done on a highway, where the undertaker, like any member of the public, already has the right to go. Powers of entry on to land tend to be subject to extra safeguards, to protect the interests of the owner or occupier of the land, and these safeguards generally apply to private roads which are not highways.

10-21   Powers under the Telecommunications Act 1984 are different from those under other Acts, in that the Telecommunications Act does not itself grant the necessary powers; rather it provides that the undertaker must obtain agreement allowing it to carry out work, or failing that obtain an order from the County Court giving it the right to do so.

---

4. For a fuller account of this area of the law see SGG Edgar, *Craies on Statute Law* (1971), p. 274 et seq.

Electricity

The Electricity Act 1989 allows OFGEM and the DTI to grant licences for the generation, transmission and supply of electricity (s. 6). Companies granted a licence are referred to in the Act as "licence-holders".

By s. 10(1) of and Schedule 4 to the Electricity Act, a licence holder is permitted to install, "under, in, on, along or across any street", electrical lines or plant, and structures for housing or covering them, and to inspect, maintain and repair all of the foregoing. A licence-holder may also carry out incidental work, including digging up any street, opening up drains and sewers, and tunnelling or boring under any street (paragraph 1(1) of Schedule 4). "Street" has the same meaning as in the New Roads and Street Works Act 1991*.

However, the power is qualified: electrical lines and plant may not be placed under a street which is not dedicated to the public (that, is, not a highway); and a structure for housing any plant or line can only be placed on or over any street with consent of the street authority or of the DTI. The term "street authority" has the same meaning as in the New Roads and Street Works Act, so in relation to a private street means the street managers*. Consent must not be unreasonably withheld by the street authority, and if there is a dispute about whether consent has been unreasonably withheld, the dispute must be referred to an arbitrator appointed by the parties or, if they cannot agree, by OFGEM (paragraph 1(3)). A licence holder must exercise its powers so as to do as little damage as possible; must pay compensation for damage caused; and must make sure that lines and plant installed do not cause a danger to the public (paragraph 1(5) and (6)). The Act provides no right of entry in order to carry out street works: a licence-holder is not entitled to enter a private street which is not a highway, but if given consent to enter may carry out street works in accordance with the Act, as explained above.

Apart from the power to carry out street works, a licence-holder may acquire a wayleave, that is, according to Schedule 4, the right to install and maintain an electric line (but not "plant", such as an electricity substation) on land. A right of entry is included in a wayleave obtained in accordance with the Act. The licence-holder must serve notice on the owner or occupier of the land*, detailing the

*See 1-19.

*See 10-6.

*See 1-43 for possession and occupation of land.

wayleave required. If a satisfactory wayleave is not granted, the licence holder may apply to the DTI which, after giving the owner or occupier the right to be heard, may grant the wayleave. The owner or occupier is entitled to compensation (paragraphs 6 and 7).

10-26 A licence-holder also has power in connection with trees which are close to electrical lines or plant, and so may obstruct or interfere with them or constitute a source of danger to children or others, whether in a street or on other land. The licence-holder may serve notice on the owner of the land on which the tree is growing, requiring him to fell or lop the tree, or to cut back its roots and lop the tree concerned. The owner or occupier of the land may serve a counter-notice, in which case the matter is referred to the DTI for decision in the same way described above; but if there is no counter-notice, and the work is not done, the licence holder may cause the tree to be felled or lopped, or its roots cut back. In so doing the licence-holder must follow "good arboricultural practice", cause as little damage as possible, and make good any damage caused to the land. "Tree" is given a special definition for this purpose, so as to include any shrub (paragraph 9).

10-27 Under Schedule 3 to the Electricity Act, licence-holders also have power to acquire land and rights compulsorily. Legislation relating to the compulsory purchase of land applies, with certain modifications, so that there are procedures by which compensation can be obtained by a landowner affected.

Gas

10-28 The Gas Act 1986[5] governs "public gas transporters" (as it terms them), that is companies authorised by the DTI to supply gas through pipes. OFGEM regulates these companies (ss. 3–7).

10-29 By s. 9(3) of and Schedule 4 to the Act, public gas transporters enjoy powers to carry out work in streets, the word having once more the wide meaning in the New Roads and Street Works Act 1991, and thus including all private roads as well as public ones[*]. A supplier may place "pipes, conduits, service pipes, cables, sewers and other works", and also "pressure governors, ventilators and other works" under any street, and also carry out any incidental work such as digging up the street, or opening any sewers, drains or tunnels (paragraphs 1(1) and 2(2)). In carrying out the work, the public gas transporter must do as little damage as possible, and must pay compensation for any damage done (paragraph 1(3)). Additionally, "structures for housing

[*] But see 10-30.

---

5. As amended by the Gas Act 1995.

apparatus" may be erected in a street, but only with the consent of the street authority (defined in accordance with the New Roads and Street Works Act[*]) which must not be unreasonably withheld. Any dispute must be referred to an arbitrator appointed by the parties, or in the absence of agreement about the arbitrator, chosen by OFGEM.

[*]See 10-6.

10-30 These provisions apply to any street which is dedicated to public use (that is, a highway) and to any street which is not dedicated to public use if the work is to be done in order to supply gas to premises abutting the street (paragraph 3). In other words, a private road which is not a highway cannot be used as a through-route for a gas main.

10-31 A public gas transporter has no right to enter land in order to install pipes and other apparatus. No right of entry is needed in a street which is a highway. In a private road which is not a highway, as noted above, pipes cannot be installed, except in order to supply a house in the street. But since there is no right of entry, permission from the owner of the street will be required in order for the public gas transporter to come on to the land. There is a power of entry, however, in order to repair, replace or alter existing gas pipes (Schedule 5, paragraph 17). Seven days' notice must be given to the occupier, except in an emergency, in which case notice must be given as soon as possible. Entry may be made by any officer of the public gas transporter, who must on entry produce "some duly authenticated document showing his authority". Where an entry is made, the public gas transporter must make good, or pay compensation for, any damage caused (paragraph 20).

10-32 Mention must also be made of the Rights of Entry (Gas and Electricity Boards) Act 1954[6], since this adds a further requirement. Except in an emergency, entry on to land can be made only if the occupier consents, or failing that if a warrant is obtained from a Justice of the Peace entitling the public gas transporter to enter. Before granting a warrant, the Justice of the Peace must be satisfied that entry is reasonably required, and that the requirements of the Gas Act 1986 have been complied with. This Act provides that powers to enter land granted by the Gas Act can only be exercised by the consent of the occupier of the land, or by a warrant, granted by a justice of the peace, who must be satisfied that the entry would be justified (ss. 1 and 2). A public gas transporter can thus obtain entry to a private street which is not a highway, where consent is not granted.

10-33 Since gas pipes will always be underground, there is no need for all the powers which licence-holders under the Electricity Act enjoy, such as the power to lop and fell trees. Schedule 4 deals only with streets. If

---

6. As its title suggests, the Act applies to some powers under the Electricity Act 1989; but it does not apply to those mentioned in this text.

a public gas transporter wishes to install gas pipes or other equipment in land which is not a street, Schedule 3 provides a power of compulsory acquisition. Using this power, a public gas transporter can acquire land, or, as appropriate, a wayleave permitting pipes to be installed. The legislation on the compulsory purchase of land applies.

Telecommunications

10-34 The Telecommunications Act 1984 applies to telephone companies such as British Telecom, and to "cable" companies, which provide telephone, television and other services by means of fibre-optic cables[7]. The regulatory body is OFTEL and the responsible government department is again the DTI (ss. 1–9).

10-35 A licence is required by a person who wishes to operate a telecommunications system. When a licence is granted, the "Telecommunications Code" may be applied to the operator of the system. The Code is set out in Schedule 2 to the Act, and, when applied to an operator, it allows the operator to install cables and other equipment under and over land belonging to others. When the Code is applied conditions may be imposed, including particularly conditions designed to protect the environment, to prevent damage to streets or interference with traffic, and to ensure that any liabilities of the operator are met (s. 10).

10-36 The Code gives power to operators to carry out work in "streets", this word having the same meaning as in the New Roads and Street Works Act 1991[*]. Operators may install telecommunication apparatus "under, over, in, on, along or across" a street; and they may inspect, maintain and adjust it, and may break up the street, or tunnel or bore under it, in order to do so (paragraph 9 of the Code). In relation to a street which is a highway maintainable at the public expense, the operator has a right to carry out the work, and needs no further permission from the owner of the street, but must comply with the procedural requirements of the New Roads and Street Works Act[*]. In relation to any other sort of street—and any land other than a street—the operator must obtain either an agreement under paragraph 2 of the Code, or an order from the County Court dispensing with an agreement under paragraph 5. Either an agreement or an order must therefore be obtained in relation to a private street, whether it is a highway or not, in order for a telecommunications operator to install

[*]See 1-19.

[*]See 10-4 onwards.

---

7. The Act also applies in certain circumstances to much smaller-scale telecommunications systems.

cables or other equipment (paragraph 9). The same is true for land which is not a street at all, because of paragraph 2, the difference being that:

- If the land is a street, the work takes place in accordance with the New Roads and Street Works Act. And

- If the land is not a street, the work takes place by virtue of the agreement or order from the Court.

10-37 In either case, then, the operator must first seek an agreement from the occupier of the private street conferring the necessary right (paragraph 2). (The Telecommunications Code provides that in the case of a private road the "occupier" is the person who is the "street manager" for the purposes of the New Roads and Street Works Act (paragraph 2(8))*. In addition, if the proposed work is going to interfere with access to property—as is likely to be the case in a private road—the operator must also seek an agreement allowing him to do this (paragraph 3). The terms of the agreement are a matter for negotiation, and the occupier may (for example) seek to obtain a one-off fee or an annual payment, or both, for the use of his land, or special terms as to the positioning of the equipment, or the payment of compensation by the operator for any loss or damage caused.

*See 10-6.

10-38 Negotiations may not prove successful; and if this is so the operator may make an application to the County Court for an order dispensing with the need for agreement, and conferring the necessary rights on the operator (paragraph 5). According to the Code:

"The court shall make an order under this paragraph if, but only if, it is satisfied that any prejudice caused by the order—

(a) is capable of being adequately compensated for by money; or

(b) is outweighed by the benefit accruing from the order to the persons whose access to a telecommunications system will be secured by the order;

and in determining the extent of the prejudice, and the weight of that benefit, the court shall have regard to all the circumstances and to the principle that no person should unreasonably be denied access to a telecommunications system."

10-39 The court may set whatever terms and conditions it feels are appropriate, but must include terms dealing with payment (whatever would have been "fair and reasonable if the agreement had been given willingly...") and with compensation for any loss or damage sustained[8].

10-40   Potential users of the telecommunications system are also given rights under the Code. If an agreement is required but has not been obtained, and if the operator does not apply to the County Court for an order, a potential user may give notice to the operator requiring the operator to apply to the court. The operator may challenge the notice on the ground that, even if an agreement were obtained, the operator would not give the person concerned access to the system, and could not be required to do so. (Whether the operator can be required to do this will depend upon the terms of his telecommunications licence.) Failing such a challenge, the potential user may apply to the County Court on the operator's behalf, for an order dispensing with the need for an agreement, and conferring the necessary right on the operator (paragraph 8). This is therefore an alternative way in which to overcome a refusal by the occupier of the street to agree to the installation of cables or other equipment.

10-41   A right created by an agreement, or by an order of the court, is in effect a wayleave, though the Act does not use the term. It is not an easement, and cannot be shown on the Land Register[*]. Although it is the occupier of the land who makes an agreement, or is the subject of an order by the County Court, the Code contains provisions by which the owner of the land, if different from the occupier, may be bound by the agreement (paragraph 2). The right does not automatically pass to a new operator of the telecommunications system, if there is a change; but the new operator may obtain an agreement, or an order from the County Court in respect of existing equipment, and may also if necessary obtain an order from the Court allowing temporary use until a new agreement is in place (paragraph 6).

[*] See 2-38.

10-42   The right allows an operator to "fly" lines over land adjoining land over which a right under the Code exists, provided the lines are at least 3 metres above the ground and 2 metres from any building over which they pass. It is not necessary for the operator to obtain the consent of the owner of the land, but the landowner has the right to object in certain circumstances (paragraphs 10 and 17).

10-43   A telecommunications operator has power, under paragraph 19 of the Code, to lop[9] a tree overhanging a street, which obstructs or interferes with wires or other equipment. The operator can serve notice on the occupier of the land on which the tree is growing, requiring him to lop the tree, and can do the work himself if the occupier does not do so. If the operator carries out the work, it must be done in a "husband-

---

8. For a case on the meaning of "fair and reasonable" see *Mercury Communications Ltd v London and India Dock Investments Ltd* (1995) 69 P&CR 135.

9. To "lop" means to remove lateral branches, not the top of the tree: see *Unwin v Hanson* [1981] 2 QB 115.

like manner", and in such a way as to cause the minimum damage to the tree. In either case, the operator may be required to compensate the occupier for loss, damage or expenses caused.

Water and sewerage

The privatisation of the industry was carried out by the Water Act 1989. Between 1974 and 1989, water authorities provided water and sewerage services; before 1974 local authorities were responsible. The privatised suppliers of water and sewerage services are now governed by legislation passed in 1991, particularly the Water Industry Act 1991. Companies may be "water undertakers" or "sewerage undertakers" or both—the Act uses "relevant undertaker" to include both. The industry regulator is the OFWAT, and the government department concerned is the DEFRA.

Water Water undertakers have power to lay a "relevant pipe" in a street, and to inspect, maintain and repair it; and to carry out any incidental work including digging up the street, tunnelling or boring under it, or opening up any sewer, drain or tunnel (s. 158(1)). "Street" has the meaning given by the New Roads and Street Works Act, and thus includes both private streets which are highways and those which are not. A "relevant pipe" is, in the case of a water undertaker, a water main, resource main, discharge pipe or service pipe. The most important of these definitions are "water main", which means a pipe belonging to the undertaker which is used to provide a general supply of water to customers, not just one customer, and "service pipe" which means a pipe connected to a water main, to supply water to a house or other premises (s. 219(1)).

Power is given by s. 159 to carry out the same sort of work on land which is not a street. The installation of water meters is catered for specifically by s. 162. A water undertaker can carry out work for the installation, maintenance or repair of a meter, and any incidental work, of a street or any other land[10]. By s. 163, a water undertaker can fit stopcocks to service pipes.

Powers of entry in connection with ss. 158, 159 and 163 are provided generally by s. 168; while linked to s. 162, dealing with the installation of water meters, is a power of entry in s. 172. In order for these powers of entry to be exercised, the person exercising them must be designated in writing. The procedures and conditions which apply

---

10. See also the Water (Meters) Regulations 1988, SI 1988/1048, which deal with the positioning of water meters and related matters.

to all the above powers are not easily summarised, but the position is briefly as follows:

- Section 159: except in an emergency, reasonable notice (a minimum of 3 months for installing a new pipe, or 42 days for repairing an old one) must be given to the owner and occupier of the land; complaints may be made to OFWAT about the exercise of the power, and OFWAT may award compensation of up to £5,000 if the water undertaker has failed to consult the owner of the land adequately or has acted unreasonably; and every water undertaker must prepare and agree with OFWAT a code of practice, which is relevant to the award of compensation.

- Sections 158 and 162: Schedule 12 applies, providing for compensation. Undertakers must do as little damage as possible, and must pay compensation for any damage they cause.

- Section 162: any dispute as to the exercise of the power must be referred to an arbitrator (to be chosen by OFWAT in the absence of agreement).

- Sections 162, 168 and 178: the rules set out in Schedule 6 Part II apply, with the result that, in order to exercise the power of entry[11], notice (usually 7 days) must be given except in an emergency, entry must be at a reasonable time, a warrant from a justice of the peace may be obtained if entry is refused, and compensation is payable if damage is caused in entering.

10-48 *Public sewers* While pipes, cables and other apparatus under a private road are generally the property and responsibility of the companies which provide the services in question, sewers and drains are an exception, in two respects. First, drains do not belong to sewerage undertakers; secondly, not all sewers belong to them. These points must first be explained.

10-49 Under the Water Industry Act 1991, the difference between a drain and a sewer is that a drain is used for draining a single building (not counting any ancillary buildings such as garages) whereas a sewer is used for draining more than one (s. 219(1)). Earlier legislation generally drew the same distinction between drains and sewers. The usual pattern in a street will thus be for drains to lead from each house, into a sewer running along the street.

---

11. These rules are broadly similar to those in the Rights of Entry (Gas and Electricity Boards) Act 1954, mentioned above.

10-50 In order to tell whether a sewer belongs to a sewerage undertaker in a given case, it is necessary to consider the history of the legislation. As explained above, water and sewerage undertakers acquired their assets, including water mains and sewers, from the bodies which preceded them—between 1974 and the privatisation of the industry in 1989, the bodies were public water authorities, and before 1974 they were local authorities. The legislation is complex, but the following summary covers most[12] cases:

- Sewers laid before the Public Health Act 1936 were subject to the provisions of the Public Health Act 1875. Ownership would generally pass to the local authority, unless the sewer was constructed for profit (as would be the case in a private street if the developer reserved the right to make a charge for use of the sewer).

- Sewers laid after the Public Health Act 1936 may have been adopted by the local authority, water authority or water undertaker, by means of a "vesting declaration", that is, a declaration transferring the sewer to the body in question. There was power to do this in the Public Health Act 1936, and there is currently power to do so in s. 102 of the Water Industry Act 1991.

10-51 The legislation was thus more generous, in passing ownership and responsibility to official bodies, in relation to pre-1936 sewers. It should be noted that, apart from the procedures mentioned above, the legislation (Part XI of the Highways Act 1980) provides for a sewer to be adopted as part of the process of making up and adoption of a private street. This was also possible under earlier legislation. Where this happens, the street becomes a highway maintainable at the public expense. Ownership of the street passes to the local authority, but the sewer passes to the sewerage undertaker, under s. 179(2) of the Water Industry Act.

10-52 Those sewers which belong to a sewerage undertaker are referred to in the Water Industry Act as "public sewers" and consist of sewers which the undertaker has acquired as part of the assets of the water authority which preceded it, and any sewers which the undertaker has itself constructed (s. 179(1) and (2)). It is the responsibility of the sewerage undertaker to maintain these sewers (s. 94). The sewerage undertaker must keep a list, open to public inspection, of public sewers (ss. 199 and 200).

---

12. Other factors may be relevant, such as whether a private street was developed in accordance with a local Act, or a scheme drawn up under planning legislation.

(10-53) The powers of a sewerage undertaker to install, maintain and repair public sewers are briefly as follows. Sections 158 and 159 apply to sewers in the same way that they do to water pipes; and the rules which apply to the exercise of these powers are the same as those described above in relation to water pipes.

(10-54) *Private sewers and drains* A sewer which is not a public sewer for the purposes of the Water Industry Act is a private sewer. Residents in a private street are likely to have a right to lay, maintain and use a private sewer, the right taking the form of an easement*. Such a right is likely to cater for the installation of drains and their connection to the private sewer. In relation to a public sewer, the drains under the street and under houses adjoining the street are the responsibility of the owner of the house. Section 108 of the Act gives the right to dig up the street in order to connect to a public sewer, or to repair drains, subject to the same conditions as apply to the sewerage undertaker. Thus the owner of a house may generally dig up a private street to repair his drains, whether the sewer is public or private.

*See 4-60.

(10-55) Some drains may be designed merely to channel surface water from a street into a sewer, and these will generally be the responsibility of the owner of the street.

The Post Office

(10-56) Mention should be made of the Post Office. The Post Office has no statutory powers to install post boxes on land, but does so by agreement. Generally post boxes are located on highways maintainable at the public expense, by agreement with the local authority.

Assessment

(10-57) The work of undertakers, in installing and maintaining their apparatus, is likely to be beneficial, and the owner and residents of a private street will generally have no reason in principle to object to the work. But there is an obvious interest in seeing that work is completed promptly and efficiently, and with the least possible disruption and damage. Furthermore, the New Roads and Street Works Act 1991 places duties on the street managers to co-ordinate work, and on undertakers to co-operate with the street managers. Contact between the street managers and undertakers, from the earliest possible stage, is thus both necessary and desirable.

10-58 Notice must be served under the Act in some, but not all cases. This need not prevent the street managers from making contact with undertakers in advance, if they are aware that work is due to be carried out. Undertakers have an obligation, by virtue of s. 60 of the Act, to co-operate with street managers, and they should be able and willing to explain what work they wish to carry out and what powers (including, where appropriate, powers of entry) they propose to exercise in order to do so. It may be useful for the street authority in a private street to check that the undertaker is aware of, and will comply with, the statutory requirements to which it is subject, particularly the requirements to cause as little damage as possible, and to pay compensation for any damage or loss.

10-59 Street managers have only a limited power to give directions as to the timing of work (s. 56); but they have a general responsibility for co-ordinating work (s. 59) and as noted undertakers have an obligation to co-operate with the street managers. This suggests that discussions should normally take place at the outset as to such matter as the date when work will commence, the placing of pipes, cables and other apparatus, and the undertaker's arrangements for keeping disruption and damage to a minimum. In some cases, it will be necessary to reach an agreement with the undertaker for the grant of a wayleave or similar rights, including any fee to be paid by the undertaker for the rights, and this applies particularly to work carried out under the Telecommunications Act.

10-60 There is no reason why the street managers should not enter an agreement with an undertaker on matters of mutual interest. It might (for example) be agreed that the undertaker should be allowed to store machinery or materials temporarily in the street, and should in return carry out work, in making good the street, beyond what was strictly required under the legislation.

10-61 If a sewer is in need of repair, the first question will be whether it is a public sewer, and hence the duty of the sewerage undertaker to repair. Enquiries of the local authority, and of the sewerage undertaker, should reveal whether this is the case.

Chapter 11: Making up and adoption

Introduction

11-0   As chapter 3 explained, a private road can cease to be private, and become a highway maintainable at the public expense, as a result of an agreement under s. 38 of the Highways Act 1980. This chapter looks at the much more complicated provisions, set out in Part XI of the Highways Act, which give local authorities some control over both new and existing roads, and which govern the processes of "making up", i.e. bringing a private road up to an acceptable standard, and "adoption", i.e. making it a highway maintainable at the public expense, and therefore no longer private.

11-1   In this chapter, the text uses "street" rather than "road", so as to follow the language of the Highways Act.

Part XI of the Highways Act 1980

11-2   Part XI of the Highways Act 1980 (ss. 203 to 237) is entitled "Making up of private streets". Within Part XI, one group of sections, ss. 205 to 218, is called "the private street works code", and another (ss. 219 to 225) is called "the advance payments code". There are also some introductory sections (ss. 203 and 204), and some general provisions (ss. 226 to 237).

11-3   The two codes (referred to in this chapter as the PSWC and the APC) serve rather different purposes. The PSWC gives local authorities powers to carry out work necessary to bring an existing private street up to an acceptable standard, the cost generally being apportioned between the premises fronting the street. The APC applies (though not in all areas) where a new private street is constructed, or where certain sorts of development take place in an existing private street, and its purpose is to see that the cost of constructing the street to an acceptable standard is provided for.

11-4   The codes are interrelated, and the way in which they work is summarised in a flow-chart at the end of this chapter. Both codes can —but do not automatically—lead to the adoption of the street. There were similar provisions in earlier legislation. The predecessor of the

PSWC was the Private Street Works Act 1892, and the predecessor of the APC was the New Streets Act 1951. The Public Health Act 1875 also contained provisions for the adoption of private streets, but these were repealed in 1972 and not replaced.

11-5 In applying the PSWC and the APC, the initiative generally lies with the local authority. In some circumstances the law requires the local authority to act; in some circumstances it is given a discretion as to whether it acts. But in some situations the residents of a private street, acting by a majority, can take action to secure the adoption of a private street.

11-6 The codes contain detailed provisions for deciding what work should be done, for determining the cost, and for apportioning it among the premises served by the street.

Some basic concepts

11-7 "Street", for the purposes of the Highways Act 1980, is given a wide definition by s. 329(1), and is likely to include all private roads*. In practice, streets will almost always be used by vehicular traffic, and when adopted will become carriageways; though the definition seems wide enough to include alleys and passages not used by vehicles—in which case adoption would presumably give rise to a footpath or bridleway, but not a carriageway. The term includes part of a street, and for most purposes the PSWC and APC can apply to part of a street. A "private street" is a street which is not a highway maintainable at the public expense, in other words, not adopted (s. 203(2)). The definition thus includes both those private streets which are highways and those which are not.

*See 1-19.

"Street works" means:

"any works for the sewering, levelling, paving, metalling, flagging, channelling and making good of a street, and includes the provision of proper means for lighting a street" (s. 203(3)).

11-8 The phrase "paving, metalling and flagging" is also dealt with in s. 203(3): this includes:

"all methods of making a footway or carriageway".

11-9 No fixed standards are set out in the Highways Act 1980 for the work which must be carried out under the two codes. Local authorities thus have a measure of freedom to decide for themselves what standards should apply. They must, however, act reasonably in exercising their powers, this being a general requirement of administrative law for public bodies*. Whether it is reasonable for a

*See 1-51.

*See chapter 9.

local authority, in exercising its powers, to insist on a tarmac surface, or some more specialised finish such as cobbles or granite setts, or whether to require street lighting or pavements, must depend upon the particular circumstances. These are likely to include the condition of nearby or comparable streets. It should be noted that the powers referred to elsewhere in the Highways Act* continue to apply here, and can be used in conjunction with the procedures under Part XI of the Highways Act. And, as explained below, Part XI Act gives local authorities some additional powers in this context. Under the PSWC, work required to be carried out may include incidental work[1], to bring the street into conformity with other streets in the area (s. 206). Under either code, the local authority may vary the relative widths of the street and the pavements; and if the street is a highway, the local authority may require it to be widened (s. 226). They may also (under other provisions in the Act) widen a highway; and where they do so in relation to a private street, this is deemed not to affect the liability of frontagers to pay for the street works (s. 227). (But for this provision the frontagers might claim that, having lost some land, their liability ought to be reduced.)

The private street works code: procedure

(11-10) The procedure for applying the PSWC can best be described as a series of steps.

(11-11) *First step: initial resolution by the local authority* By s. 205(1) of the Highways Act:

> "Where a private street is not, to the satisfaction of the [local] authority, sewered, levelled, paved, metalled, flagged, channelled, made good and lighted, the authority may from time to time resolve with respect to the street to execute street works and, subject to the PSWC the expenses incurred by the authority in executing those works shall be apportioned between the premises fronting the street."

(11-12) A resolution in general terms that street works should be executed is thus the first step. The local authority can act of its own accord or on request from a resident of the street in question, or any other member of the public, but the decision is the local authority's. The local authority can act soon after the street has been constructed, or at some later date; though if a lengthy period has elapsed since the street was

---

1. As to what work may be included as incidental, see *Pool Corporation v Blake* [1955] 3 WLR 757.

constructed, and the street has been maintained to a reasonable standard, it may be difficult for the local authority to assert that they are not satisfied with it.

Second step: preparation of specification, etc. Once the necessary resolution has been passed, it is for the staff of the local authority to draw up a specification of the street works required, with:

- Any necessary plans.

- An estimate of the probable expenses. And

- A provisional apportionment of the estimated expenses between the premises fronting the street (s. 205(3)).

Additional particulars specified in paragraphs 1 to 4 of Schedule 16 to the Act must be included; for example, the measurements of the frontages. Any other factors relevant to the apportionment must also be shown.

"Fronting" is given a definition for these purposes: it includes "adjoining" (s. 203(3)). Any land running along a private street has a frontage on that street, even though the street may be regarded as being to the side, or at the back, of the land. Land may be said to "adjoin" a street even where it is separated from the street by a narrow strip of ground; though verges and other strips of land running alongside a roadway will in any event tend to be regarded as part of the street[2]. On the other hand, a first floor maisonette does not have a frontage for this purpose[3]. A local authority may resolve to execute street works in part of a street, rather than the whole of the street. (It might properly decide to do this if that part of the street was in bad repair but the rest was not.) In this case the costs are to be apportioned among the owners of premises fronting that part of the street (s. 205(2)).

The provisional apportionment must, under s. 207, be made "according to the frontage of the respective premises", that is, according to their respective lengths. This, therefore is the main consideration in apportioning the cost[4]. But the local authority may also resolve to take into account two other factors—firstly, the greater or lesser degree of benefit to be obtained by particular premises from the street works; and, secondly, the amount and value of any work already done by the owners or occupiers of particular premises (s.

---

2. See *Warwickshire County Council v Adkins* (1968) 112 SJ 135; 66 LGR 486.
3. See *Buckinghamshire County Council v Trigg* [1963] 1 WLR 155, [1963] 1 All ER 403, 61 LGR 189
4. See *Parkstone Primrose Laundry Ltd v Poole Corporation* (1950) 48 LGR 637.

207(2)). Consideration of these matters may increase or decrease the amount due according to the frontage of the premises, and the local authority must not close its mind to these matters[5]. It is also open to the local authority to include in the apportionment any premises which have no frontage but which have access to the private street by way of a court, passage or otherwise (for example, a private driveway) and which will be benefited by the street works. Backland development can thus be taken into account. The amount of the apportionment is then fixed according to the degree of benefit (s. 207(3)).

11-17 Although the local authority is required to apportion the cost among the premises with frontages, s. 236 provides that the local authority may resolve to bear some or all of the cost itself, in which case the liability of the owners is discharged, or proportionately reduced (s. 236(1)). Furthermore, the local authority may resolve specifically to bear costs which would otherwise fall on the owners with rear or flank frontages on the street—in such cases it may appear unfair for the owners of the premises in question to pay a full share of the cost (s. 236(2)). It would no doubt be particularly appropriate for the local authority to use this power if premises with a rear or flank frontage had no access to the street, and so would not benefit from the making up of the street.

11-18 Not all premises are liable to bear the expenses of street works under the PSWC. By s. 215, places of public religious worship[6] and associated churchyards and burial grounds are exempt, and the appropriate share of the expenses must be borne by the local authority. Premises belonging to "railway undertakers", and to "canal undertakers", provided they have no communication with the private street, and are used only for the purposes of the railway or canal, are also exempt in certain circumstances; in this case the expenses have to be shared among the other premises liable to contribute (s. 216).

11-19 *Third step: resolution of approval* The specification of the street works to be carried out, with the estimate of the expenses, and the provisional apportionment, are submitted to the local authority. The latter, having made any amendments they consider necessary, may pass a "resolution of approval" (s. 205(3)).

11-20 *Fourth step: publicity* After the resolution of approval has been passed, a notice in the form specified in paragraph 5 of Schedule 16 to the Highways Act must be published in a local newspaper for two successive weeks, posted in a prominent position in or near the street

---

5. See *Carter and Another v Surrey County Council*, The Times 2 June 1989.
6. "Place of public religious worship" is defined in s. 203(3), and includes premises belonging to the Church of England, or to the Church in Wales, and premises "certified as required by law as a place of religious worship" under the Places of Worship Registration Act 1855.

in question, and served on the owners of the premises shown in the provisional apportionment (who must also be told the amount of the provisional apportionment), and, finally, made available for public inspection, free of charge, at the offices of the local authority (s. 205(5) and (6)).

Fifth step: objections There is a right of objection, under s. 208, for the owner of any premises shown in a provisional apportionment of expenses as being liable to contribute to the costs of the street works. An owner can object on any of the following grounds:

- That the street, or the part in question, is not a private street (s. 208(1)(a));

- That there is a material informality, defect or error in the local authority's resolution or the documents prepared under it (s. 208(1)(b));

- That the proposed street works are insufficient or unreasonable (s. 208(1)(c));

- That the estimated costs are excessive (s. 208(1)(dd));

- That premises ought to be included in, or excluded from, the provisional apportionment (s. 208(1)(e));

- That the provisional apportionment is incorrect on some matter of fact; or, where the local authority has taken into account considerations other than the frontage of premises, the local authority is wrong in relation to the degree of benefit to premises, or in relation to the value of work already done by residents in the road (s. 208(1)(f)).

Objections must be made in writing and within one month of the notice under s. 205, and must take the form of a notice to the local authority.

Where objections are made and are not withdrawn, the local authority may apply to a magistrates' court, under s. 209, for the objections to be "dealt with". The magistrates' court has a wide power to nullify or amend the resolution of approval, or the specification, plans, estimate and provisional apportionment, but it cannot decide that additional street works should be carried out[7].

---

7. See *Ware Urban District Council v Gaunt* [1960] 1 WLR 1364, [1960] 3 All ER 778.

11-24   The local authority may at any time amend the specifications of the proposed street works (s. 210). If they increase the estimate—but not, apparently, if they amend other details—they must publicise the amended proposal in the same way as the original, under s. 205(5) and there is a right to make objections under s. 208.

11-25   *Sixth step: carrying out of work* Once all objections have been dealt with, the local authority may proceed with the work. The consent of the owner of the street, or of residents, is not required: the Highways Act is sufficient authority for the work to be carried out. After that, the street may be adopted*.

*See 11-44 onwards.

The private street works code: financial provisions

11-26   When the private street works have been completed, the local authority must make a final apportionment, by dividing the expenses by the provisional apportionment (in its amended form, if appropriate) and notice of the final apportionment must then be served on the owners of premises affected (s. 211(1)). The owners of premises affected can object to the final apportionment on one of a number of specific grounds:

- That there has been an unreasonable departure from the specification (s. 211(2)(a));

- That the actual expenses have without sufficient reason exceeded the estimate by more than 15% (s. 211(2)(b));

- That the apportionment has not been made in accordance with s. 211; in other words that expenses have not been apportioned in accordance with the provisional apportionment (s. 211(2)(c)).

11-27   Any objections are to be dealt with by a magistrates' court, in accordance with s. 209, in the same way as objections to the provisional apportionment. Once the court has reached a decision, the final apportionment is "conclusive for all purposes" (s. 211(3)). The local authority can recover the appropriate share of the final expenses from the owners "for the time being" of the premises concerned, together with interest at a reasonable rate (s. 212(1)). "For the time being" means that if the local authority cannot recover the amount from the present owner, they may do so from successive owners of the property. Furthermore, the amount in question is deemed to be a charge on the property, so that the local authority can enforce the debt by taking action against the property, in the same way as if there was a mortgage on the property (s. 212(3)).

11-28   The local authority may declare that the amount, together with interest, is payable in annual instalments, over a period of up to 30 years (s. 212(4)). Schedule 13 sets out detailed arrangements which supplement this provision.

11-29   Owners of premises may generally borrow against the security of the premises in order to pay off the debt (s. 213). The local authority is required to keep separate accounts of money spent and recovered under the PSWC (s. 214).

The advance payments code

11-30   Unlike the PSWC, which applies throughout England and Wales, the application of the APC depends upon detailed rules in s. 204 of and Schedule 15 to the Highways Act. Enquiry should reveal whether the APC is in force in a particular area.

11-31   The APC applies where a new private street is constructed, or where there is new building in an existing private street. In either case, the advance payment code applies only where there will be a building which will have a frontage on the street—backland development is thus not included. The underlying aim of the code is that arrangements should be in place to ensure that the street is made up to the satisfaction of the local authority. Money must therefore be paid in advance to cover the cost of street works, or the appropriate amount must be secured to the satisfaction of the local authority, so that the latter can be sure the money will be available. A guarantee of the appropriate amount may thus be required. As with the PSWC, no fixed standard for the work is laid down in the Highways Act: it is for the local authority, acting reasonably, to determine what is required. There are, however, many exceptions to the APC, and where an exception applies no advance payment will need to be made. Where the APC applies, this does not mean that the street will necessarily be adopted by the local authority, but the Highways Act provides ways in which this can happen*.

*See 11-44 onwards.

11-32   By s. 219(1) of the Highways Act 1980, the payment has to be made where:

> "(a) it is proposed to erect a building for which plans are required to be deposited with the local authority in accordance with building regulations, and

(b) the building will have a frontage on a private street in which the street works authority have power under the private street works code to require works to be executed or to execute works."

11-33   If a building is erected without a payment having been made, the owner of the land, and (if different) the person erecting the building is guilty of an offence, and may be fined. It should be borne in mind that a developer laying out a new street who wishes it to be adopted may, as is often the case, prefer to reach agreement with the local authority, under s. 38 of the Highways Act for the adoption of the street*. In this case the APC does not apply (see below). The agreement will provide that the street is constructed to the satisfaction of the local authority, at the expense of the developer—who may in practice be asked to arrange for a guarantee, as part of the agreement, to ensure that the work is done—and that the street is then to be adopted by the local authority.

*See 11-44 onwards.

Exemptions from the advance payments code

11-34   Section 219(4) sets out 11 cases in which an advance payment does not have to be made. Of these the following are the most important:

*See 11-18.

- Where the owner of the land is exempt under the PSWC* from having to contribute to the expense of work (s. 219(4)(a)).

- Where the new building will be within the curtilage of, and appurtenant to, an existing building (s. 219(4)(b)). This example would apply, for example, to a garage for or extension to an existing house, but not to the erection of a new house in a garden.

- Where the builder agrees with the street works authority that he will carry out street works, on completion of which the street is to become a highway maintainable at the public expense (s. 219(4)(d)). (In other words, where there is an agreement under s. 38 of the Highways Act 1980.)

- Where the local authority is satisfied that the street is not, and is not likely to become, within a reasonable time, substantially built up or in so unsatisfactory a condition as to justify the use of powers under the PSWC, and the authority exempt the building from the liability to make advance payments. The Act does not give a definition of "substantially built up". The authority must be satisfied on both points (that the street will not become built up, and that it will not get into unsatisfactory condition) if the building is to be exempt (s. 219(4)(e)).

• Where the local authority is satisfied that the street is not, and is not likely within a reasonable time to become, joined to a highway maintainable at the public expense, and exempt the building (s. 219(4)(f)).

• Where it is possible to show that a part of the street at least 100 yards long (or all of the street if it is less than 100 yards long) including the frontage of the new building, is already built up so that frontages of these buildings, on both sides of the street, amount to at least one half the total frontages in that part (s. 219(4)(g)). The developer appears to be free to decide how to measure his 100-yard length, provided the frontage of his proposed building is included. The "frontage" of a building has the meaning given by s. 203(4), and includes the land in which the building stands. This widens the application of the exemption, which would otherwise be largely confined to terraces of buildings.

• Where the last exemption does not apply, but the local authority exempt the street on the ground that it was substantially built up on "the material date" (s. 219(4)(h)). In most cases the "material date" will be 1 October 1951, by virtue of s. 219(6)).

• Where the local authority is satisfied that more than three-quarters of all the frontages in the street, or a part of the street at least 100 yards long and including the proposed new building, consist or will consist of industrial premises, and that the authority's powers under the private street works are not likely to be exercised within a reasonable time, and exempt the street, or the relevant part of it (s. 219(4)(k)).

If the proposed development cannot be fitted into one of these exemptions, the APC will apply, and an advance payment must be made or secured. In general terms, a payment is likely to be required for new private streets and for some which are less than half built up. Some of the exemptions are a matter of discretion for the local authority: they may be applied if the local authority think it appropriate, though as noted above the local authority has a general duty to act reasonably in taking decisions*. The APC does not apply to buildings which will have no frontage on a private street, as will be the case for most backland development.

11-35

*See 1-51.

The advance payments code: financial provisions

11-36   Within 6 weeks after the approval of plans for new building, the local authority must serve on the person concerned a notice under s. 219 requiring an advance payment to be made or secured. By s. 220(3), the amount is the amount which in the opinion of the local authority would be required in respect of that frontage if the local authority were to carry out whatever street works it considered necessary under the PSWC before declaring the street to be a highway maintainable at the public expense. The local authority may take the street as a whole, for the purpose of deciding what work would be required, and specify the amount appropriate to the frontage of the new building, though they can if they think fit treat part of a street as a separate street for these purposes. The local authority must make a judgment about the work they would require under the PSWC, and if the street is already made up to a good standard, little further work may be required. The local authority may take the view that the street already meets the standard they would require, in applying the private streets work code—in which case their notice will say that there is no payment to be made or secured.

11-37   Interest is payable by the local authority, under s. 225, on money deposited. The amount may be decreased, if the local authority considers that the likely cost of the work will be less than anticipated, but it cannot be increased (s. 220(4)). If the cost is less, the appropriate part of any money paid or secured must be refunded or released. There is a right of appeal against the amount specified by the local authority, unless there is no payment to be made or secured. The appeal is to the appropriate government department, which may substitute a smaller sum (s. 220(6)).

11-38   When the appropriate sum has been paid or secured, the building work can be carried out. In relation to the making up of the street, the developer may carry out the work, or he may ask the local authority to do so—this appears to be a matter for agreement, since the local authority has no power to insist that it carries out the work. If the developer does some or all of the work, the appropriate part of the money paid under the APC will be returned, or the guarantee released, as the case may be. The money must also be refunded, or the security released, if the plans to build in the street are not proceeded with (s. 221).

11-39   The local authority's power to set in motion the PSWC is not excluded by anything in the APC. In effect, this is a reserve power: if the work is not done to the satisfaction of the local authority under the APC, the local authority can invoke the PSWC. As explained above, the amount payable under the APC is the amount which would be payable, in respect of the frontage of the new building, under the PSWC. If the PSWC is invoked, the amount payable will not necessarily be the same, but by s. 222 any sums paid or secured under the APC will reduce the liability under the PSWC.

Land designated as a private street on a development plan

Special rules are set out in s. 232 of the Highways Act 1980 for land shown on a development plan as the site of a proposed street, or as land required for the widening of an existing street. A development plan is a plan drawn up by the local authority under the Town and Country Planning Act 1990, showing how they expect the land to be developed over the coming years. (11-40)

Section 232 (2) allows the local authority to declare the land to be a private street, and the land is thereupon deemed to be dedicated as a highway, and to be a street to which Part XI of the Act, including the PSWC and the APC, applies (see s. 203(2)). (The land would not otherwise be within Part XI, since it would not be a "street" as defined in the Act because it has not yet been laid out as a way*.) The consent of all persons interested in the land is required before the local authority can make such a declaration (s. 232(3)). (11-41)

*See 1-19.

The provision thus allows land to be treated as a private street at an early stage. In particular, the APC is likely to apply, so that the owners of land fronting the proposed street will have to make or secure payments to ensure that the street is made up to the required standard. There are regulations[8] which supplement s. 232 and deal with such matters as the adoption of the new street, so that it becomes maintainable at the public expense. (11-42)

Local land charges

By s. 224, a number of steps taken under the APC are deemed to be local land charges, including the notices served by the local authority under s. 220(1) and (4), decisions by the local authority exempting buildings from the code, and refunds and releases under ss. 221, 222 (11-43)

---

8. The Town and Country Planning (Construction and Improvement of Private Roads) Regulations 1951, SI 1951/2224.

*See 2-43.

and 223. This means that a record of these matters can be made on the register maintained under the Local Land Charges Act 1975, so that subsequent owners of property, who may be affected by them, are alerted to their existence*.

Adoption after street works

11-44 After street works have been carried out, the street in question may be adopted, in accordance with s. 228. There are two ways in which the street can be adopted—on the initiative of the local authority, or on the initiative of a majority of the owners of premises in the street. The street works may be works carried out under the PSWC (which, as explained above, may be invoked either in its own right or when an advance payment has been made under the APC). But the Highways Act does not limit the operation of s. 228 to such works.

11-45 *Local authority's discretion* A local authority may adopt a private street after *any* street works have been carried out; though it would appear that minor repairs may not be enough to allow the street to be adopted by the local authority (s. 228(1)). Indeed, it may be that the street works must be works which bring the street up to a satisfactory standard, since otherwise the local authority is taking on the burden of bringing the street up to standard, when it could have made the frontagers bear the cost, under the PSWC. In any event, the local authority may quite reasonably be reluctant to adopt the street under s. 228 if the street is not made up to a standard which it considers satisfactory, since it will then be faced with a need for work to be done at the public expense.

11-46 If the local authority decides to adopt the street, it must display a notice in a prominent position in the street, declaring it to be a highway maintainable at the public expense. Then, after the expiry of one month, the street becomes a highway maintainable at the public expense (s. 228(1)). During that period, however, the owner of the street (or, if more than one, a majority in numbers of the owners) may give notice to the local authority objecting to the adoption of the street. The local authority may in turn apply to a magistrates' court for an order overruling the objection. There is a right of appeal (generally to the Crown Court, under s. 317) from the decision of the magistrates' court if they overrule the objection. If the matter is finally determined in favour of the local authority, the street becomes a highway maintainable at the public expense; otherwise it does not (s. 228(2)–(5)).

11-47 The local authority has a discretion whether to adopt the street. The Highways Act is silent on the question of how this discretion is to be exercised (and equally silent on how a magistrates' court should deal with any objections). But a local authority must act reasonably, in accordance with the principles of administrative law*. If the street is one which will be useful to the public, the case for making its maintenance at the public expense may be a good one; but it may be more debatable if the street is a cul-de-sac which the public at large will have no reason to use. As against that, there may be other cul-de-sacs in the area which are already highways maintainable at the public expense, and adoption may arguably be of some indirect benefit to the public if it serves to improve the area. It is for the local authority to weigh the arguments and decide whether it should adopt the street.

*See 1-51.

Majority of residents If the local authority does not take the initiative, the residents of a private street may require its adoption after the completion of street works to the satisfaction of the local authority (s. 228(7)). The section refers to "...all street works (whether or not including lighting)...", and the implication is that work must have been carried out, if necessary, to bring the street up to the standard required by the local authority in all the respects set out in s. 203(3)*, including sewering, levelling, metalling, paving etc, but not necessarily street lighting

*See 11-7.

It is not necessary that the work should have been done under the PSWC, though this will no doubt usually be the case: the work could conceivably have been done voluntarily, after consultation with the local authority as to what is required. The owners of a majority by rateable value of the premises in the street may apply to the local authority for the adoption of the street, and the local authority must, within a period of 3 months, display a notice in the street declaring it to be a highway maintainable at the public expense, and when the notice is displayed the street then immediately becomes a highway maintainable at the public expense (s. 228(7)).

This provision does not apply to part of a street: it is only possible for residents to require the adoption of the street as a whole. The Act makes no provision for objections or appeals in this situation, from the owner of the street or indeed anyone else.

Special procedures for urgent repairs

Section 230 of the Highways Act provides special procedures so that a local authority can act where a private street is in a dangerous condition. Under s. 230(1), where repairs are needed to "obviate danger to traffic", the local authority may serve notice on the owners of premises fronting the street requiring them to carry out repairs within a specified time. If only part of the street needs repairs, the frontagers of that part of the street must bear the cost (s. 230(2)).

11-52 A right of appeal to a magistrates court is provided for (s. 230(3)); but, subject to any appeal, if the work is not carried out by the frontagers in the time specified, the local authority may carry out the work, and may recover its reasonable expenses from the owners of the premises fronting the street. In this case, the expenses are apportioned according to the lengths of the respective frontage, and the local authority has no discretion in the matter (s. 230(4)). Money due as a result of urgent repairs is a debt owed by the frontagers to the local authority, but it seems that s. 212 does not apply, so that the premises are not charged with the debt.

11-53 Though s. 230 is intended for cases where urgent repairs are needed, it also provides a way of bringing into effect the PSWC. During the period allowed by the notice for the completion of repairs, the "majority in number or rateable value" of premises in the street may by notice require the local authority to proceed under the PSWC. The local authority must then do so. The procedure outlined above[*], including the preparation of specifications for the work and apportionments of the expenses, will apply. When the work has been completed, the local authority *must* declare the street to be a highway maintainable at the public expense, and it thereupon immediately becomes one (s. 230(5)). There is no provision for objection and appeals, as there is in s. 228[*].

[*]See 11-10 onwards.

[*]See 11-46.

11-54 The local authority may also carry out repairs which it considers are urgently required to prevent or remove danger to persons or vehicles in the street (s. 230(7)). This is a freestanding provision, under which the local authority must meet the cost of the work.

Adoption when an advance payment has been made

11-55 Section 229 allows frontagers, when at least one payment has been made under the APC, to invoke the PSWC. They can thus take the opportunity of having the street made up and adopted. There must be a majority in number of the frontagers, or as many frontagers as own more than half the aggregate length of all the frontages. The street must be "built up", the test being that land with buildings on it must represent at least half the total frontage in the street. There is a proviso, which is that the section does not apply to a part of a street unless it is a part at least 100 yards long, which the frontagers (presumably by a majority) elect to treat as a street. However, it appears that the section may apply even though the payments made related only to a part of the street.

11-56 In these circumstances, a majority in number of the frontagers may serve notice on the local authority, requesting the local authority to secure the carrying out of whatever work it considers necessary under the PSWC, and to declare the street to be a highway maintainable at the public expense. The local authority must comply, by putting into effect the PSWC. When the necessary work has been done, which may or may not be more work than was thought necessary under the APC, the local authority *must* declare the street to be a highway maintainable at the public expense (ss. 229(1)). Section 229(1) does not appear to exclude the procedure for objections and appeals under s. 228(2)–(4).

11-57 If the majority of frontagers have not taken this course, once the street works have been completed it appears that the local authority *may* if they wish proceed under s. 228, and put a notice in the street declaring the street to be a highway maintainable at the public expense. The street then becomes a highway maintainable at the public expense after the expiration of one month, subject to any objection from the owner (s. 228(2)–(4)).

Human rights issues

11-58 The Human Rights Act 1998, giving effect in the United Kingdom to the European Convention on Human Rights, protects citizens' property rights. Property may be appropriated by the State; but this must be done in accordance with the law, and must be justified in the public interest.

11-59 It seems at best doubtful whether Part XI of the Highways Act 1980 complies fully with these requirements. The owner of a private road may be a residents association or company, or one of more residents. In some circumstances Part XI may operate so as to take away ownership of the road without allowing the owner any opportunity to object or appeal. This will be the case, for example, if the owner is different from the residents, and a majority of frontagers require the road to be adopted after the carrying out of all necessary street works, under s. 228(7).

11-60 Furthermore, Part XI may operate so as to deprive the owner of the road in circumstances where there seems little public interest in doing so—for example, in a cul-de-sac which is never used by the public at large.

11-61 The fact that Part XI does not comply with the human rights legislation does not mean that the legislation cannot be used. But the higher courts are able to issue a "declaration of incompatibility", and the appropriate government department can then amend the legislation to make sure that it conforms (ss. 4 and 10 of the Human Rights Act 1998).

Assessment

11-62 It will be relatively rare for the APC (assuming it applies in the area in question) to affect an existing private street, in view of the exemptions which apply—particularly the exemption for new buildings erected within a 100-yard stretch of the street which is already at least half built-up.

11-63 The PSWC is more likely to be relevant. If, for whatever reason, the street is not maintained by residents to a reasonable standard, the PSWC provides a way in which the work can be carried out at their expense, and the street then adopted by the local authority so that it becomes a highway maintainable at the public expense.

11-64 The initiative lies mostly with the local authority. Intervention is a matter of discretion, and local authorities in different areas may quite properly take different approaches. Some may actively pursue a policy of adopting private streets. Others may prefer not to intervene if it can be avoided; and such an attitude is legally unexceptionable.

11-65 The case for adoption will generally be stronger in a private street which is a highway. The complexity of the PSWC means that operating it is burdensome for the local authority, and the PSWC may prove unpopular with residents, who will be subject to its technicalities and procedural complexities, and who may be obliged to pay for work which they do not believe to be necessary. Whether intervention is necessary is a matter of judgment, but there is no obligation on a local authority to do so merely because a private street does not meet, in every respect, the standard which the local authority would regard as appropriate for a highway maintainable at the public expense. In many cases, therefore, private streets continue for long periods to be maintained by residents.

11-66 To a lesser extent, residents may be able to take the initiative if they wish to remove their private status and turn the street into a highway maintainable at the public expense. If residents are prepared at their own expense to bring the street up to the standard regarded by the local authority as satisfactory, a majority can then force the local authority to adopt the street under s. 228(7). Section 38, explained in chapter 3, offers an alternative approach; but adoption under this provision is a matter for agreement with the local authority, not compulsion; and the initiative lies with the owner of the road, since it is only the owner who can decide to dedicate the road as a highway.

11-67 The PSWC and APC generally proceed on the reasonable assumption that those who use the street for access should pay for any necessary street works. The liability for costs is thus imposed principally on frontagers. This means, however, that the owner of the street is given little influence over the fate of her property.

11-68 Furthermore, the way in which the PSWC and APC provide for decisions to be taken will not necessarily correspond with arrangements which are in place for the ownership and management of the street; and there is no guarantee that the application of the codes will produce a result which is predictable or which is regarded by those concerned as fair. Suppose, for example, that the condition of a private street deteriorates to the point at which the local authority considers that it is dangerous, and action is required. A number of different courses are possible, including the following:

- The local authority may decide to proceed in accordance with the PSWC, and to adopt the street. The owner of the street has the right to object before adoption, though her objection may be overruled.

- The local authority may decide to proceed in accordance with the PSWC, but not to adopt the street. In this case the majority in rateable value of the owners of premises in the street may require the local authority to adopt the street, and the owner has no right to object.

- The local authority may decide that urgent repairs are necessary, and serve the appropriate notice on frontagers. It is possible to require the local authority to proceed under the PSWC, and the frontagers may wish to take this course, if there are significant numbers of residents who are not frontagers, so as to spread the cost. This decision, however, is a matter for the majority in number or rateable value of owners of premises in the street as a whole, and residents who are not frontagers may oppose the operation of the PSWC, since it is in their financial interests that the cost of the repairs should be confined to the frontagers. If the PSWC is brought into operation in this way, the owner of the street has no say in whether her property is taken away from her— though she would have done if the local authority had decided to proceed under the PSWC in the first place, as explained above.

for more information see www.barsby.com

11-69   In any situation involving Part XI of the Highways Act, careful consideration will need to be given to the possible effect of these provisions, and particularly to the options which may arise, and the liabilities which may be incurred by frontagers and others.

MAKING UP AND ADOPTION

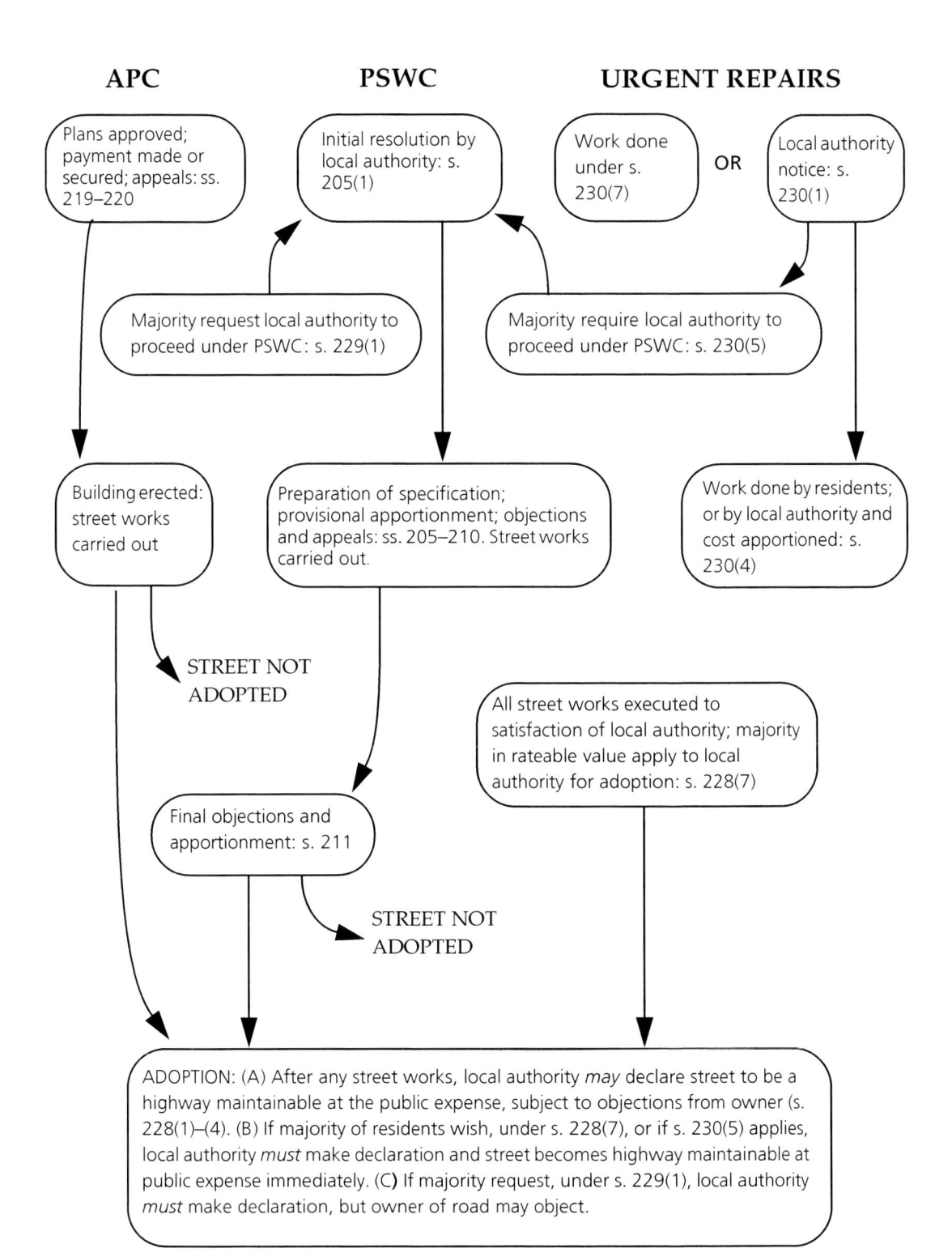

APC

Plans approved; payment made or secured; appeals: ss. 219–220

↓

Building erected: street works carried out

→ STREET NOT ADOPTED

PSWC

Initial resolution by local authority: s. 205(1)

↑ Majority request local authority to proceed under PSWC: s. 229(1)

↓

Preparation of specification; provisional apportionment; objections and appeals: ss. 205–210. Street works carried out.

↓

Final objections and apportionment: s. 211

→ STREET NOT ADOPTED

URGENT REPAIRS

Work done under s. 230(7) OR **Local authority notice: s. 230(1)**

↑ Majority require local authority to proceed under PSWC: s. 230(5)

↓

Work done by residents; or by local authority and cost apportioned: s. 230(4)

All street works executed to satisfaction of local authority; majority in rateable value apply to local authority for adoption: s. 228(7)

ADOPTION: (A) After any street works, local authority *may* declare street to be a highway maintainable at the public expense, subject to objections from owner (s. 228(1)–(4)). (B) If majority of residents wish, under s. 228(7), or if s. 230(5) applies, local authority *must* make declaration and street becomes highway maintainable at public expense immediately. (C) If majority request, under s. 229(1), local authority *must* make declaration, but owner of road may object.

for more information see www.barsby.com

Chapter 12: Organisation

Introduction

12-0   This chapter discusses the ways in which residents may organise themselves, through a residents association or a company, or some other arrangement, so that they can act collectively in managing, and perhaps owning, a private road. The question of securing an income which will be due regardless of changes in the ownership of houses in the road is considered separately at the end of the chapter.

Why be organised?

12-1   There is no legal requirement that residents in a private road should be organised, or act collectively in owning and managing the road. A resident with a private right of way will generally be entitled to maintain the surface of the road, so that he can continue to exercise his right of way*. Sewers and drains are likely to belong to a utility company; but, if not, a resident who uses them will generally have the right to maintain them.

*See 4-50.

12-2   If the road is a highway, the local authority will have an obligation to protect the public's rights over it, and will enjoy a range of powers over the road*.

*See 9-1.

12-3   The road can thus fulfill its essential function whether it belongs as a whole to one person or an organisation, or is divided into parts which belong to different people, or whether the ownership is unknown. But for residents to be organised, and to own and/or manage the road collectively, confers some important advantages:

- Maintenance can be carried out in a planned and efficient way, and provision can be made over a period of time for work such as re-surfacing.

- The use of the road, and the acquisition of rights over it, can be controlled, and residents can thus exercise a degree of control over their surroundings.

- Steps can be taken to enhance the amenity of the road, and thus increase the value and saleability of houses in it.

- Residents individually can participate in the making of decisions which affect them.

- The road has collective representation, and can deal effectively with local government and others.

There are thus powerful reasons for setting up and maintaining an effective organisation. (12-4)

Ownership and management

Ownership is desirable, since it carries with it the right to exercise full control over a road. Residents may be able to acquire ownership in one of several ways, as explained in chapter 2*. (12-5)

*See 2-30 onwards.

But even if residents cannot obtain ownership of their road, they may still look after the road. The law protects those who are in possession of land, whether with the consent of the owner or without it*. The former will often be the case on the basis that the frontagers are the presumptive owners, and give their permission for a residents association or company to manage the road*. The latter may be the case if the owner is known—perhaps a descendant of the developer, who has no wish to exercise his or rights, but will not sell the road. (12-6)

*See 1-43 onwards.

*See 2-9.

Unchallenged possession should generally be enough to allow the residents to manage the road; though if they are not owners, some of their actions may amount to a technical trespass against the true owner, who could take legal action against them and require them to stop*. (12-7)

*See also 3-12 and 4-14 for the implications in relation to public and private rights of way.

Forms of organisation

Several forms of organisation are possible, the main ones being: (12-8)

- An unincorporated association.

- A company

- A trust.

for more information see www.barsby.com

None is ideal—there is no purpose-made legal vehicle for owning and managing a private road. The following paragraphs take each of the above solutions in turn and consider how they work.

Unincorporated associations

12-9   *Nature* An unincorporated association is an association of people which has not been made into a corporation—that is, a legal "person" in its own right, such as a company registered under the Companies Act[1]. It thus has no separate legal existence of its own (though for some purposes it is treated by the law as though it has). Large numbers of clubs, societies and groups of all kinds are unincorporated associations, and residents of a private road may decide to form one. The key feature of an unincorporated association is simply that it has adopted rules which may define its purpose, the way it is to be run, the rights of members, and other matters.

12-10   *Operation* There are no special legal requirements for the formation of an unincorporated associations, as there are for companies, and the law does not supply model rules governing the running of unincorporated associations, or indeed say what matters should be the subject of rules. The position of those involved is determined by the rules of the association, which have the effect of a contract binding on all the members. A member of a snooker club, for example, may have a contractual obligation under the rules to pay an annual subscription, and a contractual right to use the club's facilities; and the club may have a committee which, under the rules, has the ability to organise snooker competitions and award prizes out of the club's funds. There is no legal requirement for the rules to be comprehensive, or to be set down in writing, and the courts are careful not to adopt too legalistic an approach in considering the rules of an unincorporated association.

12-11   However, it will obviously be difficult to establish what the rules are, and whether members have agreed to be bound by them, unless they are recorded in writing and made available to all members when they join the association. It is thus highly desirable that there should be written rules, that they should be drawn up with care and, although they may not cover every possible occurrence, that they should go into a sufficient degree of detail about how the association is to function.

12-12   In the case of a private road, then, the rules of a residents' association would be expected to deal with such things as a member's obligation to pay subscriptions and other sums, and his right to

---

1. Companies are not the only form of artificial legal "person".

participate in decisions, the responsibilities of the officers of the association (typically a Chairman, Secretary and Treasurer) and any committees to which functions may be delegated, and the objects of the association. The latter might encapsulate the association's general policy on the standard of maintenance of the road, and on encouraging or discouraging development, and the business or commercial use of property in the road. The rules might, if members wished, also deal with matters of mutual interest such as parking, noise and other issues.

12-13 Since an unincorporated association has no legal existence of its own, liability for breaches of the law falls personally upon those responsible within the association—often, one or more of its officers, or the members of a committee or sub-committee. The rules of the association may commit others within the association to share the cost; but otherwise those responsible are themselves liable to meet any legal liability; for example compensation due to a person who has been injured in the road*, or damages for breach of a contract entered into by the association.

*See chapter 6 on civil liability generally.

12-14 *Ownership of property* Land[2] owned by an unincorporated association is usually held on trust for the members of the association for the time being, in accordance with the association's rules. The trustees may be members or officers of the association. Land belonging to an unincorporated association will be shown on the Land Register as being held by the association's officers on trust for the members of the association, in accordance with the rights and obligations which the rules of the association give to the members. There will be a restriction on the Land Register, to show that the trustees do not have complete freedom to dispose of the road, but may do so only in accordance with the rules of the association*.

*See 2-40.

12-15 When a trustee of land dies, his share of the ownership passes automatically to the surviving trustees. But if a trustee wishes to retire, and be replaced, a deed will generally be necessary in order to transfer his share in the ownership of the road to the new trustee. The process will be simplified (though a deed will still be required) if the trustees are appointed by deed, since a deed appointing the new trustee, and discharging the retiring trustee, will automatically transfer ownership (Trustee Act 1926, s. 40(1) and (2)).

12-16 The need for deeds, when trustees are replaced, can be kept to a minimum by arranging for the trustees who will own the road to be long-term appointments, while the persons who act as officers and committee members of the association are appointed for shorter periods, in accordance with the rules. It may be possible to transfer ownership to a "custodian trustee", who will act as the sole owner of

---

2. Other property may include assets such as money held in an account.

the road, but take no decisions in relation to it. The Public Trustee is able to act as a custodian trustee, as are some banks and other financial organisations; but using a custodian trustee may attract charges; and insurance may also be required, since the custodian trustee will wish to be indemnified against any liability.

12-17 *Dissolution* An unincorporated association can come to an end by ceasing to function. The rules of an association may also allow a majority to decide to dissolve the association; and if there is no provision in the rules, the members of the association can unanimously decide to end it. The High Court also has the power to order the dissolution of an unincorporated association.

12-18 On dissolution, the debts of the association must be paid, and its property can then be distributed. In the case of an association owning a road, it will be highly desirable for the rules to lay down what is to happen to the road. The rules might (for example) give frontagers the right to acquire the section of road along their frontages, or for the road to be sold as a whole to the highest bidder and the proceeds distributed among members of the association.

Companies

12-19 *Nature* A company is an artificial legal "person", which can own property, transact business and take legal action, in the same way as a living person.

12-20 *Formalities* Companies are formed by registering them with the Registrar of Companies, in accordance with the Companies Act 1985, which involves sending in the necessary documents and information and paying a fee. A company must have a name, laid down by the memorandum of association (s. 25). The name must not be misleading, and must end in "limited" or "ltd" (ss. 25 and 32). There must be a registered office (s. 287). The company must have at least one director and a secretary who, if there is only one director, must be a different person (s. 282). A register of directors and secretaries must be kept, and this must be open to public inspection at the registered office (s. 288). Similarly, the company must keep a register of members, which must generally be kept at the registered office (ss. 352 and 353). The company's name must appear outside its place of business, and must be used in correspondence, together with particulars including its registered number and the address of its registered office (ss. 348–351).

12-21 Companies are required to prepare accounts for each financial year (s. 226). The accounts, together with the auditor's report, and a report from the directors which summarises the activities of the company during the year and contains various particulars, must be laid before a general meeting of the company. Copies must be sent to Companies House, where they are open to public inspection (ss. 241–244). Accounting records must be kept, and must be preserved for at least three years (s. 221).

Operation The way in which a company is to be run is set out in its constitutional documents, which consist (firstly) of a memorandum of association and (secondly) of articles of association, which legally have the same effect as though the company and its members had undertaken, in a deed, to abide by them (s. 14). The reason why there are two documents rather than just one is historical, and of no particular significance in practice. These documents, together with the provisions of the Companies Acts, provide the rules which govern the relationship between the company, its members, and its directors and other officers. Standard-form memoranda and articles of association are set out in the companies legislation[3], and anyone forming a company is required to follow these as far as possible, but can modify them in order to produce the desired result. There is thus an inherent flexibility in the rules which govern the running of companies.

12-22

The standard-form articles of association provide that the directors are to manage the company's business, may delegate specific functions to a managing director or to some other director, and at meetings may take decisions by majority vote. The members of the company have the task, at general meetings, of appointing the directors and the company's auditor (s. 385). As explained above, this division of responsibility can be varied by the persons who form the company, so that, for example, unanimity may be required of the directors for certain decisions, or some decisions may be reserved to the members of the company, to be decided by a certain majority or unanimously in a general meeting. It is possible for the company's articles of association, and in some circumstances its memorandum of association, to be varied by the members (ss. 9 and 17).

12-23

A private company may raise initial capital by selling shares[4]. A company responsible for a private road may also need a regular income from its members. There is no reason why a company's articles of association should not provide for its members to make regular payments to the company, or provide for sums to be payable in accordance with decisions taken by the directors or members of the

12-24

---

3. The Companies (Tables A to F) Regulations Act 1985, SI 1985/805, as amended by later regulations.
4. Companies may also be "limited by guarantee", rather than "limited by shares", meaning that the members each guarantee payment of a certain amount towards the debts of the company. This form of company is more suited to a philanthropic or charitable body.

company. The Companies Act 1985, however, contains several provisions which tend to restrict arrangements of this nature. The memorandum or articles of association cannot be changed so as to oblige a member to pay more to the company unless she agrees, in writing, to be bound by the change (s. 16). Furthermore, a member of a company may ask the court to intervene on the ground that the affairs of the company are being conducted in a way unfairly prejudicial to the members, or a minority of them (including himself). An attempt to levy excessive sums from members, even if it had the support of the majority and was in accordance with the articles of association, might thus be open to challenge by the minority (s. 744).

12-25   Practical considerations will in any event limit the ability of a company to raise money from its members: if the articles of association contain provisions which appear to be onerous, or allow the directors or a majority of members to impose onerous obligations, there may be a reluctance to hold the shares and the company may ultimately prove to be unworkable. Nonetheless, there is no reason why the articles of association should not make provision for the company to raise reasonable amounts from its members. Safeguards can be incorporated into the articles of association, so that, for example, sums above a specified amount require the approval of the members by a certain majority or even unanimously.

12-26   In its relations with others, the company is legally a "person" in its own right. If there is an accident, or a breach of contract, and the company is liable to pay compensation, this is an obligation which rests on the company. The directors and other officers of the company will not normally be liable in their personal capacity.

12-27   *Holding and transfer of shares*   The articles of association may lay down special rules concerning the holding and transfer of shares. In the case of a company owning a private road, there are likely to be three main objectives, namely that:

- Each resident or household should be entitled to acquire a certain number of shares.

- Each resident or household should not hold more than a certain number of shares. (Otherwise it would be possible for one shareholder to buy out other shareholders and so gain control of the company.)

- The shares should not be held by anyone other than residents.

12-28   These objectives can be achieved by drawing up the articles of association accordingly. It is common for the transfer of shares in a private company to be restricted, and the articles will provide that shares cannot be transferred to a person who is not a resident, or who already holds the maximum number of shares, and that shares are forfeited if the holder ceases to be a resident or exceeds the maximum. While the articles can give each resident the right to hold shares, residents cannot in practice be required to be members; though a legal arrangement requiring them to make payments to the company, whether or not they are members of it, is possible*.

*See 12-38 onwards.

Ownership of property A company is capable of lasting indefinitely, so that if a private road is once transferred to a company it need not change hands again, so long as the company continues in existence.

(12-29)

Winding up A company can be brought to an end by being wound up, under the Insolvency Act 1983; and it can also be struck off, by the Registrar of Companies, for failing to submit annual returns. For a company limited by shares, the standard-form articles of association allow the shareholders to decide what to do with the company's property, once creditors have been paid. They can thus decide to transfer ownership of the road to one or more shareholders, or to some other person or body. But if no arrangements are made for property to be transferred to the shareholders or sold, it will pass to the Crown, as *bona vacantia*, when the company is dissolved*.

(12-30)

*See 2-44 onwards.

Trusts

Nature Like other property, a private road may be held on trust, meaning that it belongs legally to trustees, but that any benefits flowing from the property go to the beneficiaries of the trust. A private road might thus be held by two or three residents on trust for themselves—trustees may also be beneficiaries—and other residents. Four is the maximum number of trustees permitted for trusts of land, by s. 34 of the Trustee Act 1925 and s. 19 of the Trusts of Land and Appointment of Trustees Act 1996. There is no limit on the number of beneficiaries.

(12-31)

The law imposes various restrictions on the use of trusts. With limited exceptions which are not applicable here, the law does not permit property to be held on trust for a stated purpose: it must be held for the benefit of people. It is therefore not possible to set up a trust which has the purpose of owning and maintaining a private road. Moreover, the law does not allow property to be tied up for indefinite periods in the future, and for this reason a private road cannot be held on trust for the benefit of all present and future residents of a private road. A trust for

(12-32)

the benefit of residents for the time being, however, would be lawful. The beneficiaries would be the current residents of the road, and the class of beneficiaries would change as people became, or ceased to be, residents.

12-33   *Operation* The law relating to trusts of land has been simplified by the Trusts of Land and Appointment of Trustees Act 1996, which came into force at the beginning of 1997 and which applies to existing as well as new trusts of land. (Before then, trusts of land were subject to a number of complex and artificial rules.) A trust will be created if property is transferred to someone who agrees to hold it on trust, or if the owner of property declares that he will henceforth hold it on trust. No special words are required for a declaration of trust: the essential requirement is a statement that the person concerned intends to hold the property for the benefit of others. The declaration of a trust of land must generally be proved by evidence in writing, but the courts may, exceptionally, treat conduct by the owner as being a sufficient declaration of trust. It is not necessary, in order to create a trust to go into details of how the trust will operate, since the law supplies a basic framework of rules. The Trusts of Land and Appointment of Trustees Act 1996 provides that a trustee of land has all the powers, in connection with the land, which an outright owner would have (s. 6). Trustees must, so far as is practicable, consult the beneficiaries, and generally give effect to their wishes, or (if there is a dispute) to the wishes of the majority (s. 11). Provisions in the Trustee Act 1925 cater for the retirement, removal and appointment of trustees.

12-34   While the law provides basic rules which may be sufficient for a private road to be held on trust for residents, it is likely that more rules will be required, to define more precisely the rights which residents have to participate in decisions about the road, and the duties of the trustees, including such matters as their appointment and retirement. For these purposes, a trust deed will be required, which will contain the necessary provisions. The trustees could thus, for example, be required to obtain the agreement of all or a majority of beneficiaries before taking decisions such as granting further rights of way, or raising exceptional sums of money from beneficiaries.

12-35   When a trustee is replaced, as is bound to happen from time to time, the legal ownership of the property must be adjusted, so that the outgoing trustee ceases to be an owner of the property, and the new trustee, together with the existing trustees, are the owners. For this a deed is required. The Trusts of Land and Appointment of Trustees Act allows beneficiaries in certain circumstances, acting unanimously, to require an existing trustee to retire, or to appoint a new trustee (s. 19). The law of trusts generally holds trustees accountable for the way in which they administer the trust property, and they may be liable to compensate beneficiaries for any breach of trust.

Ownership of property When land is owned by a trust, the names of the trustees will appear on the Land Register as owners of the property, and a restriction will note that the land is subject to a trust*.

(12-36)

*See 2-40.

Dissolution Just as the members of a company may always wind up the company, so the beneficiaries of a trust, acting unanimously, may always bring the trust to an end and divide the property amongst themselves. Residents might, for example, decide that their road should be organised as an association rather than a trust; and they could then, acting unanimously, call on the trustees to end the trust and transfer the road so that it was held by an association. The courts also have powers to supervise and if appropriate to wind up.

(12-37)

Securing an income

The members for the time being of a company (the shareholders) or of an unincorporated association can agree to make payments to it, to cover the cost of maintenance of the road and other expenditure, and the agreement may be binding as a contract. In the case of a company, an obligation to make payments to the company can be written into the articles of association, which take effect as a contract between the members and the company, subject to the limitation explained above on increasing the payment*. However, these obligations are not automatically binding on later owners of property in the road; and the association or company cannot be sure of an income in future years. This is likely to make it difficult to draw up long-term plans, and indeed will make the position of the association or company itself somewhat uncertain, since in the absence of a secure income its own future is not guaranteed. It is thus highly desirable for arrangements to be put in place whereby the owners for the time being of each house in the road must make contributions.

(12-38)

*See 12-24 onwards.

To some extent, the law already assists, since an obligation to contribute towards maintenance which is linked to a right of way can be enforced*. But otherwise the difficulty which presents itself is that an obligation to pay money cannot generally be passed on from one owner of freehold property to the next[5]. Some legal ingenuity is therefore necessary in order to ensure that the obligation to make

(12-39)

*See 4-49.

---

5. The difficulty does not affect leasehold property, since covenants (undertakings) in leases are generally enforceable as between the current landlord and the current tenant.

payments is binding on successive owners of property. There are two main possibilities.

12-40 *Rentcharges* A rentcharge is a legal arrangement by which a regular payment is secured on land. In its effect it is similar to mortgage, though a mortgage is an arrangement by which repayment of a loan is secured. In both cases, the person to whom money is owed can if necessary take possession of the land and obtain the income from it until he has been paid[6].

12-41 The Rentcharges Act 1977 abolished rentcharges for most purposes. But some sorts of rentcharge may still be created. These include "estate rentcharges", which can be created:

> "for the purpose.... of meeting, or contributing towards, the cost of the performance by the rent owner of covenants for the provision of services, the carrying out of maintenance or repairs, the effecting of insurance or the making of any payment by him for the benefit of the land affected by the rentcharge or for the benefit of that and other land" (s. 2(4)).

12-42 Estate rentcharges are common in relation to flats and other leased property, where the lessees are called upon to contribute to the maintenance of common parts of the building.

12-43 In the case of a rentcharge designed to secure contributions for the maintenance of a private road, the "rent owner" would be the residents association or company, which would covenant (i.e. undertake) to carry out tasks such as maintaining the road, insuring it, etc. A deed is necessary to create a rentcharge. The amount to be paid can be either a fixed sum or the product of a formula, such as a share of annual costs, but must be reasonable in relation to the covenanted services. Once created, the rentcharge applies permanently to the land, and can if necessary be enforced against the current owner of the land by the residents association or company. It should be registered at the Land Registry in its own right (since it is a form of legal property) and should be shown on the title of the land subject to it.

12-44 *Restrictions on transfer* An indirect way of achieving the same result is for the owner of a house to execute a deed by which she undertakes (firstly) to make payments to the residents association or company, and (secondly) not to transfer the house without requiring the new owner to execute a deed in the same terms. This arrangement ensures that successive owners of property will remain members of the association or company, and so be required to make payments to it. The deed restricts the owner's ability to transfer the property. The restriction will be shown on the Land Register, and the Land Registry will generally[7] decline to register a transfer unless it is clear that the

---

6. A mortgagee has other remedies too, including selling the land.

new owner has executed the necessary deed, this being confirmed by a certificate from the buyer's solicitor.

12-45 These arrangements result in a continuing obligation, which the residents association or company can enforce against the current owner of the land.

Assessment

12-46 It is in the interests of residents in a private road to establish an organisation to look after, and if possible to own, the road. The form which that organisation takes will depend on the circumstances.

12-47 A company is the best choice if the road is going to be owned collectively: ownership will then rest with the company, unaffected by the coming and going of directors and shareholders. The legislation provides model rules for running the company which can be adapted to suit. However, a company must be run in accordance with the legislation, and there will be an ongoing administrative and financial burden in holding meetings, making returns, etc.

12-48 An unincorporated association is not subject to any requirement of this sort, and is thus in some ways a cheaper and easier option. No model rules are supplied by the law, however, and the way in which land is held by an unincorporated association means that a deed will be required when there is a change in one of the owners (who as explained will be a trustee). And legal liability attaches directly to the responsible members of the association. The person, or members of a committee, responsible for (say) maintenance of the road could find themselves personally responsible to pay compensation in the event of an accident. If residents are not to be deterred, by the risk of personal liability, from acting as officers of committee members of the association, insurance will be required in order to absorb the risk. (The position can also be addressed by rules which make all the members of the association liable to share the cost. But this may well prove unsatisfactory for all except the smallest claims.)

12-49 There is no legal reason why the road should not be owned and managed by residents by means of a trust. But the nature of a trust is likely to be less well-known and understood, the duties on trustees are onerous, and the need to transfer ownership, when a trustee retires, is a significant inconvenience. For these reasons a trust will in most cases not be the solution of choice.

---

7. The Land Registry might allow the transfer to be registered if, for example, it appeared that the new owner had been unable to comply with the requirement in question.

for more information see www.barsby.com

*See Appendix 2 for a list of tasks for managers of a private road.

12-50   Whatever form the organisation takes, it will be important to draft rules attracting general support which set out what the organisation is to do, and how it is to do it. What exactly will the organisation do*? Will it concern itself just with maintenance, aiming to spend only the minimum amount necessary; or will it do more, and spend more, in the interests of amenity, regulating matters such as parking? And what will its attitude be to new development and requests for further rights of way—will it grant the rights, and use the proceeds to improve the road, or will it refuse, in the interests of amenity?

12-51   And who will decide? Will all decisions be taken by the directors or (in the case of an association) by the committee? If some decisions are reserved for residents generally—for example, granting new rights of way, or approving major expenditure—how will residents be able to vote, and what majority will be required? All these questions need to be addressed, and agreed by residents, and the organisation's rules drawn up accordingly.

12-52   Funding the organisation raises special problems. Providing a secure income for the organisation from each current resident will mean employing one of the techniques explained above. Without a guaranteed income, the organisation may well be able to continue on the basis of voluntary contributions; but its position will be weaker. Residents may decide not to support it, and even if only a small minority take this course, this will tend to undermine the efforts of the majority, and make it harder for the organisation to function, especially when it has to take unpopular decisions such as resurfacing.

12-53   As a matter of policy, the best course may be for the organisation to plan for the long term, and aim to build up funds gradually to meet major expenditure such as resurfacing. Setting up an arrangement to guarantee income is routine when a new private road is constructed: when first sold, each house is subjected to the requirement to contribute to the management company (a company is usually set up to manage the road). Thereafter, the obligation continues automatically as houses change hands. Such an arrangement may be more difficult to introduce to a road which has been in existence for some time.

*See 12-40.

12-54   If there is a willingness to provide the organisation with a secure income, this may best be done by means of an estate rentcharge* which commits each household to paying:

> ● A fixed annual amount which is modest, but can be increased in line with inflation, and which is sufficient to cover the organisation's expense and to accumulate funds slowly with a view to paying for more work such as resurfacing.

- Larger amounts, on a one-off basis, if it should become necessary and subject to appropriate safeguards, for example, approval by a majority of members of the organisation.

In the case of a company, residents should be entitled to hold shares in the company, and to participate in its running; but they should not necessarily be under an obligation to do so. Their obligation to fund the company by means of an estate rentcharge would continue regardless of whether they held shares, however, and they would therefore have an incentive to participate. (12-55)

Appendix 1: Questions and Answers

The following paragraphs give outline answers to questions which often arise in relation to private roads. They provide an initial indication of the law, and also to show how different parts of the book relate to each and may need to be consulted in order to find the answer to a single query. In square brackets are references to the appropriate paragraphs in the text, which contain a fuller explanation.

1.*Q: If the ownership of a private road is unknown, what action can be taken to trace the owner?* A: This is common. The first step should be to search the Land Register [2-41]. If the road is registered (which may not be the case [2-30]) the owner's name will be shown. Failing this, it may be possible to trace ownership from the original developer of the road, by examining title deeds for houses in the road or deeds granting rights of way in the road [4-10].

2.*Q: If the owner cannot be traced, does this mean that residents cannot manage the road?* A: No—if residents are in possession of the road, which means asserting the right to control the road, for example by regulating parking and maintaining the road, the law will protect them against all but the true owner [1-44]. There are, however, limits to what they can do if they are not in fact the owners of the road [4-14, 4-68; 3-12, 3-78].

3.*Q: Is it possible that part of the road belongs to one person and part to another?* A: Yes—like any other piece of land, a private road can be divided between different owners [2-1]. Indeed, if the ownership is otherwise unknown, it is possible to rely on the presumption that the frontagers each own half the width of the road in front of their properties [2-9].

4.*Q: If the road is owned by someone other than the residents, can he do things with which residents may disagree?* A: This is possible, but the freedom of action of any owner is very limited. The owner cannot interfere with public or private rights of way [9-1, 9-5; 4-56]. He cannot generally prevent residents with private rights of way from repairing the road [4-50]. He may, however, be entitled to give or refuse permission to park in the road [5-3, and see below].

5.Q: *How can one tell whether a road is private?* A: Local authorities are required by s. 36(6) of the Highways Act 1980 to maintain a list of roads which are "maintainable at the public expense". If a road is not on this list, it will on the face it of it be private [1-27].

6.Q: *How can one tell whether a private road is a highway?* A: A private road can become a highway by means of various statutory procedures [3-35 onwards]. If so, the local authority should have a record of the fact that the procedure in question has been applied. But in many cases private roads become highways merely through use by the public at large—the process known legally as "dedication and acceptance" [3-11 onwards]. A highway consisting of a footpath, bridleway or byway should be shown on the "definitive map and statement" for the area in question, which is, as the name suggests, definitive of the information shown on it [3-50].

7.Q: *Does it matter that people are using a private road without permission?* A: Yes, in that use by the public may lead to the creation of a highway by the process of dedication and acceptance [see above]; and use to gain access to a particular property in the road may lead to the creation of a private right of way by prescription [see above]. The possibility of civil liability to those whose use of the road is tolerated should not be forgotten [6-18 onwards].

8.Q: *Is it necessary to have a sign indicating that the road is private?* A: A sign alerts the world at large to the fact that the road is private property. It may also serve to prevent public use from leading to the creation of a highway—but to do this the sign must make clear that the road is not dedicated to the public. "Private" may not be enough to do this; whereas words such as "No public access" will do so [3-28].

9.Q: *Is there a limit or restriction on new development in a private road?* A: Not necessarily. Land in a private road (like land in a public road) may be subject to restrictive covenants which limit development, though these can in certain circumstances be modified or removed [6-44 onwards]. If the road is not subject to a public right of way for vehicles (a carriageway[3-3]), further private rights of way may be required for the land to be developed [4-6].

10.Q: *Are people who do not live in the road entitled to park there? What can be done to prevent them doing so?* A: The right to park could be granted as an easement, or in some circumstances acquired by use over time [5-5, 5-9]. If the road is a highway, or a road to which the public has access [1-20] the local authority has power to authorise use of the road for parking [9-22]. Occasionally, an owner of property ion the road may enjoy a right to park as a necessary adjunct to a right of way [5-16]. Otherwise, unless the owner of the road has given permission, there is no right to park. Doing so may be an offence in a road which is not a highway nor a road to which the public has access [7-21]. Wheel-clamping may also be considered, though it will be necessary to comply very carefully with the conditions laid down by the courts if this is not to be illegal, and it will soon be subject to regulation [5-21].

12.*Q: Who can trim trees in a private road?* A: This is primarily a matter for the owner of the road. A resident with a private right of way would be entitled to trim them if they interfered with the right of way [4-56]. Trees overhanging from adjoining land could be trimmed by the owner of the road; and trees growing in the road but overhanging adjoining land could similarly be trimmed by the owner of that land [6-38]. Note that if the trees are subject to a tree preservation order, or if the area is a conservation area, there are restrictions on what can be done to them; but that they can be trimmed if they are causing a legal nuisance (which includes overhanging adjoining land or interfering with rights of way)[8-27].

13.*Q: Can a resident in a private road construct a new crossover between the road and his land?* A: If the road is not a highway, this will depend upon the nature and terms of his private right of way [4-52]. In a private road which is a highway, residents have in principle a right to gain access to the road at any point [3-10]. Planning permission is required for the construction of access points if they involve "engineering operations"; but permission is deemed to be granted in the case of highways in certain circumstances [8-15].

14.*Q: Can a speed limit be introduced in a private road?* A: If the road is a highway, or a road to which the public has access, the general 30 m.p.h. speed limit may already apply [9-17]. If not, an informal speed limit may be introduced. Failure to observe it will not, of course, be an offence. It might be possible to make observance of an informal speed limit a condition of the exercise of private rights of way, when a right is granted [4-30]. Local authorities have the power to require the removal of unofficial traffic signs in a highway or a road to which the public has access [9-17]. In a highway, it is an offence to put up a sign without "reasonable excuse" [7-3].

© A. W. & C. Barsby 2003

15. *Q: Can road humps be constructed in a private road?* A: In view of the various offences relating to highways contained in the Highways Act 1980, it seems doubtful whether road humps could be constructed in a private road which was a highway [7-3]. In other roads, traffic-calming measures will not necessarily amount to an obstruction, and hence an interference with private rights of way [4-56], but it will be wise to ensure that all residents are content with it before starting the work. Local authorities have no power to construct road humps in a road which is not a highway maintainable at the public expense [9-4].

16. *Q: What legal points arise in resurfacing or repairing a private road?* A: First, the consent of the owner (if known) may be required; though residents with a private right of way have the right to repair the road [4-50]. An application for planning permission will generally not be required, since permission for work of this kind is granted by the planning legislation [8-9].

17. *Q: Whose responsibility is it to maintain a private road?* A: The responsibility does not automatically attach to anyone, whether the owner of the road or a resident. A resident whose house has a private right of way may have an accompanying obligation to contribute to the cost of maintenance [4-48]. And if management of the road has been put on a formal basis, the arrangements may involve an obligation to contribute to the cost of maintenance [12-39].

18. *Q: Can the local authority carry out work in a private road?* A: Local authorities have a range of specific powers, more extensive for roads which are highways, less so for roads which are not [9-3 onwards]. But there is no general power to carry out work in private roads. If a local authority considers that the condition of a private road is not satisfactory, it can in principle take action under Part XI of the Highways Act 1980 [chapter 10].

19. *Q: Can the local authority be requested or required to take over a private road?* A: Section 38 of the Highways Act 1980 allows a private road to be adopted by agreement between the owner and the local authority, so that it becomes a highway maintainable at the public expense [3-48]. If the owner cannot be traced, it will not be possible to use s. 38. Part XI of the Act provides various different ways in which a road may be adopted—and, in certain circumstances, gives residents the right to require the adoption of the road [chapter 10]. The owner, if known, may in certain circumstances have the right to object.

20. *Q: Is it worth forming a company to administer a private road?* A: If the company is—or may become—the owner of the road, and if residents are willing to devote the necessary resources to the setting up and running of the company, this will in many cases be a sensible idea. If the company will not be the owner of the road, an unincorporated association, may be better way of proceeding [chapter 11].

Appendix 2: Tasks for managers

Checklist

The following notes are intended to serve as a checklist of the tasks which may be undertaken by the managers of a private road, whether they are the directors of a company, or trustees, or the officers of an unincorporated association.

- Be aware of whether the road is subject to public rights of way (i.e. a highway) or is a road to which the public have access. If the latter, consider whether public use should continue.

- If the road is not a carriageway, be aware of the existence and extent of private rights of way.

- Resist encroachment by anyone seeking to appropriate part of the road, e.g. by fencing off part of the verge, acquiring new rights of way, or extending existing rights of way.

- Be aware of whether the road is in a conservation area, an area of special control for the purposes of outdoor advertisements, or some other area subject to special controls, such as a National Park; be aware of whether the road contains any hedgerows subject to the Hedgerows Regulations 1997.

- Be aware of any hazards which might give rise to a claim for compensation by users of the road, and take appropriate action to minimise them; make sure, if the road is managed by an unincorporated association, that those responsible are aware of their personal liability; take out public liability insurance to cover the risks.

- If not the owners of the road, try to obtain and register title to the road.

- Undertake maintenance of the road, including repair of fences, surgery to trees etc. In engaging contractors, check that they carry their own public liability insurance.

- Administer the association or other form of collective ownership; if possible, put in place arrangements so that the association's future income is guaranteed; accumulate funds in order to meet major costs such as resurfacing.

- Consider and deal with requests for further private rights of way or other rights over the road.

- Liaise with residents; keep them informed; collecting subscriptions for upkeep of road.

- Liaise with the local authority on planning, trees and other issues. Commenting on any proposals by the local authority which affect the road or the area generally.

- Act as the street authority for the purposes of the New Roads and Street Works Act 1991.

Table of Authorities

1. Acts of Parliament
    Access to Neighbouring Land Act 1992 . . . . 6-0, 6-42
    Administration of Estates Act 1925
        s. 46(1) 2-44
    Animals Act 1971 6-6
    Commons Act 1876 1-37
    Commons Act 1899 1-37
    Commons Registration Act 1965 1-38
    Companies Act 1985 12-20
        s. 14 12-22
        s. 16 12-24
        s. 25 12-20
        s. 32 12-20
        s. 221 12-21
        s. 226 12-21
        s. 241–244 12-21
        s. 282 12-20
        s. 287 12-20
        s. 288 12-20
        s. 348–351 12-20
        s. 352 12-20
        s. 353 12-20
        s. 385 12-23
        s. 656 2-44
        s. 744 12-24
    Control of Pollution Act 1974
        s. 62 7-19
        s. 74 7-20
    Countryside Act 1968 3-50
        s. 27 . . . . 3-61, 9-9
        s. 30 3-3
    Countryside and Rights of Way Act 2000 . . . . 1-39, 3-64, 4-0, 4-36
        s. 47 . . . . 3-53, 3-62
        s. 48 3-53
        s. 49 3-62
        s. 50 3-62
        s. 67 7-22
        s. 68 4-69
        ss. 53–56 3-53
        Schedule 5 3-53
        Schedule 7 7-22

Criminal Damage Act 1971 .... 5-21, 7-6
Criminal Justice and Public Order Act 1994
    s. 68 7-27
Criminal Law Act 1977
    s. 6 7-27
Cycle Tracks Act 1984 3-3
Dangerous Dogs (Amendment) Act 1997 7-33
Dangerous Dogs Act 1991
    s. 3 7-33
    s. 10 7-33
Dogs (Fouling of Land) Act 1996 7-34
Electricity Act 1989 .... 10-0, 10-22
    s. 6 10-22
    s. 10(1) 10-23
    Schedule 3 10-27
    Schedule 4 10-23
Environment Act 1995 7-10
    s. 97(8) 7-11
Environmental Protection Act 1990
    s. 33 7-10
    s. 75 7-10
    s. 87 7-7
Gas Act 1986 10-32
    ss. 3–7 10-28
    s. 9(3) 10-29
    Schedule 4 10-29
    Schedule 5 10-31
Gas Act 1995 10-28
Government of Wales Act 1998 1-54
Highway Act 1835 .... 1-6, 1-16, 7-32
    s. 72 7-32
    s. 78 7-32
Highways Act 1959 1-7
Highways Act 1980 .... 1-2, 1-7, 3-2, 3-11
    Part XI 3-0, 3-35, 10-51
    s. 25 .... 3-44, 3-60
    s. 26 .... 3-46, 3-60
    s. 27 3-47
    s. 28 3-46
    s. 30 .... 3-35, 3-36
    s. 31 .... 3-20, 3-21
    s. 31(1) 3-19
    s. 31(2) 3-19
    s. 31(3) 3-28
    s. 31(5) 3-29, 3-31
    s. 32 3-21
    s. 36 .... 1-8, 3-46

s. 36(6)	1-27, 3-26, 3-74
s. 37	3-35, 3-37
s. 38	3-35, 11-0, 11-33, 11-34
s. 38(3)	3-40, 3-41
s. 41	1-8, 3-60, 9-1
s. 47	3-69
s. 48	3-69
s. 67	9-8
s. 72	9-5
s. 79	9-7
s. 97	9-5
s. 100	9-5
s. 101	9-5
s. 116	3-66, 3-68, 9-5
s. 117	3-67
s. 124	9-5
s. 130	9-1
s. 131	7-3
s. 131A	7-3
s. 132	7-3
s. 137	7-3
s. 138	7-3
s. 139	7-3
s. 140	7-3
s. 140A	7-3
s. 141	7-3
s. 143	9-5
s. 145	9-5
s. 146	9-5
s. 147	9-5
s. 148	7-3
s. 149	9-5
s. 150	9-5
s. 152	9-8
s. 153	9-8
s. 154	9-7, 9-11
s. 160A	9-5
s. 161	7-3
s. 161A	7-3
s. 167	9-8
s. 168	7-2
s. 170	7-3
s. 172	7-2
s. 173	7-2
s. 174	7-2
s. 179	7-2
s. 185	9-8

www.barsby.com

s. 203	11-2
ss. 203–207	11-2
s. 203(2)	11-7, 11-41
s. 203(3)	11-8, 11-15, 11-48
s. 204	11-2, 11-30
s. 205	11-22
s. 205(2)	11-15
s. 205(3)	11-13, 11-19
s. 205(5)	11-20
s. 206	11-9
s. 207(2)	11-16
s. 207(3)	11-16
s. 208(1)	11-21
s. 209	11-27
s. 211(1)	11-26
s. 211(2)	11-26
s. 211(3)	11-27
s. 212	11-52
s. 212(3)	11-27
s. 212(4)	11-28
s. 213	11-29
s. 214	11-29
s. 215	11-18
s. 216	11-18
s. 219	11-36
s. 219(1)	11-32
s. 219(4)	11-34
s. 219(6)	11-34
s. 220(1)	11-43
s. 220(3)	11-36
s. 220(4)	11-37
s. 220(6)	11-37
s. 221	11-38, 11-43
s. 222	11-39, 11-43
s. 223	11-43
s. 224	11-43
s. 225	11-37
s. 226	11-9
s. 227	11-9
s. 228	11-44, 11-45
s. 228(1)	11-46
ss. 228(2)–(4)	11-56, 11-57
ss. 228(2)–(5))	11-46
s. 228(7)	11-49, 11-66
s. 229	11-55
s. 229(1)	11-56
s. 230(1)	11-51

© A. W. & C. Barsby 2003

s. 230(2)	11-51
s. 230(3)	11-52
s. 230(4)	11-52
s. 230(5)	11-53
s. 230(7)	11-54
s. 232	11-40
s. 232(2)	11-41
s. 232(3)	11-41
s. 236	11-17
s. 236(1)	11-17
s. 236(2)	11-17
s. 263	3-62
ss. 263–268	1-8
s. 287	9-8
s. 317	11-46
s. 327	1-42
s. 328	1-17, 3-6
s. 329(1)	11-7
Schedule 12	3-66
Schedule 12A	9-5
Schedule 16	11-20
Human Rights Act 1998	11-58
s. 4	11-61
s. 10	11-61
Insolvency Act 1983	12-30
Land Registration Act 1925	4-63
s. 5	2-33
s. 75(2)	2-24
Land Registration Act 2002	2-34, 4-63
s. 15	2-19
Schedule 6	2-19
Law of Property Act 1925	
s. 84	6-52
s. 84(1)	6-54
s. 193	1-38, 4-34, 4-38
Law of Property Act 1969	6-52
Limitation Act 1980	2-13, 2-20
s. 29(1)	2-16
Local Government (Miscellaneous Provisions) Act 1976	
s. 23	9-11
Local Government (Miscellaneous Provisions) Act 1982	
s. 1	9-33
Local Land Charges Act 1975	2-43, 11-43
London Building Acts	9-31
Metropolitan Police Act 1839	
s. 54	7-31
National Parks and Access to the Countryside Act 1949	3-50

www.barsby.com

s. 21	7-13
s. 57	3-61
s. 47	3-47
s. 49	3-47
s. 89	9-25
New Roads and Street Works Act 1991	1-18, 10-3, 10-36, 10-57
ss. 48–106	10-4
s. 48(2)	10-5
s. 48(3)	10-4
s. 49	10-6
s. 50	10-7
s. 51	10-7, 10-8
s. 53	10-13
s. 53(1)	10-15
s. 55	10-8
s. 56	10-10, 10-59
s. 57	10-10
s. 58	10-11
s. 59	10-15, 10-59
s. 60	10-10, 10-58
s. 61	10-15
ss. 61–73	10-14
s. 72	10-12
s. 80	10-14, 10-15
s. 86(2)	10-4
Schedule 3	10-10
New Streets Act 1951	11-4
Noise and Statutory Nuisances Act 1993	7-19
Occupiers' Liability Act 1957	1-44, 6-16, 6-18
s. 2(2)	6-22
s. 2(3)	6-23
s. 2(4)	6-25
s. 2(6)	6-20
Occupiers' Liability Act 1984	1-44, 6-16, 6-28
s. 1(3)	6-28
s. 1(4)	6-28
s. 1(7)	6-28
s. 1(3)(c)	6-28
Places of Worship Registration Act 1855	11-18
Planning (Listed Buildings and Conservation Areas) Act 1990	8-0, 8-19
s. 69	8-40
s. 72	8-41
Planning and Compensation Act 1991	8-0
Prescription Act 1832	4-0, 4-13, 4-16, 4-20
Private Security Industry Act 2001	5-23
Private Street Works Act 1892	11-4
Public Health Act 1875	10-50, 11-4

© A. W. & C. Barsby 2003

Public Health Act 1925	9-27, 9-30
s. 17	9-30
s. 18	9-30
s. 19	9-30
Public Health Act 1936	10-50
Public Health Act 1961	
s. 75	9-33
Public Health Acts Amendment Act 1907	
s. 21	9-29
Public Order Act 1994	
s. 61	7-28
s. 77	7-28
Refuse Disposal (Amenity) Act 1978	9-21
s. 2	7-8
s. 3	7-9
s. 4	7-9
Rentcharges Act 1977	12-41
s. 2(4)	12-41
Rights of Entry (Gas and Electricity Boards) Act 1954	
s. 1	10-32
s. 2	10-32
Rights of Way Act 1932	3-50
Road Traffic Act 1930	4-69
Road Traffic Act 1988	1-28, 1-29, 7-21
s. 2	7-21
s. 3	7-21
s. 5	7-21
s. 19	5-27
s. 22	5-27, 7-21
s. 28	7-21
s. 29	7-21
s. 34	3-17, 3-62, 4-34, 4-38, 5-21, 7-22, 7-27, 7-36
s. 34A	7-24
s. 143	7-21
s. 170	7-21
s. 185(1)	10-8
s. 192(1)	1-20
Road Traffic Act 1991	7-21
Road Traffic Regulation Act 1984	1-29, 3-70
s. 1(1)	9-15
s. 2	9-16
s. 23	9-22
s. 32	9-22
s. 45	9-22
s. 46	9-22
s. 65	9-17
s. 69	9-18

s. 81 9-17
s. 82 9-17
s. 84 9-17
s. 85 9-17
ss. 99–103 9-20
s. 142 9-14
s.101 9-21

Supreme Court Act 1981
    s. 50 6-36

Telecommunications Act 1984 .... 10-21, 10-34, 10-59
    s. 10 10-35
    ss. 1–9 10-34

Theft Act 1968 7-5

Town and Country Planning Act 1990 .... 8-0, 8-2
    s. 55 8-6
    s. 55(1) 8-1
    s. 55(2) 8-2
    s. 172 8-20
    s. 183 8-21
    s. 198 ....8-23, 8-24
    ss. 198–214D 8-22
    s. 198(6) 8-27
    s. 201 8-25
    s. 207 8-31
    s. 208 8-31
    s. 209 8-31
    s. 210(1) 8-29
    s. 210(2) 8-30
    s. 210(4) 8-30
    s. 211 8-42
    s. 214A 8-31
    s. 215 9-23
    s. 220 8-33
    s. 222 8-34
    s. 224(3) 8-39
    s. 225 8-39
    s. 258 3-70
    s. 324 6-3
    s. 336 8-15
    s. 366 8-4

Town Police Clauses Act 1847 7-29
    s. 28 7-30

Towns Improvement Clauses Act 1847 9-27
    s. 64 9-28
    s. 65 9-28

Trustee Act 1925 12-33
    s. 34 12-31

© A. W. & C. Barsby 2003

s. 40(1) 12-15
s. 40(2) 12-15
Trusts of Land and Appointment of Trustees Act 1996 12-33
    s. 6 12-33
    s. 11 12-33
    s. 19 .... 12-31, 12-35
Vehicles Excise and Registration Act 1994
    s. 62 7-26
Water Act 1989 10-44
Water Industry Act 1991 .... 10-44, 10-49
    s. 94 10-52
    s. 102 10-50
    s. 108 10-54
    s. 158 .... 10-47, 10-53
    s. 158(1) 10-45
    s. 159 .... 10-46, 10-47, 10-53
    s. 162 .... 10-46, 10-47
    s. 163 .... 10-46, 10-47
    s. 168 10-47
    s. 172 10-47
    s. 179(1) 10-52
    s. 179(2) 10-51, 10-52
    s. 199 10-52
    s. 200 10-52
    s. 219(1) 10-45, 10-49
    Schedule 6 10-47
    Schedule 12 10-47
Wildlife and Countryside Act 1981 3-74
    Part III 3-50
    s. 28 7-13
    s. 53 3-54
    s. 54A 3-53
    s. 56(1) 3-51
    s. 61(1) 3-52
    Schedule 14 3-54
    Schedule15 3-54

2. Delegated legislation

    Builders' Skips (Markings) Regulations 1988, SI 1988/1933 7-3
    Commons (Schemes) Regulations 1982, SI 1982/209 1-37
    Companies (Tables A to F) Regulations Act 1985, SI 1985/805 12-22
    Control of Dogs Order 1992, SI 1992/901 7-35
    General Permitted Development Order 1995, SI 1995/418 8-3, 8-8, 8-14, 8-15,
        .... 8-18, 8-19, 8-20
    Hedgerows Regulations 1997, SI 1997/1160 7-11
    Highways (Road Humps) Regulations 1999, SI 1996/1025 9-4

Highways (Traffic Calming) Regulations 1999, SI 1999/2056 9-4
Land Registration Rules 1925, SR&O 1925/1093 . . . . 2-33, 4-63
Local Authorities (Transport Charges) Regulations 1998, SI 1998/948 . . . 7-3
Removal and Disposal of Vehicles Regulations 1986, SI 1986/183 9-20
Street Works (Registers, Notices, Directions and Designations) (Amendment No 3)) Regulations 1995. SI 1995/2128 10-4
Street Works (Registers, Notices, Directions and Designations) (Amendment) Regulations 1995, SI 1995/990 10-4
Street Works (Registers, Notices, Directions and Designations) (Amendment) Regulations 1999, SI 1999/1049 10-4
Street Works (Registers, Notices, Directions and Designations) Regulations 1992, SI 1992/2985 10-4
Town and Country Planning (Construction and Improvement of Private Roads) Regulations 1951, SI 1951/2224 11-42
Town and Country Planning (Control of Advertisements) Regulations 1992, SI 1992/666 8-33
Town and Country Planning (General Development Procedure) Order 1995, SI 1995/419 . . . . 8-3, 8-17
Town and Country Planning (Trees) Regulations 1999, SI 1999/1892 . . . 8-22
Vehicular Access Across Common and Other Land (England) Regulations 2002, SI 2002/1711 . . . . 4-34, 4-36
Water (Meters) Regulations 1988, SI 1988/1048 10-46
Wildlife and Countryside (Definitive Map and Statement) Regulations 1993, SI 1993/12 3-50

3. Cases

Adams v Commissioner of Police of the Metropolis [1980] RTR 289 9-40
Arthur v Anker, The Times 1 December 1995, [1996] 2 WLR 602, [1996] 3 All ER 783 5-21
Attorney General v Beynon [1965] Ch 1 2-28
Bakewell Management v Brandwood, The Times 5 February 2003 4-15
Barvis Ltd v Secretary of State for the Environment (1971) 22 P&CR 710 8-5
Batchelor v Marlow [2001] EWCA Civ 1051 5-11
Benn v Harding (1993) 66 P&CR 246, *The Times* 13 October 1992 4-59
Bracewell v Appleby [1975] 2 WLR 282, [1975] 1 All ER 993 6-36
Bridle v Ruby [1988] 3 WLR 191, [1988] 3 All ER 64 4-19
Buckinghamshire County Council v Trigg [1963] 1 WLR 155, [1963] 1 All ER 403, 61 LGR 189 11-15
Burton v Winters [1993] 1 WLR 1077 [1993] 3 All ER 847 6-40
Carter and Another v Surrey County Council, The Times 2 June 1989 11-16
Celsteel Ltd v Alton House Holdings Ltd [1985] 1 WLR 204, [1985] 2 All ER 562 . 4-56
Central Midland Estates Ltd v Leicester Dyers Ltd, The Times 18 February 2003 . 5-11
Co-operative Wholesale Society Ltd v British Railways Board, The Times 20 December 1995 6-39

AUTHORITIES

Cornwall County Council v Blewett [1994] COD 46 9-5
Cowen v Peak District National Park Authority [1999] 3 PLR 108 8-11
Das v Linden Mews [2002] EWCA Civ 590, *The Independent* 9 May 2002 ...4-28
Director of Public Prosecutions v Jones [1999] 2 WLR 65 3-8
Giles v County Building Constructors (Hertford) Ltd (1971) 22 P&CR 978 ...4-33
Graham v Philcox [1984] QB 747 5-16
Guise v Drew (2001) 82 P&CR DG25 4-33
Gwilliam v West Hertfordshire Hospital NHS Trust [2002] EWCA Civ 1041, 24 July 2002 6-26
Hale v Norfolk County Council, The Times 19 December 2000 2-28
Halsall v Brizell [1957] 2 WLR 123, [1957] 1 All ER 371 4-49
Handel v St Stephen's Close Ltd [1994] 1 EGLR 70 5-7
Hanning v Top Deck Travel Group Ltd (1994) 68 P&CR 14 4-15
Hogg v Nicholson [1968] SLT 265 1-21
Holden v White [1982] QB 679 6-21
Holmes v Bellingham (1859) 7 CB (NS) 329 2-10
Horne and Horne v Ball [1995] CLY 1841 4-56
Hubbard v Pitt [1975] 3 WLR 201, [1975] 3 All ER 1 3-8
Investors Compensation Scheme v West Bromwich Building Society [1998] 1 WLR 896 4-10
JA Pye v Graham [2002] 3 WLR 221 2-15
Jacques v Secretary of State for the Environment, The Independent 8 June 1994 .3-32
Jaggard v Sawyer [1995] 1 WLR 269, [1995] 2 AER 189 6-36
Jalnarne v Ridewood (1991) 61 P&CR 143 4-57
Jones v Portsmouth City Council [2003] 1 WLR 427 6-12
Jones v Price (1992) 64 P&CR 404 4-20
Keefe v Amor [1964] 3 WLR 183, [1964] 2 All ER 517 4-25
Kreft v Rawcliffe, The Times 12 May 1984 1-21
Lock v Abercester Ltd [1939] Ch 861 4-32
London & Blenheim Estates Ltd v Ladbroke Retail Parks Ltd [1994] 1 WLR 31, [1993] 4 All ER 157 5-7
London and Suburban Land and Building Co (Holdings) Ltd v Carey (1991) 62 P&CR 480 5-14
London Borough of Hounslow v Minchinton (1997) 74 P&CR 221 2-17
Massey v Boulden Court of Appeal, 14 November 2002, EWCA Civ 1634 4-28, ...7-24
McGeown v Northern Ireland Housing Executive (1995) 70 P&CR 10 6-30
Mercury Communications Ltd v London and India Dock Investments Ltd (1995) 69 P&CR 135 10-39
Mills v Silver [1991] 2 WLR 324, [1991] 1 All ER 449 ....4-18, 4-50
Ministerial Planning Decision [1996] 1 JPL 70 8-10
Overseas Investment Services Ltd v Simcobuild Construction Ltd, The Times 21 April 1995, [1995] EGCS 63, (1995) 70 P&CR 322 .3-41
Palmer v Bowman, The Times 10 November 1999 6-10
Pardoe v Pennington (1993) 73 P&CR 26 2-10
Parkstone Primrose Laundry Ltd v Poole Corporation (1950) 48 LGR 637 ...11-16

www.barsby.com

Patel v W H Smith (Eziot) Ltd [1987] 1 WLR 853, [1987] 2 All ER 569 5-13
Peacock v Custins [2002] 1 WLR 1815, [2001] 2 All ER 827, 21 November 2001 . 4-28
Pettey v Parsons [1914] 2 Ch 653 4-52
Poole Corporation v Blake [1955] 3 WLR 757 11-9
Prudential Assurance v Waterloo Real Estate (1999) 17 EG 131 2-14
Pugh v Savage [1970] 2 WLR 634, [1970] 2 All ER 353 4-13
R (on the application of Beresford) v Sunderland City Council [2001] EWCA Civ 1218, [2002] 2 WLR 693 . . . . 3-15, 4-18, 5-4
R v Shorrock [1994] QB 279, [1993] 3 WLR 698, [1993] 3 All ER 917 7-4
Ramblers Association v Kent County Council (1990) 154 JP 716, (1990) 60 P&CR 464 3-67
Robinson v Adair, The Times 2 March 1995 3-17
Robinson Webster (Holdings) Ltd v Agombar [2002] 1 P&CR 20 3-21
Sargeant v Macepark (Whittlebury) Ltd, The Times 29 March 2003 4-28
Scott v Westminster County Council [1995] RTR 327, 93 LGR 370 9-5
Secretary of State for the Environment, Transport and the Regions v Baylis (Gloucester) Ltd, The Times 16 May 2000 3-18
Simpson v Fergus (1999) 79 P & CR 398 2-18
South Lakeland District Council v Secretary of State for the Environment [1992] 2 WLR 204, [1992] 1 All ER 573 8-41
Spittle v Kent County Constabulary [1985] Crim LR 744 9-17
Stonebridge v Bygrave [2001] All ER (D) 376 5-7
Torbay Borough Council v Cross (1995) 159 JP 682 7-3
Unwin v Hanson [1891] 2 QB 115 . . . . 8-24, 10-43
Vine v Waltham Forest London Borough Council, The Times 12 April 2000 . . 5-21
Voice v Bell (1994) 68 P&CR 441 4-1
Wandsworth London Borough Council v Lloyd 96 LGR 607 9-8
Ware Urban District Council v Gaunt [1960] 1 WLR 1364, [1960] 3 All ER 778 . . 11-23
Warmhaze Ltd v Soterios Aspris [2001] All ER (D) 196 5-13
Warwickshire County Council v Adkins (1968) 112 SJ 135, 66 LGR 486 11-15
Westley v Hertfordshire County Council [1995] COD 414 3-66
Wheeldon v Burrows (18790 12 Ch D 31 4-46
Wheeler v JJ Saunders Ltd [1995] 3 WLR 466, [1995] 2 All ER 697 6-10
White v Grand Hotel, Eastbourne Ltd [1913] 1 Ch 113 4-11
White v Richards (1994) 68 P&CR 105 4-24
Worcestershire County Council v Newman [1974] 1 WLR 938, [1974] 2 All ER 867, 72 LGR 616 9-5
Wycombe District Council v Secretary of State for the Environment [1994] EGCS 61 8-13

© A. W. & C. Barsby 2003

Index

A

Access
    removing hedge to form 7-14
    stopping up 9-5
    to highway 8-15
Access to neighbouring land 6-42
Access to private road
    highway 3-10, 4-8
    planning permission 8-15
    road which is not a highway 8-16
Accident 7-2
    liability for 6-23
Accommodation road 1-15
Act
    consolidating 1-7
    local 7-29
Administrative Court
    jurisdiction 1-51
Administrative law 1-51
Adoption of road 3-35
    meaning 1-6
    by agreement 3-36, 3-41
Advance payments code
    meaning 11-2
Adverse possession
    meaning 2-13
    Crown land 1-42
    law 2-15
    registration of title 2-35
Advertisement
    hoarding 8-34
Advertising control 8-33
Alcoholic drink 9-36
Amenity
    advertisement 8-38
    powers of local authority 9-23
    restrictive covenant 6-51
    tree preservation order 8-23
Arbitrator 10-29
"As of right"
    meaning 4-15

B

Barbed wire
    removal 9-5
Barrier 1-21, 3-30, 3-65, 7-2, 8-13
Beneficiary
    of trust 12-32
BOAT
    meaning 3-52, 3-63
    definitive map and statement
    marking 9-9
    private road as 3-62
    signpost 9-9
Bona vacantia
    meaning 2-44
    Crown ownership of 2-44
    property of dissolved company 12-30
    title to road 2-35
Boundary
    marker 2-14
    of curtilage 7-13
    of parish or township 7-15
    of road 8-10
    vegetation overhanging 6-10, 6-38
Breach of condition notice 8-21
Bridge
    highway passing over 3-6
Bridleway 3-3, 3-67, 3-74
    adoption 11-7
    disturbing surface 7-3
    gates and stiles 9-5
    meaning 3-3
    private road subject to 3-58
    signpost 9-9
British Telecom 10-34
Builder's skip
    in highway 7-3
Building
    meaning 8-4
    listed 8-19
Building lease
    meaning 2-6
Building operation
    meaning 8-4, 8-6
Burial ground 11-18
Byelaw 3-3
    cyclists 3-3
    dogs 7-34
    prohibiting vehicles 4-38

Byway open to all traffic
    see BOAT

C

Cable company 10-34
Camping and caravanning
    unauthorised 7-28
Canal undertaker 11-18
Car
    dumping 7-8
Car boot sale 8-35
Caravan
    restrictive covenant 6-49
Careless and inconsiderate driving 7-21
Carriageway 3-12, 3-35, 4-5
    meaning 3-3
    made-up 9-5, 11-7
    stopping up 3-67
Caution
    on Land Register 2-40
Cellar
    under street 7-2
Children
    danger to 10-26
    duty of care owed to 6-19, 6-61
    playing in road 3-9, 4-60
Church 3-24
Churchyard 11-18
Cobbles 11-9
Commercial waste
    meaning 7-10
Common land 4-38
    meaning 1-36
    hedgerows 7-12
Common law
    meaning 1-3
Community council 1-7, 3-36
Company
    articles of association 12-22
    memorandum of association 12-22
    winding up 12-30
Compulsory purchase 9-37, 10-27, 10-33
Conservation area 8-40
    tree within 8-42
Controlled waste
    meaning 7-10
Cornwall, Duchy of 2-44
County Council
    as highway authority 1-7
County Court
    jurisdiction 1-49
    order under Telecommunications Act 1984 10-36
Crossover
    meaning 3-10
    right to construct 4-52
Crown 12-30
    ownership of *bona vacantia* 2-35, 2-44
    ownership of land 2-46
Crown Court
    jurisdiction 1-49
Crown Estate Commissioners 1-41
Crown land
    meaning 1-41
Cul-de-sac 3-68, 11-47
    as highway 3-24
Curtilage
    hedgerow 7-13
Custodian trustee 12-16
Cyclist 3-12

D

Damages
    meaning 6-34
Danger
    on land adjoining street 9-8
    warning of 6-25
Dangerous driving 7-21
Dedication and acceptance
    meaning 1-3
    notices to prevent 3-28
    presumption 3-23
    voluntary dedication 3-35
Deed 4-3
    transfer of land 1-34
Definitive map and statement 3-74
    generally 3-1
    purpose 3-49
DEFRA
    meaning 1-55
    confirmation of modification order 3-55
    creation of public paths 3-46
    definitive map and statement 3-57
    hedgerows 7-16
    regulations under CROW 4-36

© A. W. & C. Barsby 2003

INDEX

Delegated legislation
   meaning 1-53
Demolition
   need for hoarding 7-2
Derelict land 9-25
Development
   meaning 8-1
   control over 4-31
   in conservation area 8-40
Development plan 8-48, 11-40
DfT 10-6
   meaning 1-55
   highway authority 10-6
   street works 10-10
District Council
   highway functions 1-7
Dog
   collar 7-35
   stray 7-35
   trespassing 6-6
   walking 4-60
Dominant tenement
   meaning 4-1
Door bell
   maliciously ringing 7-30
Door or gate opening on to street 9-8
Drain
   easement 4-60
   ownership 10-1, 12-1
   private 10-54
   repair 8-18
   under road 10-49
Driveway
   parking on 5-16
   private 11-16
Driving with excess alcohol 7-21
DTI
   meaning 1-55
   electricity lines 10-26
   gas and electricity 10-0
   telecommunications 10-22, 10-34
Dumping
   motor vehicles 7-8
   things other than motor vehicles 7-9

E

Easement
   meaning 4-1
   characteristics of 4-2
   creation 4-9
   creation by prescription 4-12
   different sorts of 4-60, 6-42, 10-54
   grant 4-9
   interference with 6-9
   types of 4-4
Election
   notice of 8-36
Electricity 8-18
Enforcement notice 8-20
Engineering operation
   access to highway 8-15
Entry
   right of 10-47
   rights of 6-3, 6-20, 10-20, 10-31, 10-32, 10-47
Estate rentcharge 12-42
Estate road 1-15
European Convention on Human Rights 11-58
Excavation
   danger from 6-28

F

Failing to stop after accident 7-21
Fences, hedges, walls 8-46
   alteration 8-14
   barbed wire 9-5
   hedge in highway 7-3
   maintenance 8-12
   regulations for hedgerows 7-11
   relaying hedge 7-14
   tree preservation order 8-23
   trimming hedge 7-14
Fences, hedges, walls
   adverse possession 2-14
Fire 7-3
Firework 7-3
Flat
   block of flats 1-13
   maintenance 12-42
   road servicing 1-14
Flowers 7-6
Fly-posting
   local authority powers 8-39
Foliage 7-6
Footpath 3-44

adoption 11-7
agreement for 3-44
creation 3-24
crossover across 10-4
disturbing surface 7-3
gates and stiles 9-5
over private road 3-74
private road subject to 3-58
signpost 9-9
Forecourt
    parking on 5-14
Frontager 11-52
    adoption of road 11-52
    application to register title 2-36
    cost of making up road 11-67
    ownership of road 2-10
    street works 11-9
Fruit 7-6
Fruit tree 8-27
Fumes 6-10

G

Garden
    development in 11-35
    fête 9-34
    waste from 7-10
Gas 10-4
Gate 3-30
    alteration to 8-14
    dedication and acceptance 3-31
    maintenance 8-12
    right of way 4-24
Gate on highway
    widening 9-5
GPDO
    Hedgerows Regulations 1997 7-14
Graffiti 7-6
Granite setts 11-9
Grass
    cuttings 7-10
    mowing 2-26
    verge 2-25, 3-10
Greater London
    road names 9-27, 9-31
Green lane
    meaning 3-53
Guard-rails 9-8

H

Hedgerow
    access 7-14
    protection 7-11
    replacement 7-17
    site of special scientific interest 7-13
Hedgerow removal notice
    meaning 7-15
Hedgerow retention notice
    meaning 7-15
High Court
    jurisdiction 1-49
Highway
    meaning 1-17
    access to 8-15
    classes of 3-3
    depositing things on 7-3
    maintainable at the public expense, list of 1-27, 3-26
    making mark on 7-3
    obstructing 7-3
    planting hedge in 7-3
    playing games in 7-3
    public's right to use 3-8
    removal of nuisance 9-5
    stopping up 1-9, 3-0, 9-5
    trading on 7-3
    tree or shrub in 7-3
    verge 7-3
    widening 9-5, 11-9
Highway authority
    meaning 1-7
Highway maintainable at the public expense
    meaning 1-8
    footpaths and bridleways 3-47
    history 1-2
    ownership of verges, etc 2-28
    parking 5-1
Horse-drawn vehicle 3-12
House
    extension to 11-35
    number and name of 9-27
    services for 10-0
Household waste
    meaning 7-10

© A. W. & C. Barsby 2003

I

Industrial estate
    road on 1-13
Industrial waste
    meaning 7-10
Injunction 6-37
    planning control 8-21
    principles applied by courts 6-36
    protection of hedgerow 7-17
    right of way 4-56
    tree preservation order 8-31
    trespassing 4-55, 5-19
Insurance
    contractor 6-26
    public liability 12-48

J

Justice of the Peace
    licensing 9-36
    warrant for entry 10-32

K

Kerbstones
    replacement 8-11
Kite
    flying 7-30

L

Lancaster, Duchy of 2-44
Land
    compulsory purchase 9-37
    Crown 1-41
    derelict, neglected or unsightly 9-25
    fencing off 2-14
    used for breeding horses and ponies 7-12
Land Charges Register 2-43
Land Register 2-19
    adverse possession 2-13
    effect of registration 2-33
    filed plan 2-42
    Index Map 2-42
    office copy 2-42
    prescriptive right 4-21
    restriction on 12-14
    restrictive covenant 6-48
    searching 2-41
    unincorporated association 12-14
    wayleave 10-41
Land registration 4-63
    easement 4-63
    ownership of private road 12-36
    restriction on transfer 12-44
Lands Tribunal
    restrictive covenant 6-52
    vehicular access to land 4-43
Leaves 7-10
Leaving vehicle in dangerous position 7-21
Legal fiction 4-13
Levelling road 11-8
Licence 4-7
    revocation 1-47
Licence to use land
    meaning 2-3
Lighting
    absence of 6-59
    improving road 4-50
    installation 6-25, 9-5
    liability for 6-25
Limitation period
    meaning 2-13
Listed building 8-19
Local Act 7-29
Local authority powers
    generally 9-0
    road signs 9-18
    traffic regulation generally 9-14
Local land charge
    tree preservation order 8-26
Lost modern grant
    meaning 4-13

M

Made-up road
    meaning 1-25
Magistrates' court
    creation of highway 3-37
    highway 3-38
    maintenance of highway 3-69
    making up and adoption 11-23
    renaming road 9-30
    stopping up highway 3-66
Major project
    meaning 10-8
Making up and adoption

meaning 3-0
Manorial system 1-36
Map
    evidence of highway 3-21
    existence of highway 3-31
Metropolitan District Council
    as highway authority 1-7
Modification order
    meaning 3-54
    application by public 3-56
Motorised trespassing
    in private road 7-25
    offence of 4-34, 7-22
Mushrooms 7-6

N

Neighbourhood watch
    sign 8-37
Noise
    in street 7-19
    nuisance 6-10
    rules of residents association 12-12
Notice
    dangers in a road 6-60
    naming of street 9-30
    public rights of way 1-21, 3-13, 3-28, 3-30, 3-37
    removal of vehicles 7-9
    under private street works code 11-20, 11-46, 11-49, 11-57
Nuisance
    meaning 6-8
    abating 6-39
    in highway 6-30
    in street 7-30
    interference with private rights of way 5-20, 6-9
    overhanging vegetation 6-10
    public 6-8, 6-13, 7-4
    roots encroaching 6-10
    self-help 6-38

O

Occupation and possession of road 6-5, 6-15, 6-17, 7-5
Occupation of land
    meaning 1-43
Occupation road 1-15

ODPM
    meaning 1-55
    tree preservation order 8-26
OFGEM 10-22
    meaning 1-55
    function 10-0
OFTEL
    meaning 1-55
    functions 10-34
OFWAT
    meaning 1-55
    functions 10-47
"Once a highway, always a highway" 3-2, 3-24
"Once a highway, always a highway" 3-65
Overriding interests in land
    meaning 2-38
Ownership
    collective 12-1

P

Parish council 1-7, 3-36
Parking
    as ancillary right 4-42, 5-14
    authorisation 9-22
    control of 8-48
    in dangerous position 5-27
    licences to park 5-3
    local authority powers 9-22
    no general public right 3-9
    obstruction 4-56
    on driveway 5-16
    on forecourt 5-14
    on verge 5-27
    unauthorised 7-9
Pavement 3-59, 6-59, 11-9
Paving, metalling and flagging
    meaning 11-8
Pedestrian 3-12
Pedestrian crossing
    construction 9-22
Pets
    restrictive covenant 6-49
Plan
    evidence of highway 3-21
Planning contravention notice 8-21
Planning permission
    and rights of way 8-44

© A. W. & C. Barsby 2003

INDEX

maintaining private road 8-10
Plant
    theft of 7-6
Possession of land
    meaning 1-43
Post box 8-18, 10-56
Post Office 8-18, 10-56
Premises
    entry by force 7-27
Prescription 4-9
    lost modern grant 4-13
    right of way 4-12
    under Prescription Act 1832 4-13
Presumption 3-12
Private road
    meaning 1-1
    adoption 1-16, 1-52
    dangerous condition 11-51
Private street works code
    meaning 11-2
Projection in street
    removal 9-8
Protected land
    hedgerows 7-13
Protected street
    meaning 10-15
Public entertainment
    licence for 9-33
Public gas transporter 10-28
Public house 3-24
Public liability insurance 12-48
Public nuisance
    meaning 6-8
Public path creation agreement 3-44
Public path creation order 3-46
Public right of way
    contrast with private right of way 4-7
Public sewer 10-52
Public Trustee 12-16

R

Railway undertaker 11-18
"Rave" party 7-4
Registrar of Companies 12-30
Rentcharge
    meaning 12-40
    registration 12-43
    rent owner 12-43

Residential area
    nuisance in 6-10
Restricted byway
    meaning 3-53
Restricted road
    meaning 9-17
    speeding in 9-17
Restriction
    on Land Register 2-40
Restrictive covenant
    entry on Land Register 2-39
    legal requirements for creating 6-47
    powers of Lands Tribunal 6-52
    significance 6-0
Retaining wall
    by street 9-8
Right of way, private
    registration 4-63
    restrictions on 4-11
Road
    levelling 11-8
    metalling 11-8
    occupation 1-15
    paving 11-8
    traffic sensitive 10-8
Road (in Road Traffic Act 1988)
    meaning 1-20
Road humps 9-4
    impeding right of way 4-56
    in public road 9-4
    in public roads 9-4
    installation 8-11
Road sign
    dimensions 8-37
Root
    growing across boundary 6-10, 6-38
RUPP
    meaning 3-52
    private road as 3-62
    reclassification 3-53

S

Security camera 8-19
Security Industry Authority 5-23,
Servient tenement
    meaning 4-1
Sewer
    easement 4-60

www.barsby.com

ownership 10-1, 12-1
private 10-54
public 10-52, 10-54
under road 10-49
Sewerage undertaker
   meaning 10-44
   development by 8-18
Share
   in company 12-27
   transfer 12-28
Shop 3-24
Sign
   defacing 7-6
   misleading or distracting 9-19
   neighbourhood watch 8-37
   sale of property 8-37
   to prevent dedication and acceptance 3-13
Signpost
   BOAT 9-9
   bridleway 9-9
   footpath 9-9
   on footpath 3-61
Skip
   in highway 7-3
Sleeping policemen 9-4
Slide in the snow 7-30
Slip-road 1-13
Smells 6-10
Smoke 6-10
Speed limit 9-17
Statutory declaration
   meaning 3-31
   easement 4-64
Statutory undertaker
   meaning 10-0
Stop notice 8-21
Stopping up
   meaning 3-65
   access to highway 9-5
   consequences 3-71
   effect 1-9, 3-0
   powers 3-70
Storage and refuse bins
   in street 9-8
Street
   meaning 1-18
   danger on adjoining land 9-8
   emergency barriers 9-8

refuse and storage bins 9-8
removal of projection 9-8
retaining wall 9-8
Street authority
   meaning 10-6
   duties 10-10, 10-13, 10-29
Street lighting 9-5, 9-17, 9-39, 11-8, 11-9
Street managers
   meaning 10-6
   duties 10-57
   in private road 10-37
Street works
   meaning 11-8
Street works licence
   meaning 10-7
Structure
   adjoining highway 6-14
Structure on highway
   removal 9-5
Surveyor of highways 1-7

T

Tax disc
   vehicle without 7-26
Telecommunication apparatus
   installation 10-36
Telecommunications Code
   meaning 10-35
Television camera 8-19
Theft of land 7-5
Time immemorial 4-13
Tort
   meaning 6-1
Trader
   on highway 7-3
Traffic
   commercial 4-56
Traffic regulation order 1-29, 9-15
Traffic sign
   as advertisement 8-36
   local authority powers 9-17
   unofficial 9-19
Traffic-calming 4-56, 9-4
Treasury Solicitor's Department 2-44, 2-45
Tree
   adjoining highway 6-14
   damage to 8-24
   dangerous 9-11

INDEX

dead, dying or dangerous 8-27
electrical lines 10-26
fruit 8-27
lopping 10-26, 10-33, 10-43
replacement 8-28
within conservation area 8-42
Tree preservation order 8-22
hedgerows 7-11
procedure 8-23
registration as local land charge 2-43
Trees and shrubs
in highway 7-3
obstructing view 9-7
on verge 4-25
overhanging 9-7
planting by local authority 9-25
trimming 6-58
Tree-surgeon 6-24
Trespass
meaning 6-2
by dog 6-6
compensation 4-55
criminal 6-7
disruption 7-27
duty of care 6-60
occupier of land 1-44
occupiers' liability 6-21
on highway 3-9
parking 5-4
prescription 4-15
Trustee
custodian 12-16
death of 12-15
replacement of 12-15
Tunnel
highway passing through 3-6

U

Unadopted road
meaning 1-6
Unadopted street
meaning in GPDO 8-10
Unincorporated association
nature 12-9
ownership of property 12-14
Utility company
functions 12-1
power of entry 6-2

V

Vegetation
overhanging 6-10
Vehicle
horse-drawn 3-12
leaving in dangerous position 7-21
removal 9-20
unloading in highway 3-8
Verge
adverse possession 2-26
crossover crossing 3-10
development and 8-14
hedge along 7-3
maintaining 2-26
minor work involving 10-8
mowing 6-18
right of way over 4-25
Vibration 6-10
Violence
entry to premises 7-27

W

Wall
alteration 8-14
maintenance 8-12
retaining 9-8
Water
damage caused by 6-10
main 8-2
Water main
meaning 10-45
Water meter
installation 10-46
Water undertaker
meaning 10-44
Wayleave
meaning 4-7, 10-25
gas pipe 10-33
Land Register 10-41
nature of 10-41
Welsh Assembly 1-54
Wheelclamping 5-21
Widening
gate on highway 9-5
highway 9-5, 11-9
Woodland
tree preservation order 8-23
Works for road purposes

www.barsby.com

meaning 10-4